Mental Health Social Work in Ireland

Comparative issues in policy and practice

Edited by
JIM CAMPBELL
ROGER MANKTELOW

Ashgate

Aldershot • Brookfield USA • Singapore • Sydney

Published by
Ashgate Publishing Ltd
Gower House
Croft Road
Aldershot
Hants GU11 3HR
England

Ashgate Publishing Company
Old Post Road
Brookfield
Vermont 05036
USA

British Library Cataloguing in Publication Data
Mental health social work in Ireland : comparative issues
   in policy and practice
      1.Mental health services - Ireland 2.Mental health services
      - Government policy - Ireland 3.Psychiatric social work -
      Ireland
      I.Campbell, Jim II.Manktelow, Roger, 1948-
      362.2'0425'09415

Library of Congress Catalog Card Number: 98-70982

ISBN 1 85972 694 1

Printed and bound by Athenaeum Press, Ltd.,
Gateshead, Tyne & Wear.

Contents

Tables

List of contributors

Shane Butler is a lecturer in the Department of Social Studies, University of Dublin where he teaches in the areas of mental health social work, addictions and HIV/AIDS. He has published widely in the fields of substance misuse and social work, and gender and substance misuse.

Jim Campbell worked as a mental health social worker in Northern Ireland before becoming a lecturer in the Department of Social Work in The Queens University of Belfast. He has published in the fields of mental health social work, and social work and social conflict in Northern Ireland.

Janet Convery is presently a community care worker and family support coordinator with the Eastern Health Board. She lectures part-time at Trinity College Dublin on aspects of social work with older people, and is a member of the National Council for the Elderly and IASW. She has published in the field of community care for older people.

Faith Gibson is an emeritus professor of Social Work at the University of Ulster at Jordanstown and a member of the National Council for the Elderly. Her practice and research interests include the use of reminiscence theory with older people and social work for people with dementia.

Paul Guckian is senior social worker, Clare Mental Health Services, Mid-Western Health Board and current chairperson of Social Workers in Psychiatry (SWIP), a special interest group of the Irish Association of Social Workers. In recent years he has been involved in setting up Service Users/Carers Groups in County Clare and is currently involved in research into current service needs.

Stanley Herron was formerly employed as a psychiatric social worker in Belfast before becoming a social services inspector in the DHSS in Northern Ireland, and later, assistant director of the Northern Ireland Association for Mental health. He has published in the fields of mental health social work and social work in Northern Ireland.

Máire Leane lectures in social policy at University College Cork, teaching courses on family policy, deinstitutionalisation, gender and health. She has published in the fields of gendered assumptions in the care of older people and aspects of community care for older people.

Roger Manktelow worked as a mental health social worker at Holywell Psychiatric Hospital before becoming a lecturer in the Department of Applied Social Studies at the University of Ulster at Magee. He has published in the areas of the sociology of mental illness and community care for people with mental health problems.

Augusta McCabe is Social Work Adviser, Department of Health and Children, Dublin. She previously worked as a social worker in child and family psychiatry, and in community care. She was President of the Irish Association of Social Workers and elected President of the International Federation of Social workers from 1986 to 1988.

John Park is Social Services Inspector, Department of Health and Social Services, Belfast. He previously worked in North and West Belfast Social Services where he was responsible for the development of community mental health services. His current interests include the British Association of Social Workers and the Northern Ireland Association of Mental Health

Fred Powell lectured in the University of Ulster at Coleraine before taking up his current post as Professor in the Department of Applied Social Studies, University College Cork. He has written on various aspects of social policy in the Republic of Ireland.

Pauline Prior practiced social work at the Royal Victoria Hospital Belfast and was later a social work trainer in the Northern Health and Services Board. She currently lectures in the Department of Social Policy at The Queens University of Belfast and has published widely in the field of mental health policy.

Lydia Sapouna worked as a psychiatric social worker in Greece before joining the Department of Applied Social Work in University College

Cork. She teaches and researches in the fields of community care, disability-equality issues, family and health care and European social work.

Barbara Ward has worked as a social worker in the Western Health and Social Services Board. Since 1989 she specialised in addictions field and more recently in health promotion with a special interest in alcoholism and drug misuse in the Western Board area.

Acknowledgements

Both of us enjoyed periods of study leave during the writing and editing of this book. We would like to thank our colleagues at the School of Social and Community Sciences at the University of Ulster at Magee and the Department of Social Work at the Queen's University of Belfast for allowing us the time to engage in what we believe is an important project. The book would not have been possible without the kind and efficient assistance provided by Ruth Dilly, we would like to thank her for this.

Foreword

Augusta McCabe and John Park

The inspiration for this welcome collection of chapters sprang from the success of a series of DHSS(NI) publications on the theme of mental health social work (Campbell, J. and Herron, S. (1993), Campbell, J., Park, J. and Manktelow, R. (1995), Manktelow, R., Campbell, J. and Park, J (1997). In recent years contributions have expanded to include views from the South as well as North of Ireland. The conferences have clearly demonstrated that workers in both parts of Ireland have much to learn from each other. This book examines the similarities and differences in the role of mental health social work and mental health policy between the Republic of Ireland and Northern Ireland. As the reader will learn in great detail throughout the chapters, mental health services in Ireland, North and South, share a common history. Despite three-quarters of a century of separation between the two jurisdictions, there are still many similarities in the approach of the respective administrations to the provision of mental health services.

In the Republic of Ireland, *Shaping a Healthier Future: A strategy for effective healthcare in the 1990s* (DOH, 1994) spelt out a number of priorities which coincided with similar action areas in Northern Ireland's *Health and Well-being: Into the Millennium - Regional strategy for health and social well-being 1997-2000* (DHSS(NI), 1996). Both administrations continue to grapple with the challenge of shifting the focus of mental health services from the vestiges of the old Victorian asylum system to the modern target of developing community-based services. Shared priorities include, amongst other things, promoting positive mental health and developing close integration between the primary and secondary mental health services. Both documents are based on the principle of restoring people with a mental illness to as independent and as normal a life-style as possible and of involving them and their families in the planning of services.

Social workers in the mental health services are well placed to make a unique and valuable contribution to the achievement of the objectives identified in both strategies - North and South. Many of the objectives set out in both documents coincide with the fundamental aims of the social work profession. The International Federation of Social Workers in its Human Rights policy document (IFSW, 1996) states very simply that, "Human rights condense into two words - the struggle for dignity and fundamental freedoms which allow the full development of human potential." In acknowledgement of this core maxim, both the British Association of Social Workers (BASW, 1996) and the Irish Association of Social Workers (IASW, 1995) include in their respective codes of ethics a basic principle of the social work profession which is:

> the recognition of the value and dignity of every human being, irrespective of origin, race, status, sex, sexual orientation, age, disability, belief, or contribution to society. The profession accepts a responsibility to encourage and facilitate the self-realisation of each individual person with due regard to the interests of others.

This book, *Mental Health Social Work in Ireland: Comparative Issues in Policy and Practice,* is a valuable contribution to the growing body of knowledge about this important subject, presented most ably by a distinguished array of contributors.

References

British Association of Social Workers, (1996), *The Code of Ethics for Social Work,* BASW: Birmingham.

Campbell, J. and Herron, S. (1993), *Mental Health Social Work in Northern Ireland:* Policy and Practice since 1986, Queen's University Belfast/SSI(NI).

Campbell, J., Manktelow, R. and Park, J. (1995), *Social Work in Mental Health -Proceedings of the second Northern Ireland Conference,* SSI (NI).

Department of Health (1994), *Shaping a Healthier Future: A strategy for effective healthcare in the 1990s,* GOS: Dublin.

DHSS(NI), *Health and Wellbeing Into the Millenium - Regional Strategy for health and social wellbeing 1997-2000,* DHSS: Belfast.

International Federation of Social Workers (1996), *Human Rights.* IFSW: Oslo.

Irish Association of Social Workers (1995), *Code of Ethics of the Irish Association of Social Workers,* IASW: Dublin.

Manktelow, R., Campbell, J. and Park, J. (1997), *Social Work in Mental Health - Proceedings of the third Northern Ireland Conference*, SSI(NI).

1 Introduction

Roger Manktelow and Jim Campbell

A changing practice environment

As we approach the millennium it can be argued that exciting times of change and opportunity are emerging for those working in the mental health field. For so many years in the twentieth century professionals who worked within the psychiatric services were often represented as essential components of an enclosed social world, immune from outside change and influence. The retraction of the former mental hospitals, the development of community based alternatives, the breakdown in professional boundaries, the growth of the user movement and the rapidly growing public interest in the promotion of mental health and personal growth therapies - these are all factors which have encouraged a new openness about mental disorder both outside and within psychiatric institutions. However piecemeal, these shifts in policy and perception have changed the way professionals and laypersons think and behave towards those who become involved in the psychiatric system. Although discourses on 'madness' still shape popular ideas about the identities of people with mental health problems, sufferers are no longer automatically removed from society nor their rights always disregarded.

It is of some comfort that these changes mean that the mental health service user's traditional role of passive dependency has been challenged by service users themselves. It would be wrong, however, to assume that progress has been consistent and unproblematic. Social change brings with it paradox and contradiction; the relative strength or weakness of the position of service users crucially hinges on choices which can be made by policy makers and professionals. The challenge for mental health social workers is to construct a professional identity which is flexible enough to meet the problems and opportunities which have emerged in the past decade. These themes emerge in the following chapters, but with special reference to mental health social work and social policy in the North and South of Ireland. This book provides a unique opportunity for practitioners, researchers and trainers to discuss and critically analyse key issues which affect contemporary practice both sides of the Irish border. What makes the text important is not just the fact that very little has been said about mental health social work in Ireland to date; for the first time material from the two jurisdictions have been set alongside each other to allow for international comparisons between the North and South of Ireland.

The opportunity for such comparative analysis seems even more pressing given the pace of political and social change in Ireland, Europe and the rest of the world. In both the UK and Ireland the impact of globalisation and membership of the European Union in the 1990s has had a considerable effect both in Northern and Southern Ireland. For example, the entry of the Republic of Ireland into the European Community in 1973 created the circumstance for economic growth and began a process of political and social flux which eventually led to changes in policy towards divorce, contraception and the liberalisation of homosexuality. The impact of membership of the European Community and other international factors on Northern Ireland arguably has been less tangible in terms of legislation, but nonetheless substantial. Not only has Northern Ireland received regional assistance through a succession of European Union Poverty Programmes, the 'peace process' which followed cease-fires in 1994 and 1997 has been influenced by political and economic interests in Europe and the USA.

As new forms of production, consumption and lifestyle emerge as a result of international pressures, Irish and Northern Irish social workers have to adjust their practice to keep pace with change. Although there may be common issues which affect social workers both sides of the border, divergence has also occurred. For example, in Northern Ireland professional training lasts only two years in common with other UK regions whereas three year courses exist in the Republic of Ireland; this appears to reflect a closer identification on the part of the Republic of Ireland with a common policy identified by the European Community and espoused by other member states. It remains to be seen whether more radical concepts of pedagogy, *animation* and empowerment can find their way into social work approaches which tend to be more traditional on both sides of the border (Lorenz, 1993).

The political context of social work practice

Competing 'histories' permeate analyses of Irish social, political and economic life and influence the way in which mental health social work is practised on both sides of the border. When Ireland was partitioned in 1921 two separate jurisdictions were created and sustained diverse social formations. The predominantly catholic South eventually became an independent republic whereas the North, within which a large catholic minority coexisted with a Protestant majority remained as part of the United Kingdom. With the outbreak of the civil disturbances in 1969 in Northern Ireland the discriminatory nature of the Stormont administration became widely visible. For many years, provincial and local government had been allowed to decide the allocation of social opportunities - employment, housing and social services- often on the basis of religious affiliation rather than need. As an acknowledgement of the failure of successive Northern Irish and British governments to address sectarianism, Direct Rule was imposed by Westminster in 1972.

A great deal has been written about the causes of the political violence which has marred social life in Northern Ireland during the last twenty five years (Whyte, 1991), but little has been said about the impact of the conflict on welfare services generally, and services to people with mental health problems in particular. It is now seventy five years since the partition of Ireland, and some interesting comparisons as well as contrasts can be made between the two systems of welfare. Inevitably, such comparisons have implications for the way we understand mental health social work in Ireland, North and South. In Northern Ireland new bureaucracies were established in the early 1970s to manage housing (through the Northern Ireland Housing Executive), health and social services (through Health and Social Services Boards) and education and library services (through Education and Library Boards). What was interesting about the Health and Social Services Boards was that they comprised a parallel management structure for health and social care within a single body, commonly known as the 'integrated service'. This is a unique development in the context of the UK welfare state.

Whilst political conflict created the conditions for change in the delivery of health and social welfare in the North, other factors influenced service delivery in the South. As part of a process of state centralisation of health and social welfare, eight Regional Health Boards were established in 1970 with a significant bias towards a medical model of care. Unlike their counterparts in Northern Ireland, social workers in the Republic of Ireland lacked clear lines of professional management and were accountable ultimately to the County Medical Officer.

Mental health services

If political conflict and social change influenced the general structure of social welfare in Ireland then it is hardly surprising that psychiatric services and mental health social work would also be affected. During the nineteenth century an enthusiastic policy of asylum building throughout Ireland produced a total of thirty six asylums. What happened in Ireland mirrored the British experience where excessive resources were used in the provision and massive expansion of mental hospitals and numbers of available mental hospital beds (Robins, 1986). Finnane (1981) has argued that, because of the level of investment in asylums, a bureaucratic inertia developed which made it difficult for other forms of organisational provision to develop as the twentieth century moved on. This helps explain why the Republic of Ireland continues to have one of the highest rates of psychiatric hospitalisation in Europe.

As with other welfare regimes worldwide, the deinstitutionalisation of long-stay psychiatric patients and their resettlement in community facilities has also occurred in Ireland, but the particular social and cultural contexts of an island which was divided politically during the twentieth century makes this process somewhat unusual. Although political division in Ireland is along a North-South dimension, there is also a natural geographical division between the east and west of the island. The eastern seaboard is largely urban and industrialised and contains the two major conurbations of Dublin and Belfast. In the East, the pattern of psychiatric hospital admissions is similar to that of urban areas of Britain. In contrast, the West of the country is rural with a distinctive traditional culture of emigration, small farms and bachelorhood. A strikingly different pattern of mental disorder in the West is characterised by high rates of hospital admission, particularly for schizophrenia occurring in single, middle-aged men. Prior (1996) suggests that the existence of particular forms of family life and the absence of legislation which allowed for adequate protection of the rights of patients, led to specific patterns of admissions in the course of the twentieth century. Interestingly his research focused on the example of the Omagh Asylum which was left in Northern Ireland after partition.

Prior (1993) has noted how the creation of the post-war welfare state in the UK caused divergence between mental health services on either side of the Irish border. In the North services increasingly followed the general UK approach which, at least embraced the rhetoric of universal provision, delivered by state bodies and administered at a local level by county welfare authorities and hospital authorities. This allowed for the development of systems of psychiatric care which were centrally organised and largely managed by professionals employed by the state. In contrast, in the South of Ireland, the main provider of personal services remained the voluntary sector, particularly those administered by religious and lay organisations. Mental health social workers were scarce and often lacked professional identity, largely because they were a small group working within a much larger medical system, and employed directly by hospital authorities. Interestingly, recent, new management approaches have created a dual structure of medical and non-medical hierarchies in the Republic of Ireland, but psychiatric social workers continue to struggle to achieve recognition in the face of a predominant medical hierarchy. The result is that psychiatric social workers remain working either within the Special Hospital Programme or as part of the Community Care programme.

As in other parts of the world deinstutionalisation has led to the development of various types of community care for people with mental health problems in Ireland, the different mix of economy of welfare in the South has meant that voluntary and privately organised community-based services predate those which have developed only relatively recently in the North. In the South the State has never taken a primary role in the provision of such services, with Regional Health Boards acting as purchasers of services from the voluntary and independent care sectors. In contrast, it is only with the advent of community health and social services trusts and hospital trusts in Northern Ireland in the last five years which has led to similar arrangements in the community care field.

Finally perhaps one of the most fascinating comparative aspects is the relative position of mental health social workers within their respective service networks. In the Republic of Ireland, social workers in psychiatry are not numerous and outside Dublin they are geographically scattered. However, social work has been a relatively high status profession with restricted graduate entry, a considerable degree of autonomy and salaries significantly higher than in the North. In contrast, Northern mental health social workers are numerous, firmly established in multi-disciplinary teams with a clear role and function, and carry exclusive statutory responsibilities under the 1986 Mental Health Order (N.I.). In Northern Ireland mental health services have been frequently reorganised but remain administered, albeit now in a more inter-disciplinary fashion, by a hierarchical management structure.

Conclusion

These are some of the major themes which are explored below. The book is organised into six different subject areas. In Chapter Two Stanley Herron provides an historical overview of the development of the psychiatric social worker in the USA, UK and Northern Ireland. In the course of his discussion he traces the various strands which preceded Seebhom and led eventually to the creation of the ASW in the UK. He argues that, although there was some loss of professional identity with the advent of generic training, there is room for optimism for the future of mental health social work.

Features of mental health policy within the two jurisdictions are highlighted in two chapters by Pauline Prior and Fred Powell. In Chapter Three Pauline Prior provides an overview of the key policy issues which influenced the development of mental health services in Northern Ireland post-partition. What emerges from this account is a picture of convergence with an agenda driven by Westminster, yet some of the nuances of policy designed particularly for the Northern Ireland situation can be identified. She concludes that mental health social workers should be aware of the profound policy changes which have occurred in the last decade, and be prepared to develop and protect good practice as a way of professional survival. Fred Powell, in Chapter Four uses a social constructionist critique to explain the context of mental health policy in the Republic of Ireland. In his account, he argues that much of the ideology and discourse of mental health policy over the last hundred years serves to reproduce systems of inequality and disadvantage for people who have used the psychiatric system. The importance for practitioners is that they should seek to examine the underlying meaning of this discourse if they are to fulfil an empowering role for clients.

Jim Campbell and Paul Guckian examine the legal context of mental health social work in the North and South of Ireland in Chapters Five and Six. In Chapter Five Jim Campbell reviews the development of the Approved Social Worker in Britain and Northern Ireland. He then discusses the general role of the mental health social worker in the context of policy themes which emerged in the 1980s and 1990s. In conclusion, it is argued that mental health social workers in Northern Ireland need to refine their skills and knowledge bases if they are to preserve the gains by the profession in the last decade. Paul Guckian, in Chapter Six, traces the history of the psychiatric social worker in the context of legislation and organisational arrangements in the Republic of Ireland. In particular, he describes and analyses the new proposed mental health legislation and the concern that the statutory role be shared by social workers alongside clinical psychologists and public health nurses. There may well be lessens learnt from the operation of the Northern Ireland Mental Health Order for psychiatric social workers in this debate in the South.

The topic of community care for people with severe mental health problems is dealt with in Chapters Seven and Eight. Maire Leane and Lydia Sapouna report their research on resettlement programmes for long-stay patients moving into the community in the Republic of Ireland. They propose a sociological understanding of the policy of deinstitutionalisation as both a process and an outcome. Roger Manktelow uses a symbolic interactionist framework to illuminate the difficulties in social integration for former long-stay psychiatric patients now living outside hospital. There are important lessons for practice in the findings that former patients are vulnerable to social exclusion and he reports on a community project, Rehability, which operates a social club to promote social inclusion.

Chapters Nine and Ten contain a comparative perspective on mental health social work with addictions in Northern and Southern Ireland. In Chapter Nine, Barbara Ward explores how treatment outside hospital is offered by Community Addiction Teams in Northern Ireland. These teams offer the possibility for innovative multi-disciplinary working outside the medical model of treatment. Shane Butler, in Chapter Ten, traces the evolution of treatment responses to alcohol and drug misuse in the Republic of Ireland within the policy context of developing mental health services. He explores the reasons why social workers in the South have not participated in the growth of addiction services.

Faith Gibson and Janet Convery provide an assessment of mental health social work with older people in Chapters Eleven and Twelve. The authors emphasise the importance of dementia as a growing problem in an ageing population in both jurisdictions. In Chapter Eleven, Faith Gibson provides a critical overview of policy for people with dementia and their carers. She makes detailed recommendations to improve social work and other professional practice in this area in Northern Ireland. Janet Convery, in chapter Twelve, outlines the position of mental health social work with older people in the Republic of Ireland and is critical of the lack of resources and the low priority awarded such work in community care programmes.

In conclusion, we believe that this collection of chapters breaks new ground in reporting on how mental health social work has responded to the demands of the changing policy and social context in late twentieth century Ireland, North and South. What the material suggests is that, where political and legal processes diverge, then so too will some aspects of mental health social work practice between jurisdictions. On the other hand, common issues of professional identity and the needs of clients are transferable across national borders and bureaucratic barriers. We believe that the interests of people with mental health problems, and the role of mental health social workers in preserving social and legal rights for services users can both be enhanced if the profession is encouraged to look beyond the narrow boundaries of agency and nation state. By learning through the experiences of others, elsewhere, our vision of what is valid and purposeful practice will expand accordingly.

References

Finnane,M. (1981), *Insanity and the Insane in Ireland,* Croom Helm: London.

Lorenz, W. (1993), *Social Work in a Changing Europe*, Routledge: London.

Prior, L. (1996), 'The appeal to madness in Ireland' in Dylan Tomlinson and John Carrier (eds), *Asylum in the Community,* Routledge: London.

Prior, P. (1993), *Mental Health and Politics in Northern Ireland,* Avebury: Aldershot.

Robins, J . (1986), *Fools and the Mad. A History of the Insane in Ireland,* Institute of Public Administration: Dublin.

2 A history of mental health social work in Northern Ireland

Stanley Herron

Introduction

In this chapter the history of mental health social work in Northern Ireland is described using a chronological and narrative approach. This framework allows for the classification of broad periods in the development of the profession during the twentieth century. What emerges is a rich history which reveals contradictions and continuity in training and practice. From the early beginnings to current practice issues, there is a focus, using comparisons between Northern Ireland and Britain, on how mental health social workers have changed and adjusted practice according to the legal and policy imperatives of each era.

Establishing an identity (1900-1920)

There are two 'tributaries' which merge to create an identifiable entity for mental health social work in the twentieth century: one geographical and the other professional. Although social work has its roots in England, for example, in the Charitable Organisation Society and the Settlement Movement, it appears that it was only when it was transplanted to America that a serious debate about professionalism began in the early 1900s. The professional tributary refers to the 'professional' aspect of social work which became most apparent in the context of collaboration with other professions, notably medicine and, more particularly, psychiatry. Even then, the development of mental health social work took place alongside work with the families of children who had mental health problems; medical social work and mental health social work proper. Thus Richmond (1917, p.35) quotes Dr Richard C.Cabot, the founder of the Medical-social service department in Massachusetts General Hospital in 1905 describing the role:

9

In our own casework in the social service department of the hospital we are accustomed to sum up our cases in monthly reports from the case records by asking about each case four questions: What is the physical state of this patient? What is the mental state of this patient? What is his physical environment? What is his mental and spiritual environment? The doctor is apt to know a good deal about the first of these four things; a little about the second but about the other two almost nothing. The expert social worker comes with these four points in mind in every case.

The development of child guidance services and family casework agencies in America also began under a 'charities and corrections' umbrella. Thus the psychological clinic established at the University of Pennsylvania in 1896, and the subsequent clinic in Chicago, were staffed by doctors, psychologists and social workers, and mainly concerned with the study of juvenile delinquents. The first psychiatric hospital provision for children was in Boston in 1912. However, it was not long before some psychiatric social workers adopted the new psychoanalytic approaches of Freud and others to herald what Taft (at that time director of the child study department at the Children's Aid Society of Pennsylvania) described as "the birth of an epoch-making movement" (in Courtney, 1992, p.202). That this was no idle boast was illustrated by the establishment of the American Association of Psychiatric Social Workers in 1926, although this had been pre-dated by the first summer school in psychiatric social work which had taken place in Smith College in 1918.

Developments in Great Britain followed a somewhat similar path. In the elitism which was prevalent in early psychiatric social work it was often considered that psychiatric social workers were somehow 'superior' to medical social workers. Historically, however, psychiatric social work owed its origins, at least in part, to medical social work. As early as 1907 the Hospital Almoners Council (later to become the Institute of Almoners) initiated training courses, at first lasting 12 to 18 months but, by 1921, extending to two years. Four months were spent full-time in a Charity Organisation Society office in London; nine months' theoretical study at the London School of Economics and 11 months at a hospital training centre under the direction of an experienced almoner. It was proposed to add a further three months post-graduate training in mental health to the course but this initiative was short-lived, being overtaken by developments in the child guidance field (Yelloly, 1980, p.49).

A Child Guidance Council had been set up in 1927 and contributed to the establishment of the Mental Health course at the London School of Economics and Political Science in 1929 (Yelloly, 1980, p.47), the same year in which the British Association of Psychiatric Social Workers was set up, with 17 members. By 1939 there were 30 child psychiatric or child guidance clinics in Great Britain and this number had grown to 350 by 1958 (Mayer-Gross et al., 1969, p.635). Most of these were established in close liaison with childrens' hospitals or with the paediatric department of general hospitals. Even then a division occurred between 'centres' provided by the local education authority, often under the direction of educational psychologists, and 'clinics' staffed by what became the standard 'core-team' of psychiatrist, psychologist and psychiatric social worker. The style of training provided for psychiatric social work set a standard which it is difficult to improve on:

For the small groups of carefully chosen students of the Mental Health Course there were advantages not hitherto experienced in any other British training of social workers. Their practice was undertaken in centres charged with professional education as well as service. There were learners and practitioners from the other disciplines. Leisured supervision was given by social workers who themselves had recently undertaken training for this purpose in America. Fieldwork and study were concurrent and there was frequent consultation between tutor and supervisors. (Brown, 1970, p.24)

Developments in Northern Ireland (1920-1950)

In retrospect, the period between the establishment of Northern Ireland as a separate political and administrative entity in 1921 and the administrative and legal changes brought about by the immediate post-war reforms from 1948 led to few changes in mental health social work. During these three decades mental health services remained largely institution-bound (Prior, 1993, p.15, and Appendix 1).This reliance on institutional care did not mean that there were not equally challenging demands in the community. For example, during the interwar years 1922-34 there were consistently high levels of unemployment in Northern Ireland, varying between 13% and 28% of the population (Evason et al., 1976).This, and other adverse social conditions, obviously created a demand for social work services but the Poor Law was still in operation and continued to be administered by Relieving Officers. Poor Law relief in Northern Ireland doubled in the period 1932 to 1936, the large increase in 'exceptional distress' in the 1930's was attributable to high levels of unemployment (Evason et al., 1976. p.24).

Post-war developments (1950-1970)

It is difficult to over-estimate the extent of the changes brought about by a series of Acts of Parliament during the years 1946-48. Faced with the inheritance of 500 workhouses and the Poor Law system staffed by untrained Relieving Officers the National Health Service Act (1946), the National Assistance Act (1948) and the Children Act (1948) provided the legal framework for hospitals authorities, local authority health and welfare departments and childrens' departments. The legislation enabled the development of services for elderly people, people with physical and sensory disabilities, mentally ill people, people with a learning disability, homeless people and families with children. Although the new National Health Service and community Health and Welfare Services provided an overarching structure, there continued to be organisational divisions within it. One of these was the distinction between the role, functions and training of Mental Welfare Officers who were employed by local authority health departments, and Psychiatric Social Workers who, in the main worked in hospitals and in child guidance clinics. Younghusband (1951,p.87) describes the role of Mental Welfare Officers as follows:

> They are occupied in social work for patients in mental hospitals as well as in after-care and in acting as duly authorised officers under the Lunacy and Mental Treatment Acts 1890-1930 [i.e. being involved in compulsory admission to hospital].

> The vast majority are ex-relieving officers or others who started as clerks in the local authority service and have in due course been promoted, normally without training, to do this work. For example, one local authority with a population of over 750,000 employs 20 workers in its mental health service, all of whom are untrained.

> Many local authorities are using their health visitors for all the work, other than that of the duly authorised officers. On the whole it is probably true to say that many local health authorities are fully satisfied with this situation. They are apt to prefer the local man or woman who has risen through the ranks in their service and medical officers of health certainly have a preference for health visitors who not only visit homes continuously for a variety of health purposes but also, having been trained in hospitals and in the nursing tradition, have a proper regard for their relation to the doctor.

Younghusband (1951, p.85) also describes the role of psychiatric social workers:

In a mental hospital, a psychiatric department in a general hospital or an out-patient clinic she usually takes social histories and is responsible for maintaining contact between the patient and the community, for allaying the anxieties of relatives and for explaining procedures to them. It is also her task...to encourage the patient with the help of his relatives to become re-established in the community.

In child guidance centres and clinics she usually takes a social history from the parents as part of the diagnostic procedure. As a rule she sees the parents and, in close co-operation with the psychiatrist, helps them to understand the possible causes of the child's problems, the nature of the treatment given by the clinic and the part which the inter-action between the child and his family may be playing in the causation and treatment of those problems. As in adult work it is the responsibility of the psychiatric social worker to maintain contact with social agencies outside the clinic.

There is also a demand for them in a variety of other social work where their special training and skill is the most appropriate available; thus, for example, all the tutors in charge of child care courses in university social science departments are psychiatric social workers.

By the early 1960's little had changed:

Mental Welfare Officers in all areas were far more often in communication with personnel in the health services, particularly psychiatrists and general practitioners, than with other social services. Apart from their own colleagues they were seldom in contact with other social workers, even those in the psychiatric hospital service....We found Mental Welfare Officers providing too much intermediary service - statutory admissions, arranging treatment or making investigations as a preliminary to treatment - and too little social care during and after treatment. Most of the work was of a short-service, infrequent contact variety. It seemed to us that social work energies were being dissipated in these ways. Mental Welfare Officers were responding to situational demands in which their traditional role, their generally inadequate training and their low status combined to inhibit their recognition of 'casework' opportunities and to reduce their power to seize them. Hospital-based workers, who were better trained, functioned in ways in which they were not making the fullest use of their skills. This suggested a redeployment of psychiatric social workers from hospitals into local authorities where they could provide leadership, help the less well-trained, and utilise their higher social status and greater interpersonal competence to resist or change the inappropriate expectations of G.P.s and psychiatrists for perfunctory intermediary or auxiliary service.(Martin and Rehin, 1969, p.230)

By 1950 the balance of professional social workers in Britain was as follows:

Table 1.1
Membership of professional and other associations (1950)

Association	Membership
Institute of Almoners	1380
Association of psychiatric social workers	361
National Association of Authorised Officers	500

Source: Younghusband (1951, pp.84,87,89)

The position in Northern Ireland was similar in many ways but different in others. The divisions between employees of the Northern Ireland Hospitals Authority (this meant the small number of psychiatric social workers), local authority health departments and local authority welfare departments (which inherited the 'duly authorised officer' role) were also present in Northern Ireland. Welfare departments had at least the potential to provide a more integrated service since, for example, they did not have a separate childrens' department. Nevertheless, the distinction between professionally qualified psychiatric social workers working in hospital and child guidance settings and, generally speaking, unqualified staff working in an under-developed community mental health service in welfare departments held true. This position was not made any easier by the fact that the only social work training course which was available in Northern Ireland in 1950 was the two-year Diploma in Social Studies course at Queen's University Belfast with 22 places. The course offered the opportunity for two months practical work but did not lead to a recognised professional qualification. The Hospitals Authority, on the other hand, recruited a number of trainee psychiatric social workers and seconded them to professional, post-graduate courses in England and Scotland, of which, in 1950, there were three:

London School of Economics   (35 places, established in 1929)
Edinburgh University   (12 places, established in 1944)
Manchester University   (10 places, established in 1949)

In 1954 Liverpool University was added to this list. In addition to teaching on theory, all the courses emphasised supervised practice, usually consisting of three days per week for four months at adult psychiatric out-patient departments and a similar period at child guidance clinics and a block placement. The training included the full range of services, for example in the learning disability field and in the criminal justice system.

As the post-war health and welfare legislation continued to make an impact on practice it became clear that university training courses of this kind would be unable to meet the increase in demand, particularly in local authority social services departments. Consequently Dame Eileen Younghusband, who had reviewed social work and social work training in 1945 and again in 1950, was invited to chair a Working Party on Social Workers in Local Authority Health and Welfare Services which reported in 1959. (Note that the Working Party's remit was limited to local authority social work). Partly because local authority welfare departments had such a wide remit and range of staff, the Younghusband Committee adopted a kind of matrix within which to analyse the training which might be required. This included the range of situations in which social work could be relevant - with individuals, with groups, with communities. On the other hand the complexity of the needs which were to be addressed included -complex problems which required the skills of a trained and experienced social worker, more straightforward problems which nevertheless required a basic training in social work and routine problems which could be dealt with by an untrained but mature member of staff working under the supervision of a trained social worker.

It was recognised that current courses could not meet the ever-increasing demand so the Working Party recommended the establishment of a crash programme of two-year courses to be taken at Colleges of Further Education and leading to a new qualification: the Certificate in Social Work (CSW). The first of these in Northern Ireland was set up in Rupert Stanley College in Belfast in 1964. Unfortunately, from being a short-term expedient to improve levels of training in local authorities, the CSW soon acquired recognition as being equivalent to a qualification acquired through a 4-year honours degree, followed by one-year's post-graduate specialist training. In addition, the newly baptised 'Welfare Assistants' (the third category of staff in the Younghusband Report) rapidly became the 'specialists' in the field of work with elderly people. Partly as a result of these developments welfare departments in Northern Ireland showed a steady increase in social work staffing from about 250 in 1966 to 553 in

1974 (Evason et al.,1976,p.157). However, these figures are for all fieldwork staff. Of the 553 staff shown in 1974, half (281) were social work assistants (the new name for Welfare Assistants) or trainee social workers. Walker et al. (1972) carried out a 'snapshot' study of social workers in Northern Ireland welfare departments in 1970 as part of a national study of social work caseloads. **Table 1.2** gives some details of the qualifications (if any) of the 267 staff in post.

Table 1.2
Qualifications of social work staff (including welfare assistants) in welfare departments in Northern Ireland in 1970

Qualification	Number
Psychiatric social work	13
Medical social work	11
Child care or probation	17
Certificate in social work	35
All with professional qualifications	76
Home Teacher's Certificate	35
Diploma in Deaf Welfare	3
University Degree or Diploma	102
All with relevant qualification	140
Letter of Recognition	11
Others (Welfare Assistants)	122
All with no formal qualifications	133

Even allowing for the low representation of psychiatric social workers (17% of staff with professional qualifications) Walker et al.'s study shows that only 38% of their caseload consisted of clients with mental health problems (other clients being, for example, children (28%) and elderly people (11%) (Walker, 1972, p.46).

A decade of change (1970-80)

Despite these problems in training, some new developments were taking place in psychiatric services. The first psychiatric day-hospital opened in Clifton Street - a working-class area in North Belfast in 1961. Because of a geographical quirk the initiative came from Holywell Hospital in Antrim rather than Purdysburn Hospital in Belfast, but the project was extremely innovative in seeking to bring a broadly psychoanalytical approach to bear on the mental health problems of a working-class community. The day-hospital was well-staffed and, in addition to three consultant psychiatrists, had a full-time experienced psychiatric social worker. A further innovative aspect was that the day-hospital held two evening out-patient clinics per week to ensure that people who were working would not have to take time off work - something unheard of in this day.

A second day-hospital opened in 1963 in East Belfast, also serving a working-class area. Because of re-development Clifton Street Day-hospital moved to a more middle-class area in North Belfast (actually the former headquarters of Country Antrim Welfare Committee in Alexandra Gardens) in 1971. The opportunity was taken to incorporate the lessons which had been learned at Clifton Street and in East Belfast into the design and modus operandi of Alexandra Gardens Day-hospital and in its early days it was a clear model of good practice. In particular, it provided an ideal multi-disciplinary setting for the training of students, including social work students who worked under the supervision of experienced psychiatric social workers.

Unfortunately the day-hospital movement in Northern Ireland declined and further developments - for example those associated with the Early Treatment Unit at Craigavon Area Hospital, the Mater Hospital, Whiteabbey Hospital, Daisy Hill Hospital, Newry, Ards Hospital, Roe Park Hospital Limavady and at Belfast City Hospital - represented a withdrawal from a community-based service and a return to a hospital environment. Despite this, by 1985 there were nine day-hospitals in operation. (DHSS (NI), 1985, p.12).

The psychiatric hospital system in Northern Ireland was preserved at a time when deinstitutionalisation was happening elsewhere. At no point was there a firm policy decision, as there was in England, to close any of these former asylums. Indeed, in the period 1974-83 there was a net increase in hospital beds, from around 4,300 to 5,300 (DHSS (NI), 1985).

In the child guidance field the Main Committee (Dr Main was the Ministry's Chief Medical Officer) reviewed the service in Northern Ireland in 1958 and there were further reviews in 1967 and again in 1971. By this last date there were 16 child guidance centres in Northern Ireland. Seven of these were hospital-based (the Royal, the City, the Ulster, Downe, Whiteabbey, Altnagelvin and South Tyrone) and nine local authority-based (Braniel, Newtownards, Armagh, Portadown, Enniskillen, Omagh, Strabane, Magherafelt and Coleraine). However, of the 35 whole-time and five part-time consultant psychiatrists working in Northern Ireland at this time, only three claimed a comprehensive knowledge of child psychiatry, and one of these worked part-time. The projection made at that time was that 12 psychiatric social workers would be required to establish an adequate child guidance service for Northern Ireland. The 1971 review group debated the pros and cons of a hospital-based as compared with a community-based service but came down firmly in favour of the former.

Mental health social work continued to reflect this hospital/community split. There was a sense that divisions were narrowing to some extent as increasing numbers of psychiatric social workers were being employed by local authorities (welfare departments in Northern Ireland). Yet there continued to be a qualitative difference between, on the one hand, high standards of professional practice and the training of social work students in clinical settings (aided by close contact with consultant psychiatrists and other members of the multi-disciplinary team) and, on the other hand, psychiatric social workers in the community facing some dilution of their skills because of the varied demands being made on them. A small example of this difference was that only welfare department staff could be designated as 'duly authorised officers' under the mental health legislation.

It has already been mentioned that the position was worse in England since there were various departments responsible for different client-groups: families with children, people with disabilities, elderly people, homeless families and people with mental health problems (Seebohm, 1968, p.27). Given the variegated nature of these services and the multiplicity of social work roles within them, the time was clearly ripe for a review. This was duly carried out by the Seebohm Committee (1968), their terms of reference being:

> ...to review the organisation and responsibilities of the local authority personal social services in England and Wales, and to consider what changes are desirable to secure an effective family service.

It should be noted that, like the earlier Younghusband Report (1959), the sole concern was with local authority departments. The Report had a number of things to say about mental health social work. For example, an attempt was made to predict demand:

> at a very conservative estimate, a population of 100,000 will on average contain 1,500 people with severe mental disorder, chiefly psychosis or sub-normality, who should be offered social help of various kinds: many want and need it sorely. The entire social work staff now available to many local authorities could be usefully occupied solely in trying to support patients; helping them, their families and local communities to readjust. (Seebohm, 1968, p.109)

Seebohm (1968, Appendix F) calculated that there were 622 psychiatric social workers in England and Wales in 1967, the broad distribution being 37% in child guidance; 37% in hospital services and 26% in local authority health departments. Put slightly differently, of a total mental health social work workforce of 3,060, twenty percent were psychiatric social workers and only 5% were psychiatric social workers employed in local authority health departments.

Specialist training for psychiatric social work had been expanding, and these courses were all university-based:

Table 1.3
Psychiatric social work training courses in the United Kingdom (1967)

One-year course for social science graduates:

Belfast, Birmingham, Bristol, Dundee, Edinburgh, Leeds, Liverpool, LSE, Manchester, Southampton, South Wales and Monmouthshire (seven in England, one in Wales, three in Scotland, one in Northern Ireland)

Two-year course for graduates in subjects other than social sciences:
Aberdeen, York (one in England, one in Scotland).

Honours degree/professional course lasting four years:
Bradford, Keele, Hatfield (three in England)

Higher degree/professional training for honours graduates:
two in England
(Seebohm, 1968, p.331)

All the courses were approved by the Association of Psychiatric Social Workers and continued the traditional emphasis on supervised practice, mainly in hospitals and child guidance clinics thus reinforcing the divide between high standards of professional practice in clinical settings and, arguably, more diluted practice in local authority departments. In spite of this increase in training places, demand continued to outstrip supply in the child guidance field:

Table 1.4
Demand and supply of psychiatric social workers in child guidance
(1963-69)

Year	No.	qualifying	Vacancies
1963	69	111	252
1964	69	155	277
1965	69	173	317
1966	86	193	339
1967	101	144	362
1968	111	143	358
1969	143	131	361

Source: Child Guidance Special Interest Group (1975, Appendix B)

The central recommendation of the Seebohm Committee was the creation of a single social services department covering all client-groups and the services surrounding them. It has already been pointed out that, in Northern Ireland, integrated social services departments (known as Welfare Departments) already existed but in parallel with a separate Northern Ireland Hospitals Authority which, among other things, was responsible for psychiatric hospitals (and the Special Care service). The debate here, therefore, was more concerned with the integration of these two parts of the system: health services and social services rather than integration within social services.

To consider this issue of the integration of health and social services a firm of management consultants was retained. They carried out a systematic review of the existing services and proposed an innovative framework entailing 'programmes of care' (Booz, Allen and Hamilton, 1972). Unfortunately, and in spite of a series of implementation seminars, the concept of a 'programme of care' was poorly understood. It was intended to be a flexible planning tool involving programme planning teams with horizontal and vertical representation which could come together to plan the service and then disband, perhaps to be re-constituted in a different form to review progress and adjust the plans accordingly. For example in the case of mental health the 'horizontal' representation on the programme planning team might have been across disciplines, for example,

Psychiatry, nursing, social work, occupational therapy, psychology and administration

The 'vertical' structure of the organisation would ensure representation from different staffing levels and would not consist exclusively of senior members of staff. It could also include users of the service and their carers and, where relevant, representatives of other agencies, such as housing, employment services or voluntary organisations could be added. Predictably the proposals rapidly became converted into traditional, fixed bureaucratic structures - four Health and Social Services Boards were created (Northern, Southern, Eastern and Western) and they were responsible for managing 17 Districts. Each of the two levels (Board and District) was led by a four person team consisting of the professional head of each of the four main disciplines which existed at:

Health and Social Services Board level

Director of Social Services
Chief Administrative Medical Officer
Chief Administrative Nursing Officer
Chief Administrator

and at District level

District Social Services Officer
District Administrative Medical Officer
District Administrative Nursing Officer
District Administrative Officer.

A potential benefit which these changes might have created was the 'forced marriage' between hospital and community services; they were now managed as a single unit and, for example, psychiatric hospitals were subsumed under the totality of health and social services. In practice, however, many doctors opted out of the process and a number of the District Administrative Medical Officer posts remained unfilled.

From the point of view of mental health social work, there were some damaging aspects. It has been pointed out that, generally speaking, traditionally high standards of psychiatric social work were to be found within psychiatric hospitals and child guidance clinics rather than in the community. Now there was considerable pressure to dismantle the professional (rather than administrative) hierarchy within hospital and child guidance settings. This was a hierarchy which functioned on the principle that the head of department would ensure that regular, structured supervision from appropriately trained and experienced staff was available for staff and social work students. The manager might also maintain a small caseload and take an interest in research and development work. Very professional staff in these settings with a wealth of experience were inevitably sucked into purely administrative posts and - on the whole - were lost to professional social work.

What emerged from Younghusband (1959) and Seebohm (1968) was that community-based services concentrated in local authorities had not managed to build a solid foundation of professional practice. This was largely because of the speed with which staff returning from professional courses were promoted to more senior posts which, on the whole, involved administration rather than direct contact with clients. Consequently such staff were not in a position to become the professionals of the future. This fact was already acknowledged by Seebohm (1968, p.332):

The main limitation on the increase of the scale of training is the availability of staff to supervise students undertaking field training.

and reinforced by Younghusband:

In order to teach casework, people must exist who can teach casework. To learn casework involves practising casework under supervision. And good supervision necessarily implies that good casework is being done in the agency where training is given. Thus we arrive at a vicious circle because in order to improve casework practice casework itself must be better taught but it cannot be better taught until there is better practice. Younghusband (1969, p.76)

Approval and competence (1980 - 90)

Fortunately this rather pessimistic view is not reflected in the opinions of other professionals, legislators and policy-makers. On the legislative front, during the late 1970s, Gostin, then Legal and Welfare Rights Officer for MIND (the National Association for Mental Health) had been arguing forcibly for an enhanced status for social workers in order to provide a meaningful counter-balance to the alliance between G.P., psychiatrist and, on occasions, relatives: "The fact that his (the social worker's) opinion carries no more weight than that of a relative speaks volumes on Parliament's view of his status."(Gostin, 1977, p.37, in Goodman, 1987, p.144). This was borne out by a study which showed that, in 1977, only one-third of London boroughs and 43% of all other authorities in England and Wales required their mental welfare officers to hold a professional social work qualification (Dunn, 1977 in Goodman, 1987, p.144). Via the rather tortuous route of a Mental Health (Amendment) Act 1982 followed rapidly by the consolidating Mental Health Act 1983, this demand for greater professionalism led ultimately to the notion of 'approval' and social workers needing to be able to demonstrate their competence in order to be able to act as independent professionals.

The process whereby social workers could become 'approved' turned out to be equally problematic. Inevitably there had to be a two-year transition period to enable existing untrained staff to reach the required level. Somewhat reminiscent of the Younghusband 'crash' courses of the 1960s, but shaped by the Central Council for Education and Training in Social Work (CCETSW)'s desire to carve out a role for itself, 'approval' initially was based on success in written examinations set and marked by CCETSW. The National Association for Local Government Officers (NALGO), on the other hand, argued that additional competence and additional standing entitled approved social workers (ASWs) to a higher salary, and instructed its members to boycott the CCETSW examinations. As a result, by December 1984 some 938 candidates had successfully completed their examination out of an estimated requirement for ASWs of between 4,500 and 6,500 (CCETSW, 1984). Ultimately a compromise was reached with CCETSW setting down requirements for selection and training but employing authorities carrying out the assessment and approval.

The mental health legislation in Northern Ireland arrived three years behind that in England, but the Mental Health (N.I.) Order 1986 was arguably a more progressive piece of legislation than the English 1983 Act. Although mental health social workers in Northern Ireland had played a much less significant part in compulsory admissions to psychiatric hospital than was the case in England (where it had been an important aspect of the former Mental Welfare Officer's role) the review of the mental health legislation here, as in England, echoed Gostin's call for an enhanced status for social workers:

> We consider that this [whether to proceed with a compulsory admission] is a decision which should be taken by the social work profession...To avoid a wide variation in standards of practice we would suggest that those social workers who are approved for the purposes of the new statute must have experience and expertise in the psychiatric field. (DHSS(NI), 1981, p.10)

The Order imposed a duty on Health and Social Services Boards to

> Appoint a sufficient number of approved social workers...No person shall be appointed...as an approved social worker unless he is approved by the Board as having appropriate competence in dealing with persons who are suffering from mental disorder. (DHSS(NI), 1986, Article 115)

Health and Social Services Boards co-operated well in developing ASW training. Running alongside these events was a new approach to education and training (linked to the introduction of National Vocational Qualifications). The approach is based on designated and demonstrable 'competencies' and health and social services boards in Northern Ireland were in the forefront of developing CCETSW-approved competencies for approved social work. Whether competence-based training produces professional social workers who are able to exercise independent judgement rather than become dependent on a 'checklist mentality' is open to question. What can be said is that CCETSW's requirement for 60 days specialist training and experience is a pale shadow of the professional psychiatric social work courses described above.

While there was an absence of formal workforce planning, there was a gradual initial structured policy of training approximately 30 approved social workers each year in Northern Ireland with the result that, according to the most recent official figures, by 1994 there were 254 fully approved social workers in Northern Ireland (DHSS(NI), 1995). This represents 1 ASW per 6,478 head of population, a figure which is more favourable than those for authorities in England and Wales, which vary between 1:8,870 (Northern Region) to 1:15,761 (Mersey) (Huxley and Kerfoot, 1993).

People first - or last ? (1990 - 1997)

In reviewing the development of social services over the past 100 years, and given the accelerating speed of change, it is not surprising that health and social services underwent yet another upheaval at the beginning of this decade. The events leading up to the production of the second Griffiths report(1988), and its aftermath, have been described extensively elsewhere (Lewis and Glennerster (1996). From the point of view of mental health social work, perhaps the most significant aspect was the confusion which arose surrounding 'case management' and 'care management' (Huxley 1993, Simiç 1995, Burns 1997). The Griffiths Report was quite clear about what was required:

> At local level the role of social services authorities should be reoriented towards ensuring that the needs of individuals within the specified groups are identified, packages of care are devised and services co-ordinated; and where appropriate a specific care-manager is assigned. (Griffiths, 1988, p.10)

While Griffiths fully acknowledged that the response to identified needs would be constrained by the budget available, the emphasis was on the sequence: identify need; agree a package of care; if necessary, assign a care-manager to co-ordinate care review; re-assess and adjust if necessary. By the time the White Paper *Caring for People* (DHSS, 1989) and the policy guidance accompanying it, *Community Care in the Next Decade and Beyond* (DHSS, 1990)) had appeared, the context in which care-management was to be implemented had changed, to some extent as a result of measures to contain social security expenditure. Consequently, care-management moved from being a needs-led process to being one concerned with budgetary management. Furthermore, the introduction of the purchaser/ provider split effectively meant that social workers who were carrying out the assessment of needs were beholden to 'care-managers', essentially budget-holders who were not in contact with clients. Not unlike the bureaucratic transmutation described in Northern Ireland, post-1972, this again meant that some experienced social workers became sucked into purely administrative, accountancy roles and were lost to professional social work (Simiç (1995). Even this point assumes that care-managers in Northern Ireland are predominantly social workers. The Northern Ireland policy paper *People First* is notably coy on this point: "He or she should be the person best fitted to help the client with those problems which are predominant at the time, <u>regardless of his or her particular professional career background</u>." (DHSS(NI), (1991), p.29, author's emphasis).

Meanwhile, 'reforms' continue apace: the Health and Personal Social Services (Northern Ireland) Order, 1994 (DHSS(NI), 1994), devolved powers - including the power to appoint ASWs - have been given to the twenty-plus Northern Irish Health and Social Services Trusts. Not only does this make the maintenance of uniform practice standards more difficult, it could also contribute to a continuing dilution of professional mental health social work. Additional fragmentation may happen as a result of 'locality-sensitive purchasing' which could lead to the employment of non-professional staff. For example, from April 1996, a small number of pilot GP practices in Northern Ireland will be involved in the specific commissioning of mental health services. Experience in England suggests mental health social workers are not a significant feature of GPs' 'shopping-lists' (Sibbalb, 1993).

Conclusion

It has been argued in this chapter that mental health social work in Northern Ireland has undergone many changes in the course of the twentieth century. Practice in Northern Ireland during this period was subject to policy and legislative changes which sometimes mirrored the British experience, yet at other times represented the unique practice experiences of this part of Ireland. There have been many demands and pressures on the profession over this time-span: these include administrative changes, the pressure to recruit care-managers from professions other than social work, failed bids by community mental health nurses to take on statutory duties and the changing nature of the 'mental health industry' (Walker, 1996). Despite this, there remains an identifiable core of professional mental health social work throughout this period which has helped maintain high standards of practice. The configuration of this core as it changed in history can be debated - some would say that it should show expansion at some points, others that there has been a real reduction in professional mental health social work practice.

The main conclusion of the chapter is that, amidst these changes, a cadre of well-trained, professional, experienced approved social workers still exist in Northern Ireland. Contributions to and participation in the recent series of Social Workers in Mental Health conferences organised over the past few years jointly by Queen's University, the University of Ulster and the Social Services Inspectorate for Northern Ireland demonstrate this commitment to practice. The time has now come for ASWs to establish an association which will help them to consolidate their practice and maintain the high professional standards which some of their predecessors aspired to.

References

Booz, Allen and Hamilton (1972), *An Integrated Service: The Reorganization of the Health and Personal Social Services in Northern Ireland*(2 vols), Ministry of Health and Social Services: Belfast.

Brown, S.C. (1970), 'Looking Backwards', *British Journal of Psychiatric Social Work*, Vol. X, No. 4, pp.20-26.

Burns, T. (1997), 'Case management, care management and care programming', *British Journal of Psychiatry*, Vol.170, pp.393-395.

Caul, B. and Herron, S. (1992), *A Service for People*, December: Belfast.CCETSW (1984), *Report of the Examinations Board 1983/84*, CCETSW: London.

Child Guidance Special Interest Group (1975), *The Child Guidance Service*, BASW: Birmingham.

Courtney, M. (1992), 'Psychiatric social workers and the early days of private practice', *Social Service Review* Vol.64, No.6, pp.199-214.

DHSS (1989), *Caring for People*, HMSO:London

DHSS (1990), *Community Care in the Next Decade and Beyond,* HMSO: London.

DHSS(NI) (1981), *Review Committee on Mental Health Legislation,* HMSO: Belfast.

DHSS(NI) (1985), *Northern Ireland Review Committee on Services for the Mentally Ill,* HMSO: Belfast.

DHSS(NI) (1991), *People First,* HMSO: Belfast.

DHSS(NI) (1994), *Health and Personal Social Services (NI) Order, 1984* HMSO: Belfast.

DHSS(NI) (1994a), Annual Report for 1994, HMSO: Belfast.

DHSS (NI) (1995), *Annual Report of the Chief Inspector Social Services Inspectorate for Northern Ireland,* HMSO: Belfast.

Dunn, D. (1977), 'Looking at Mental Health Practice', *Social Work Today,* Vol.8, No. 40.

Evason, E. Darby, J. and Pearson, M. (1976), *Social need and social provision in Northern Ireland* , New University of Ulster: Coleraine.

Goodman, L. (1987), 'The Mental Health Act 1983: The Approved Social Worker', in Brenton, M. and Ungerson, C. (Eds) *Yearbook of Social Policy 1986-7,* Longman: London.

Gostin, L.O. (1977), *A Human Condition,* vol. 1, MIND: London.

Griffiths, R. (1983), *NHS Management Inquiry* DHSS: London.

Griffiths, R. (1988), *Community Care: An Agenda for Action,* HMSO: London.

Huxley, P. (1993), 'Case Management and Care Management in Community Care', *British Journal of Social Work,* Vol.23, pp.365 - 81.

Huxley, P. and Kerfoot, M. (1993), 'The Mental Health Workforce in the Community', *Health and Social Care,* Vol.1, pp. 169-74.

Lewis, J. and Glennerster, H. (1996), *Implementing the New Community Care,* Open University: Buckinghamshire.

Martin, F.M. and Rehin, G.F. (1969), 'Towards community care', *Planning,* March, p.226-244.

Mayer-Gross, W., Slater, E. and Roth, M. (1969), *Clinical Psychiatry,* Bailliere, Tindall and Cassell: London.

Prior, P. M. (1993), *Mental health and politics in Northern Ireland,* Avebury: Aldershot.

Richmond, M. (1917), *Social diagnosis,* Sage: New York.

Seebohm, F. (1968), *Report of the Committee on Local Authority and Allied Personal Social Services,* HMSO: London.

Sibbalb, B. et al. (1993), 'Counsellors in English and Welsh General Practices: their nature and distribution', *British Medical Journal,* Vol.306, pp.29-33.

Simiç, P. (1995), 'What's in a word: from social work to care 'manager', *Practice,* March, pp.5-18.

Walker, R. (1972), *Social Workers and their workloads in Northern Ireland Welfare Departments*, National Institute for Social Work Training: London.

Walker, J. (1996), 'The Mental Health Industry', *The Salisbury Review*, Autumn, pp.4-8.

Williamson, A.P. (1992), 'Psychiatry, Moral Management and the Origins of Social Policy for Mentally Ill People in Ireland', *Irish Journal of Medical Science*, Vol,161,pp.556-558.

Yelloly, M. (1980), *Social work theory and psychoanalysis*, Van Nostrand Reinhold: New York.

Younghusband, E. (1951), *Social work in Britain*, Carnegie United Kingdom Trust: Edinburgh.

Younghusband, E. (1959), *Report of the Working Party on Social Workers in the Local Authority Health and Welfare Services*, HMSO: London.

Younghusband, E. (1969), *Social Work and Social Change,*. Allen & Unwin: London.

3 Mental health policy in Northern Ireland

Pauline Prior

Introduction

The social work task changes constantly, due not only to developments in knowledge, but also to ideological shifts in the general policy environment. These shifts often go unnoticed until a new policy begins to disrupt everyday practice. In Northern Ireland, social workers have worked in an integrated health and social service structure since the early 1970s, and though there have been many changes in health policy, very few have had an immediate impact on the delivery of social services. However, the situation has changed since 1990, as there have been a number of radical developments in the way health care is viewed and delivered. These, in turn, have had far reaching effects on the ways in which social care is delivered.

Because Northern Ireland is politically part of the United Kingdom, welfare state provisions similar to those in Britain have applied here since 1948 - a comprehensive health care system free at the point of delivery, and a basic structure for the delivery of social services within local government. However, many of the later developments in the British system of health and social services did not necessarily affect Northern Ireland. The reasons include the fact that health services (and especially mental health services) in Northern Ireland had their roots in Irish legislation and policies and that political turmoil and civil unrest have affected all stages of the policy making process, resulting in a distinctive pattern of service provision. The most obvious difference is the integrated system of health and social services introduced at the same time as Direct Rule (from Westminster) in 1972. During the past ten years, however, there has been greater convergence between Northern Ireland and other areas of the United Kingdom in all spheres of public policy (Connolly and

29

Loughlin, 1990) and delays in applying recent policies (for example child care and health legislation) have been due to the fact that legislation drawn up for England and Wales had to be rewritten for Northern Ireland. Because the time between the introduction of a policy in Britain and its application to Northern Ireland is getting shorter, it is absolutely essential that social workers be alert to the wider political environment. The aim of this chapter is to identify and discuss recent developments in health policy in terms of their impact on services for people with mental illnesses in order to highlight areas of concern to users of mental health services and to social workers involved in their care.

Current trends

The establishment of the four integrated Health and Social Services Boards in Northern Ireland in October 1973 [based on the Health and Personal Social Services (NI) Order 1972] was regarded until recently as the most radical change which occurred in the delivery of health and social care since the introduction of the welfare state in 1948. However, this view can now be challenged, as the recent package of changes, resulting from the extension of the NHS reforms to Northern Ireland, may have an even greater effect on the direction and size of publicly funded mental health provision in the future. These changes include the separation of 'purchasers' from 'providers' of services, the emergence of self regulating Trusts (hospital and community), the introduction of GP fund-holding, and the ideological shift towards a model of health and social service delivery based on a 'mixed economy of care'. In Britain, the statutory basis for most of the initiatives are included in the NHS and Community Care Act 1990. This Act does not apply to Northern Ireland because of the differences in the statutory basis of services (with social services being the responsibility of Health and Social Services Boards in Northern Ireland and of local authorities in Britain). Instead, the legal basis for changes are to be found in the two Health and Personal Social Services (NI) Orders, the first in 1991 and the second in 1994. The task of establishing a legal basis for the emergence of self governing trusts in the health sector was not an easy one, but that of transferring the concept to social services was fraught with difficulty. The final version of the legislation reflects the intensive lobbying by the social work profession (through the Northern Ireland branch of its professional association, the British Association for Social Workers) and by child care organisations (under the umbrella of Child Care NI), to ensure a proper recognition of the specific statutory obligations held by social workers in relation to children and adults at risk.

Over the past two decades, policy documents from the Department of Health and Social Services [DHSS(NI)] have prioritised mental health services. The *Regional Strategy for Health and Social Services (NI) 1975-82*, sets itself eight major objectives, two of which were 'the development of community health and social care for the mentally ill' and 'the relief of overcrowding in psychiatric hospitals' [DHSS(NI), 1983, p.25]. Mental health services did not feature among the top five priority areas in the *Strategy* for the following period, although the need for the development of adolescent psychiatry and a medium secure unit for mentally ill offenders was acknowledged. However, these are two areas which continued to be neglected both in terms of research and service development, primarily because very few mental health professionals are involved in either service. In contrast, reducing hospital beds became the dominant concern of the next *Regional Strategy 1987-92*. One of the three objectives of the strategy was to bring about a shift in the balance of care from institutional care to care in the community, with a planned reduction of 20 per cent in the numbers of people in psychiatric hospitals [DHSS(NI), 1987, p. 22-4]. It also called for 'substantial changes in the utilisation of resources, primarily by a transfer of spending from hospitals to community services (and) an annual rate of re-deployment of at least one per cent of revenue spending, equivalent to about £28 million over five years '. The message was stronger in the next *Regional Strategy 1992-7*, which had mental health as one of its 'target areas of concern' and stressed the need to further reduce the number of people in psychiatric beds to 1,500 by the year 1997 - a target which has been achieved [DHSS(NI), 1991 p. 35 and p.46].

Because the term 'community care' means different things to different people, it is important to remember that its association in the 1990s with the transfer of long stay psychiatric patients from hospital to supported care in the community is relatively new. During the 1950s, the emphasis was on the provision of community based services, which were supplementary to hospital treatment, as preventive measures or as after-care services. This changed in the following decade due to the influence of the anti-psychiatry movement which alerted the public to the inherent dangers of institutionalisation, and to the strength of political rhetoric which indicated that community-based services were cheaper than hospital care. As a result, policies in Britain during the 1970s and 1980s emphasised the need to facilitate the movement of patients from hospital to community. In Northern Ireland, the pace of change was slow, though the integrated health and social services structure should have made it easier. The Review Committee, set up within the DHSS(NI) to make proposals for changes in services in line with the important White Paper *Better Services for the*

Mentally Ill (HMSO, 1975) proposed little that was new. The report, *The Way Forward*, published in 1984, called for an 'improved range of residential accommodation', closer relationships between statutory agencies to ensure effective use of work placements and between psychiatric hospital services and social services in the provision of day care, and the involvement of the voluntary sector and of volunteers in the 'promotion of mental health education and the development of preventive strategies' [DHSS(NI), 1984: par. 4.51-4.75]. The policy shift taking place in Britain had not yet begun to make an impact. During the second half of the 1980s, a number of influential policy documents were published in tandem with the imposition of new limits on public expenditure, emphasising the need to move resources from the hospital to the community sector to make community care work. These included *Making a Reality of Community Care* (Audit Commission, 1986), the Griffith's Report, *Community Care* (Griffiths, 1988), and the White Paper, *Caring for People* (HMSO, 1989). Legislation to facilitate the transfer of the responsibility for care of certain groups of people, including those with mental illnesses, from the health sector (predominantly the NHS) to social services (predominantly local councils) was necessary in Britain but not in Northern Ireland. All that was necessary was a new policy document (with special funding attached) to emphasise the need for immediate action. The philosophy of this new document, *People First*, was clear:

> It has been said that the best measure of a civilised society is how well it cares for those of its members who for whatever reason cannot live totally independently ... The government's vision of care needed in the community at large has three central principles: first, to help such people to lead, as far as possible, full and independent lives; second, to respond flexibly and sensitively to the needs and wishes of individual people and the relatives and friends who care for them; and third, to concentrate professional skills and public resources on those who need them most. [DHSS(NI), 1990:I)

In spite of the integrated health and social services structure, changes in the balance between hospital and community were not happening fast enough. A number of initiatives were proposed, including the following:

1) The strengthening of the role of Health and Social Services Boards as purchasers, co-ordinators and quality controllers relative to their well established role as providers;
2) The introduction of systematic assessment methods to ensure proper targeting of resources;

3) The full use of the independent sector in the provision of social services;

4) The extension of Income Support and Housing Benefit to all participants in community care programmes regardless of their living arrangements i.e. in independent sector nursing or residential homes as well as those in their own homes;

5) The establishment of registration and inspection units within Boards to monitor standards in statutory and non-statutory provision;

6) The improvement of planning procedures to focus more clearly on the development, monitoring and evaluation of community care services.

Here, for the first time, we see the influence of the NHS reforms on policies in Northern Ireland. Boards are no longer expected to provide all the necessary health or social care services, but rather to develop a mixed economy of care, in partnership with the 'independent' sector, which consists of voluntary, not-for-profit and private/commercial organisations. As purchasers of services, the Boards have primary responsibility for monitoring and evaluating services - quite a change in role from being the primary provider of health and social care services. This change is reflected in the strategy for 1997-2002 *Health and Well-being into the next Millennium* [DHSS(NI), 1996, pp. 90-1]. The need for the development of a framework for assessing the extent and burden of mental illness in Northern Ireland as a whole is stressed. The importance of health promotion, with media involvement, to increase understanding about mental illness, is also emphasised, as is the primacy of the community mental health team in delivering treatment, the urgency of finding alternatives to traditional psychiatric hospital environments for people who need long term care, and the need to include users and their carers in planning services.

Hospital services

Since 1825, when the first district asylum was opened at Armagh, services for mentally ill people in Northern Ireland have been dominated by hospital in-patient treatment. In 1961 the number of psychiatric beds available in the Province reached a peak of 6,486 or 4.5 per 1,000 of the population (Prior, 1993, p.78). Since 1961, in spite of the fact that admissions to hospital continued to increase, there has been a steady downward trend in the resident hospital population. Between 1965 and 1983 the number of patients resident in mental illness hospitals fell from over 5,400 to fewer 4,000, and by the mid 1990s the targets in *Regional* Strategies had been met and number of patients in psychiatric beds reduced to 1,500. The second half of the 1990s saw increasing pressures on psychiatric beds, with both consumers of the service and professionals calling for a reconsideration by the DHSS(NI) of the policy to continue reducing bed numbers.

Of course in-patient numbers are not the only measure of use of psychiatric services or indeed of the level of mental health need in society. The number of people presenting for help with mental health problems continues to increase. Over 100,000 people seen by GPs are diagnosed as having some form of mental illness. Both out-patient and day-patient numbers have grown over the past decade, with over 11,000 new referrals to out-patient clinics and 7,814 people attending day hospital in the year ending March 1994 (DHSS(NI), Information Office). Perhaps the more interesting of these statistics is the day hospital figure, which gives some idea of the continued need for a treatment-based (as opposed to a care-based) day service.

With regard to financial targets, it was envisaged by health planners throughout the United Kingdom that reduced bed usage would lead to a release of funding for community services. In Northern Ireland in the 1982/3 financial year, out of £39 million (seven per cent of the total HPSS budget) devoted to services for mentally ill people, some £26 million (almost two thirds) was spent on in-patient services in the major psychiatric hospitals. When psychiatric beds in general hospitals were added, the cost was almost £30 million, which meant that less than a quarter of the programme budget was available for other services. The *Regional Strategy 1987-92* made explicit the need to speed up the process of transferring resources from hospital to community. The target for 1992 was a growth in the proportion of HPSS revenue devoted to community services to around 30 per cent. By 1990, when the DHSS(NI) undertook its mid-term review of the *Strategy*, it was clear that shifting the balance from hospital to community was not easy. Although there had been a slight increase in the proportion of health and personal social services expenditure on community services, there had been no reduction in the proportion of expenditure on psychiatric in-patient services. This was in spite of the fact that bridging funds of £25 million had been allocated by the DHSS for schemes aimed at facilitating the discharge of long-stay patients including those with mental illnesses. In an effort to expedite progress in the development of community based services, the DHSS allocated a further £8.5 million between 1990 and 1992. These bridging funds were used to facilitate the discharge of 509 long-stay patients from psychiatric hospitals and 497 patients from mental handicap hospitals between 1987 and 1992 (Donnelly et al., 1994). Since then further funds have been made available to Boards to facilitate discharges and rehabilitation. While it is clear that long-stay patients are being discharged into the community and that money has been available to facilitate this transfer, it does not follow, however, that a reduction in psychiatric beds has led to the release of resources for community based services nor is it clear that there has been a sufficient increase in these services to meet the needs not only of the discharged long-stay patients but of the remainder of the adult population with mental health problems.

Community services

Community services for people with mental illnesses are particularly difficult to quantify. This is partly due to the inclusion (sometimes) of services for people with dementia or with a learning disability. The difficulty is compounded by the fact that, since 1990, there has been a radical shift in models of service provision. Traditionally, services were provided primarily by the statutory sector, complemented by the voluntary and private/commercial sector. Recent changes in the health care market (due to the NHS reforms) offering substantial incentives for co-operation between the statutory sector and other providers, have resulted, in the short term at least, in a greater reliance by all sectors on government funding. Current community mental health services include traditional services, such as day centres, hostels and the community psychiatric nursing and social work services, as well as the newer resource centres, multi-disciplinary teams of mental health workers, sheltered housing projects, employment projects and be-friending and advocacy schemes.

The recent evaluation of the impact of community care policies on individuals who, prior to 1987, were resident in the hospital sector, provides detailed information on the impact of this policy change on the individual (Donnelly et al., 1994). One of the most interesting findings was that although for most of the 509 people included in the study, there was little change in their life-style, in terms of daily activities, patterns of friendship and community involvement, they were generally very happy with their new lives. However, one must not ignore the somewhat worrying finding that staff in community based accommodation have been slow to engage in activities which might lead to greater independence among residents (because of the risks involved) and that patients in private nursing and residential homes (unlike those living in voluntary and statutory accommodation) made relatively little use of extra-mural and peripatetic services such as social workers and community psychiatric nurses. In other words, bridging funds may have been used in some cases to facilitate what the Americans term 'trans-institutionalisation', leading to a narrowing rather than a broadening of the individual's life experience.

In the early phase of the development of community mental health services, the focus was on the development of existing statutory services - residential care, day care, and domiciliary social work and nursing services. Residential services were based on the hostel provision which began in the 1960s. Current residential accommodation includes a much broader range of housing - from highly staffed units to sheltered housing and supported flats. In spite of policy statements on the importance of community care during the 1980s, there was very little expansion in this sector before 1990. At that time there were 270 hostel places in Northern Ireland, representing 17 per 100,000 of the population In England for the same year, the number of hostel places was 24 per 100,000, which reflected an increase of 100 per cent since 1980 (Prior, 1993, p.139). In Northern Ireland, the expansion had not yet begun, in spite of the availability of bridging funds during the late 1980s. However, since then developments have been rapid, due primarily to changes in the model of health service delivery and the injection of *People First* money (£29.4 million transferred from the Social Security budget in 1993/4). The promotion of a mixed economy of care and the separation of purchasing from providing responsibilities within the Boards have made it possible for the statutory sector to share the burden of the most expensive services (residential) with providers in the private/commercial and voluntary sectors. A number of voluntary organisations such as Praxis, NSF (National Schizophrenia Fellowship) and NIAMH (Northern Ireland Association for Mental Health) are now involved in providing or managing housing schemes which offer homes for life to former long-stay patients and to new clients with chronic mental illness. By the mid 1990s for example, the Northern Ireland Association for Mental Health had 20 schemes for 120 residents throughout Northern Ireland. Because of the diversity of providers and different methods of categorising projects, a total figure for residential care places for Northern Ireland is not currently available. However, information from the Western Health and Social Services Board can be presented as a good example of the rapid development which took place during the 1990s in all areas of mental health care. Community residential places increased from 66 (9 schemes) in 1990 to 180 (14 schemes) in 1993, with plans for a further five schemes before the end of the decade.

Mental health resource centres throughout the Province have developed from existing statutory day care services. In 1990, with the exception of three day centres in Belfast specifically designated for mental health, Tamar Street, Ravenhill and Whiterock, all statutory day centres were for mixed client groups. Seven years earlier it was estimated that 697 (or 14 per cent) of all those attending day centres were there because of mental illness (NIAMH, 1984:23). This was the equivalent of approximately 50 places per 100,000 of the population, a figure well below the norm (60 per 100,000 population) set in *Better Services for the Mentally Ill* (HMSO, 1975). By 1993 policies had changed and Boards were under pressure to show that they were providing community services. DHSS (NI) statistics for the year ending March 1993 showed 1,115 people with mental health problems attending statutory day care facilities (including adult centres and workshops), indicating a ratio of 70 places per 100,000 of the population. However, this may be a misleading statistic as some people with learning disability were included. In the Western Board, which presents a more accurate picture of mental health services, statutory day care places, including work therapy programmes managed in co-operation with ITO (Industrial Therapy Organisation), NSF (National Schizophrenia Fellowship) and NIAMH (Northern Ireland Association for Mental Health), increased from 336 in 1990 to 579 in 1993.

A note of caution is needed in evaluating day care provision as it is not always appropriate for individual needs. Traditionally, day centres have catered for a predominantly elderly population. Existing services, therefore, are not always suitable for young adults with mental health problems or indeed for the very different needs of older people with dementia and those with chronic mental illness. Designating a former statutory day centre as a mental health resource centre can mask rather than solve the problem. Neither does the expansion of traditional day care provided by voluntary organisations guarantee the desired outcome. The two largest voluntary organisations providing traditional though quite different day care are the NIAMH and ITO. In 1993, NIAMH had 30 local branches, of which 14 were staffed Beacon Centres with organised programmes for over 1,100 members. In 1994, ITO provided day care with an emphasis on work as therapy for 600 clients in seven centres. ITO, which relies for only one quarter of its funding from government health budgets, makes a valuable contribution to the process of integrating patients into the world of work. However, one of the difficulties inherent in both types of provision is the fact that even a large voluntary organisation often cannot provide the infrastructure of professional support necessary for a comprehensive day care service.

The importance of continuing to build this infrastructure of professional care and treatment is undisputed, and perhaps one of the most dramatic changes in statutory community services is in the availability of full multi-disciplinary community mental health teams (CMHTs) based in designated mental health resource centres. This has been due mainly to the re-allocation of existing medical, psychology and social work staff to locality based teams and to an increase in the number of community psychiatric nurses (CPNs) in Northern Ireland, from 60 in 1990 to 110 in 1993 [DHSS(NI), Information Office].

Current issues

As we approach the end of the twentieth century, the issues of concern to people with mental health problems are still largely connected to the care versus control debate and are often couched in the language of rights and citizenship. The following is a summary of some of these.

A right to care and treatment

One hundred years ago, mental health legislation was necessary to ensure that individuals were not unnecessarily treated, particularly being confined to a mental hospital with the consequent loss of civil rights. As over 90 per cent of current psychiatric patients in Northern Ireland are under no legal jurisdiction, but rather seek treatment and care voluntarily as they do any other health service, the situation is quite different. The government is not under the same legal obligation to provide services for those who are 'voluntary' as opposed to 'compulsory' patients. In the context of a shrinking statutory sector in health service provision in general, and the run-down of psychiatric beds in particular, many users of services express their fear of being unable to access treatment at times of crisis. The fear is also articulated by carers of individuals with mental health problems, who feel tricked by community care policies, which do little except move the burden of care back onto family members.

A right to an adequate income

Research has shown a significant link between poverty and mental illness. Whether poverty precipitates mental illness or vice versa, the outcome is the same - an extra burden of stress due to lack of money. In a context of increasing unemployment during the past two decades, people with mental health problems are less likely to be attractive to employers. It is to be hoped that the latest disability legislation, the *Disability Discrimination Act 1995*, will make a difference by increasing employment opportunities for everyone with a disability of any kind. However, this will only happen if advocacy services are offered to vulnerable individuals who wish to challenge employers acting in a discriminatory manner. But, even if some people manage to secure employment, many rely on the benefit system for an adequate income. Research by Hirst and Sainsbury (1996) has shown the particular difficulties experienced by people with mental health problems in their encounters with the social security system, in particular at times of transition such as moving in or out of employment or in or out of hospital. Recent changes in the benefit system have increased these difficulties. The replacement of the Invalidity Benefit by the Incapacity

38

Benefit, with its much narrower criteria for eligibility, has already increased anxiety and caused extra hardship among claimants with mental health problems. The social security system makes little allowance for the particular problems associated with mental illness, but there are positive signs that this may change in the future under the Labour Government.

A right to safety and protection

This issue is expressed quite differently by those experiencing mental health problems, their carers and the public at large. The former feel the need for protection from a society which is increasingly intolerant and discriminatory towards people who are different from the mainstream. The latter, frightened by media coverage of murders by 'psychiatric' patients, demand a reduction in risk taking by professionals. Some of the solutions under consideration are for supervision orders (which will take away the right of the patient to refuse medication), for risk registers (with names of any person who might present any danger to the public), and for more secure units (for offenders with psychiatric histories). In Northern Ireland, the public have been scared by the murder of a seven year old boy by a man who had just been discharged from a psychiatric hospital and by the flame-throwing incident in a high school, by a man with a known psychiatric history. Although the psychiatric services have been exempted from any responsibility for these incidents, the public is not convinced. Perhaps the planned opening of a medium secure unit in Northern Ireland for offenders with mental illnesses will allay the fear, though it may not necessarily decrease the risk of another tragedy occurring. There will always be tension between the rights of the individual to freedom of movement and the obligation on the state to protect the public from known risks.

Conclusion: current concerns for social work practitioners

Policy changes affecting the law or service delivery have a direct impact on social work practice. If, as is envisaged by those close to policy makers, there is a move to legislate for compulsory powers to oblige people to take medication or to attend out-patient centres, it is likely that social workers (ASWs) will be asked to take part in the proceedings serving to reinforce the view that the social control function is beginning to outweigh that of care. If the trend towards a further reduction in hospital beds continues, the pressure on social workers to find suitable community placements will increase. Without a greater financial commitment by government to community based services this will undoubtedly mean increasing marginalisation for people who are already poor and vulnerable. Though there is no documented increase in mentally ill people among the homeless or the prison population in Northern Ireland during the past twenty years, it is only a matter of time before this appears. In the USA, for example, the combination of decarceration policies in the 1960s and 1970s, and the easing of the barriers to 'involuntary' hospital admission in the 1980s, has led to a decrease in the number of 'voluntary' patients in the public mental health care system, and the appearance of psychiatric ghettos, as former hotels become home for psychiatric patients with no family to return to. In Northern Ireland, none of the six large mental hospitals (built in the nineteenth century) have closed, although most are no longer fully operational as treatment centres, but this also is only a matter of time. The provision of alternative accommodation for discharged patients has shown that there is nothing cheap about community care, but the question of where the financial burden will fall has not adequately been answered. Social workers often find themselves in the position of broker between the patient or carer and the service provider. In the face of dwindling resources, there are bound to be difficult decisions.

The restructuring of health and social services, which has led to the establishment of hospital and community trusts and to the development of an integrated programme approach (to client groups) means that many social workers specialising in mental health find themselves on multidisciplinary teams with a manager from a different professional value base - often nursing. This sometimes leads to a serious reconsideration of the role and value base of social work as decisions about individual clients are debated. Social work which prides itself on being on the side of the consumer, of being committed to empowering the client and carer, and of striving to ensure the least restrictive treatment plan for the individual with mental health problems, can now find itself isolated and dominated by other value systems. Some experienced workers, who have developed skills in confidently presenting what is often a different perspective on the client's situation to that of medicine and nursing, can cope well in these circumstances. Others, particularly newly trained workers, find it very difficult. It is essential for the future development of community based mental health services that social workers remain convinced of the importance of their contribution in ensuring that policies in the future enhance the opportunities available for both users and carers within the mental health care system.

References

Audit Commission (1986), *Making a Reality of Community Care*, A report of the Audit Commission for Local Authorities (England and Wales), HMSO: London.

DHSS(NI) (1983), *Regional Strategic Plan for Health and Social Services in Northern Ireland 1983-87*, DHSS: Belfast.

DHSS(NI) (1984), *Mental Health - The Way Forward: Report of the Review Committee on Services for the Mentally Ill in Northern Ireland*, DHSS: Belfast.

DHSS(NI) (1987), *Health and Personal Social Services: A Regional Strategy for Northern Ireland 1987-92*, DHSS: Belfast.

DHSS(NI), 1990 *People First: Community Care in Northern Ireland for the 1990s*, DHSS: Belfast.

DHSS(NI) (1991), *Health and Personal Social Services: A Regional Strategy for Northern Ireland 1992-7*, DHSS: Belfast.

DHSS(NI) (1997), *Health and Well-being into the next Millennium: Regional Strategy for Health and Social Well-being 1997-2002*, DHSS: Belfast.

Donnelly M. Mc Gilloway S. Mays N. Perry S. Knapp M. Kavanagh S. Beecham J. Fenyo A. Astin J. (1994), *Opening new doors: An evaluation of community care for people discharged from psychiatric and mental handicap hospitals*, HMSO: London.

Enthoven, A. (1985), *Reflections on the management of the National Health Service*, Nuffield Provincial Hospitals Trust.

Griffiths, Sir Roy (1988), *Community Care - Agenda for Action*, HMSO: London.

HMSO (1975), *Better Services for the Mentally Ill*, White Paper, Cmnd. 6233, London: HMSO.

HMSO (1989), *Caring for People*, White Paper, Cm. 849, HMSO: London.

Hirst, M. and Sainsbury, R. (1996) *Social Security and Mental Health: the impact of Disability Living Allowance*, Social Policy Research Unit: University of York.

NIAMH (1984), *Mental Health Statistics for Northern Ireland*, Northern Ireland Association for Mental Health: Belfast.

Prior, P.M. (1993), *Mental Health and Politics in Northern Ireland*, Avebury: Aldershot.

4 Mental health policy in the Republic of Ireland: backwards into the future

Fred Powell

Introduction

Foucault (1967, p.58) has asserted that in early modern society the "community acquired an ethical power of segregation, which permitted it to eject, as into another world, all forms of uselessness". The impotent poor, which included syphilitic and orphan children, the sick, aged and infirm as well as the insane, were excluded from the society through a policy of confinement. The social significance of confinement has been identified by Foucault. He asserted, in reference to the recipients of this form of treatment, "between him and society an implicit system of obligation was established: he had the right to be fed, but he must accept the physical and moral constraint of confinement" (Foucault, 1967, p 48).

The inter-dependent themes of segregation and confinement have been taken up by subsequent social control theorists. Doerner (1981, p.163) has referred to "the European wave of the sequestration of the poor". Scull (1979, p 27) has observed in this context "pressures developed to differentiate and institutionalise the deviant population". Furthermore, he has asserted that "clearly, the adoption of an institutional response to all sorts of problem populations greatly increased the pressures to elaborate the distinctions amongst the deviant and dependent (Scull, 1979, p.41). In this chapter, the development of mental health policy in Ireland will be reviewed from the perspective of social control theory. The argument will be that while styles and practices of social control may have changed, the implementation of policy has been guided by exclusionary social practices in modern society, whether through institutional confinement or care in the community.

Table 4.1
Changes in mental health policy

	Phase One (19th C)	Phase Two (mid 19th C - mid 20thC)	Phase Three (mid 20thC-present)
1. State Role	largely non-existent, mainly private provision of goals	dominant, in large public institutions - asylums/ hospitals	main provider of community care - out-patient clinics, day hospitals, hostels, primary care
2. Treatment Mode	non-existent	medicalization and segregative; social control through institutional confinement	deinstitution-alisation and further medicalization through use of psychotropic drugs to control behaviour in the community.
3. Categor-isation & classification of problem population	underdeveloped	established and imposed	deinstitution-alisation maintained and developed.
4. Professional Role	non-existent	established	maintained and refined, despite ideological attack from anti-psychiatry movement.
5. Exclusionary Practice	domestic confinement or abandonment by family.	segregation and confinement in asylums/ hospitals	despite ideological policy emphasis on inclusion, neglect and ghettoization due to decline in provision

Population and bio-politics

Foucault has argued that the State experienced a further significant accretion of power during the eighteenth century which devolved on the regulation of the health of the population. He attributed this development to "the great eighteenth century demographic upswing in Western Europe" which stimulated a technological pre-occupation with the management and measurement of population (Foucault, 1980, p.171).

Bio-politics constitutes the population as a field of (State and non-State) regulation through the collection of statistics and census taking, coupled with the strategic management of the health, hygiene and welfare of the population. Foucault (1979, pp.142-3) regarded this twin policy of constituting population a source of knowledge and a focus of government as marking the crossing of "the threshold of modernity in the West and the beginning of an era of governmentality". He further noted that State intervention into the management of population can be best understood as the "govermentalisation" of the State.

Knowledge of the incidence of disease had begun to be accumulated on an increasingly systematic basis. The individual commentaries of medical practitioners, which found resonance in a wider public discourse, had become the concern of Government in the early nineteenth century. Inherent in this process was the emergence of medicine as a science and the doctor as an expert. The expertise of the doctor was not, however, confined to physiological matters. The doctor also emerged as a pioneer of sociological method carefully recording details germane to the health of the population. This was not a world characterised by compassionate concern but an empirical one in which society was confronted with the facts of its own biology. In this new reality the inter-dependence of the health of the rich and poor was unmasked. Consequently, the move towards systematically documenting and classifying disease in the population coupled with the location of its aetiology in the problem of popular hygiene led to important administrative developments devolving on the family and urban communities.

Foucault has observed that the new climate of awareness of hygiene and disease led to the entry of the temporal powers into the previously sacred domain of charity. As he put it, "the new noso-politics inscribes the specific question of the sickness of the poor within the general problem of the health of populations, and makes the shift from the narrow context of charitable aid to the more general problem of 'medical police', imposing its constraints and dispensing its services" (Foucault, 1980, p.171).

At first sight, it may seem ironic that a preoccupation with the augmentation of the wealth and power of the State through the fostering of population growth should form the backdrop to the inauguration of public provision. But this apparent paradox becomes more understandable in terms of the growth of a secular morality based on the work ethic. The advocates of a statutory system of health provision were not primarily inspired by religious sentiment or humanitarian motives but by scientific knowledge about the health of the population which was in their view the basic source of its wealth.

The axis of the system of family and community based health services, which emerged in 1805, was the dispensary. According to Foucault (1980, p.178) the "aim of the dispensary system in Europe was to retain the technical advantages of hospitalisation without its medical and economic drawbacks". These drawbacks, which included the spread of contagion and cost of hospitalisation, help to explain the prodigious growth of the dispensary system throughout early nineteenth century Ireland. By 1833 there were 452 dispensaries in Ireland: 151 in Leinster; 132 in Munster; 121 in Ulster; and 50 in Connaught. Phelan (1835, p145) estimated in 1835 that "the number of whom relief is annually afforded by dispensaries alone, is probably not less than 1,376,000 annually".

Despite these provincial variations, the inauguration of the dispensary system palpably extended the State's regulation of health to encompass much of the population. This was a major development in social control terms. Through the family doctor appointed to each district, the State introduced "medical police" into the lives of a large number of poor families in many communities throughout Ireland. Donzelot (1980, p.18) has averred that "this organic link between doctor and family was to have profound repercussions on family life". He argued that the provision of community based health care for the poor was part of a wider normalisation process which enticed the family into co-operation with the State through the provision of a form of out-door relief. Inherent in this policy was an attempt to promote new social and economic attitudes including the value of hygiene (Donzelot, 1980, pp.88-90). The doctor was an indispensable part of the process. Foucault (1980, p.76) has commented in this regard that doctors "have the task of teaching individuals the basic rules of hygiene which they must respect for the sake of their own health and that of others: hygiene of food and habitat, exhortations to seek treatment in case of illness". The dispensary consequently had a pivotal function in the political economy of the developing system of health provision.

Public health and state control

The emergence of the dispensary system was paralleled by the appearance of public health services through the inauguration of Boards and Officers of Health. Boards of Health were instituted in 1818. Their powers were defined in terms of the prevention of communicable diseases, the promotion of improved sanitary conditions, and the identification of houses infected by fever. Officers of Health were instituted in the following year. The Officers of Health were required to keep the streets "cleansed and purified" and to oversee "the ventilation, fumigation and cleansing of any house whatever, in which fever or other contagious distempers shall have occurred, and for washing and purifying the persons and clothes of the inhabitants of every such house" (59th George III C.41, 1819).

The existence of Boards and Officers of Health normally appears to have been temporary in nature. A notable example was the Cholera epidemic in 1832 when the *Dublin Evening Post* on 21 April, 1832 was led to comment "the Board of Health appears to have done its duty with vigour and effect". The use of the singular is worthy of note. It appears that there was one central board located at Dublin Castle called the Central Board of Health for Ireland. It produced daily reports on the spread of cholera throughout the country in 1832 which were reproduced in the newspapers.

The development of embryonic public health services represented an attempt to interpose the State's authority into the regulation of the urban environment even if at first only in times of crises. As Foucault (1980, p.175) put it: "the city with its principal spatial variables appears as a medicalization object". In other words, the congestion of population in urban centres which was an inevitable outcome of population growth, made urban space a principal focus for hygiene.

Inglis, during his tour of Ireland in 1834, commented on the phenomenon of urban growth. He exclaimed:

> several of the first queries refer to the increase of towns in size and population, and to those queries, it may be answered, that almost all the seaports, and all the towns commanding a navigation are advancing in size and population rapidly; and that even the towns deficient in those advantages are not in general retrograding" (Inglis, 1835, p.312).

At the centre of this process of urbanisation stood Dublin with an estimated population of 170,000 in 1798 which had risen to 232,000 by the year 1842. McDowell has neatly encapsulated the remarkable importance of eighteenth century Dublin. He declared "Prominent amongst Irish cities, being about trice the size of Cork and eight times as large as Belfast,

Dublin was undoubtedly the second city of the British Isles, having twice the population of its nearest rivals, Edinburgh and Manchester" (McDowell, 1979, p20).

Inglis (1835, p.315) was also led to comment on the related phenomenon of the growth of a large problem population of outcasts in the towns and cities of Ireland:

> In all the large towns, the number of helpless and diseased paupers, and of aged and infirm women, and destitute children, is fearfully great. They are supported by voluntary alms, - by mendicancy - and by public societies; but they are supported just on the verge of starvation; and it is the opinion of the medical men of Limerick, Waterford and other large towns, that at least seventy-five per cent of the infirm poor die through destitution, either by the gradual wasting of nature, or by the ravages of epidemics, to which destitution renders them liable".

It was the danger posed by this problem population of outcasts which led to the development of an institutional segregative system of social control for victims of fevers and contagious diseases, the elderly and orphan and syphilitic children. In the normative language of the time these groups were regarded as the 'deserving' poor, as opposed to the unemployed and vagrant population who were regarded as the 'undeserving' poor.
Scull (1993, pp.34-5) has observed in this regard:

> The notion of an institutional response to problem populations can be traced to the underlying structural transformations of their society. But what were the sources of the increasing tendency, not only to institutionalise the deviant but also to depart from the traditional practice of treating the indigent, troublesome, and morally disreputable as part of a single amorphous mass? More specifically, given my present concerns, how and why did insanity come to be differentiated from the previously inchoate mass of deviant behaviours, so that it was seen as a distinct problem requiring specialised treatment in an institution of its own, the asylum?

Undoubtedly, as Scull (1993, p.35) recognises, it was the new rationality of the market economy that sought to differentiate between the economically useful able-bodied poor and the socially and economically useless, who were to be excluded through a policy of institutionalisation.

Madness and confinement

The movement towards the segregation of the victims of physical diseases was paralleled by the development of facilities for "lunatics and idiots". The treatment of the insane had been a major focus for the attentions of social control theorists. In 1967, the publication of Foucault's *Madness and Civilisation* laid the ground work for subsequent scholars. In this study, he argued that the insane were the archetypal outcasts asserting, "to inhabit the reaches long since abandoned by the lepers, they chose a group that to our eyes is strangely mixed and confused" (Foucault, 1967, p.45). The import of Foucault's argument was that madness in the Age of Reason came to be perceived as a fundamental social threat requiring the erection of a barrier between the insane and the rest of humanity.

Foucault's work has been developed by other scholars. Doerner's European study *Madmen & The Bourgeoisie,* published in 1981, concentrated on the development of psychiatry in the context of "the sequestration of unreason". Scull (1979, p.30) in a study of the emergence of public asylums in England during the nineteenth century, has emphasised the importance of the transition to capitalism which led to the "ever more thorough-going commercialisation of existence". Whereas Ireland, unlike England, did not experience an industrial revolution during this period, the major impetus towards the confinement of the insane coincided with a transition to consolidated capitalist farming in the Irish economy.

The historiography of the treatment of insanity in Ireland has been the subject of a study by Finnane (1981, p.21) in which he has concluded that "specialised confinement of any sort for the insane was scarce in eighteenth century Ireland". The evidence suggests that the insane poor in early-modern Ireland experienced a harsh fate. A witness reported to the *Select Committee on the Lunatic Poor in Ireland* 1817, p.23:

> There is nothing so shocking as madness in the cabin of the peasant, where the man is labouring in the fields for his bread, and the care of the woman of the house is scarcely sufficient for attendance on her children. When a strong young man gets the complaint, the only way they have to manage is by making a hole in the floor of the cabin, not high enough for the person to stand up in, with a crib over it to prevent his getting up. The hole is about four feet deep, and they give the wretched being his food there and there he generally dies. Of all the human calamities I know of none equal to this in the country parts of Ireland I am acquainted with.

Those who were abandoned by their kinsfolk to fate lived a life that was scarcely better according to the *Report of the Select Committee on the State of the Poor* (1830, p.28) which recorded that "wandering lunatics were dispersed over the country in the most disgusting and wretched state".

Some of the lunatic poor were confined in houses of industry, gaols and infirmaries. As late as 1834, Phelan (1835, p.233) calculated that there were 476 "lunatics" in the Dublin House of Industry, 323 in the Cork House of Industry, 52 in the Tipperary (Clonmel) House of Industry, 116 in the Waterford House of Industry, 47 in the Wexford House of Industry, and 67 in the Limerick House of Industry. In addition, there were 105 lunatics incarcerated in gaols in 1837 around Ireland (Report of Inspector of Gaols, 1837, p.11).

The only evidence of voluntary provision which Finnane (1981, p.21) was able to detect in Ireland prior to 1838 were Swift's Hospital, St. Patrick's, established in Dublin in 1857 with 150 inmates, and a private institution in Cork in 1799. In fact, there were three other private asylums in Dublin, namely: Bloomfield, Hampstead and Finglas. Furthermore, there was a private asylum at Armagh called "The Retreat". In addition, Finnane (1981, p.26) noted that there were two "successful" public asylums in Dublin and Cork.

Private asylums were important because they pioneered the moral treatment approach, associated with Tuke's Retreat opened at York in 1792 and the appointment of Pinel as head of the Bicêtre at Paris in 1793. Moral treatment has been attributed with more "humane" attitudes towards the insane "aiming at minimising external physical coercion" (Scull, 1979, p.68). The Retreat at Armagh evoked Tuke's more illustrious institution at York. The most prominent Irish advocate of moral treatment, Dr. William Saunders Hallaran, founded the Cork private asylum (Robins, 1986, p.57). But Foucault had denigrated the reformism of the moral treatment movement. In reference to Tuke's new, reformed asylum at York, which symbolised Quaker benevolence, Foucault (1967, p.244) remarked that "the religious and moral milieu was imposed from without in such a way that madness was controlled, not cured". With equal force, he dismissed Pinel's asylum as "an instrument of moral uniformity and of social denunciation" (Foucault, 1967, p.259). In Foucault's judgement, the transformation in the lives of the insane attributed to the moral treatment movement represented "a gigantic moral imprisonment which we are in the habit of calling, doubtless by antiphrasis, the liberation of the insane by Tuke and Pinel". He averred that "our philanthropy prefers to recognise the signs of benevolence towards sickness where there is only a condemnation of idleness" (Foucault, 1967, p.46).

The presence of private asylums in Ireland during the period under investigation is important because the private market provided the model and legitimacy for the establishment of public asylums (Doerner, 1981, p.27, Scull, 1979, p.25). Finnane has argued that the development of public asylums in Ireland was strongly influenced by English example, where the market economy was more developed. But this was an indirect influence. The evidence indicates that Ireland had her own tradition of private asylums to legitimate and inspire the statutory system. Furthermore, in the mid 1830s the *Royal Commission on the State of the Poorer Classes in Ireland* (1835, p.31) cited French experience as a direct influence on the Irish system noting that the Belfast District Lunatic Asylum modelled its regime for incurables directly on the Bicêtre of Paris.

The first detailed Irish examination of the condition of the insane poor was undertaken by the *Select Committee on the Lunatic Poor in Ireland, 1817* which favoured the expansion of public asylums. Finnane (1981, p.27) has observed that "two of the most forceful arguments for a system of lunatic asylums turned on the crucial issue of separation and classification". First, Finnane (1981, pp.27-8) noted that "the presence of lunatics hindered the classification principles in gaols, was disruptive in workhouses and retarded the treatment of the physically ill in infirmaries". Second, Finnane (1981, p.28) stated that "in addition to the lunatics already confined, there were considerable numbers of insane who required suitable control". In addition, Finnane (1981, p.29) observed that "lunatic asylums were accepted as a legitimate provision for relief of the poor with a degree of consensus which contrasts sharply with the controversy over the establishment of the Irish poor law". Furthermore, Finnane (1981, p.27) observed that moral treatment" readily won approval from the Irish committee of 1817".

The 1817 Select Committee's recommendations were quickly passed through Parliament initially by a Statute in 1817. However, the major Statute responsible for the establishment of a system of district lunatic asylums was enacted in 1821. It was amended by a number of subsequent measures in 1825 and 1826. By 1835 nine "district lunatic asylums" had been established in Ireland: Armagh (1825); Limerick (1827); Belfast (1829); Londonderry (1829); Carlow (1831); Maryborough (1833); Connaught (1833); Waterford (1835) and Clonmel (1835). Connaught was proportionately under-resourced. Its district lunatic asylum had 150 beds for a population of 1,343,914, compared with Waterford which had 100 beds for a population of 177,054. The median figure for beds in Irish "district lunatic asylums" in 1835 (excluding Cork) was 104. Phelan (1835, p.233) calculated that there were 1175 inmates in the "district lunatic asylums" (including Cork) in 1834. A transformation in the treatment of the "lunatic" poor had demonstrably begun. Whether this change can be regarded as a progressive social reform has been seriously questioned by Foucault's penetrating critique. But in terms of classification and segregative control an important development had occurred. It was to become the paradigm for the treatment of mental disorder for the next century until it began to be challenged by a new paradigm "community care" in the second half of the twentieth century.

Community care and social exclusion

The standard account favoured by the medical profession of the transformation of mental health policy in post-war society is that the discovery of psychotropic drugs made the institutionalisation of the mentally disordered redundant. Social reformers, on the other hand, point to a more progressive social environment in which the mass institutionalisation of the mentally disordered became unacceptable. Both of these perspectives have been challenged by social control theorists, who view the emergence of community care as simply a new style in the exclusionary practices that have guided mental health policy in the modern world. This critique informs a movement known as the "anti psychiatry" school. While its critique has been powerful it has failed to alter the fundamental of mental health policy which remains firmly under the tutelage of the medical profession. While the anti-psychiatry movement is associated with psychiatrists, notably Ronald Laing and Thomas Szasz, who offered a penetrating critique from inside during the 1960s and 1970s, academics influenced by structuralist discourse analysis have developed this ideation into an important intellectual perspective within a much deeper social and cultural resonance.

Scull (1984) in his important study *Decarceration* has provided a penetrative critique of community care. First, he challenged the claim that the introduction of psychotropic drugs has facilitated the development of community care. These drugs did not begin to be used until the mid-1950s. Community care initiatives were already under way. However, as Scull (1984, p.81) observes

> Not surprisingly, in the circumstances (and given the coincidence in the timing and introduction of thorazine and the reversal of the upward trend in the number of mental patients), an explanation of a policy of early release and the consequent decline in mental hospital population, which has enjoyed considerable popularity in some psychiatric and official circles, simply attributes the transformation to the growing use and effectiveness of psychoactive drugs.

Scull (1984, p.85) also cast doubt on the effectiveness of psychotropic drugs "after all, even those who most strenuously defend the idea that drugs are responsible for the current policy of deinstitutionalization do not contend that phenothiazines *cure* their patients - merely that they provide a measure of symptomatic relief". Scull's conclusion is that the policy of deinstitutionalization that led to community care is not guided by a progressive agenda. Rather, Scull (1984, pp.152-3) concluded that it was simply a development from institutional repression to community neglect:

> In the circumstances, it is scarcely surprising to learn that decarceration in practice has displayed remarkably little resemblance to liberal rhetoric on the subject ..... Clearly a certain proportion of the released inmates are able to blend unobtrusively back into the communities from whence they came. After all, many of those subjected to processing by the official agencies of social control have all along been scarcely distinguishable from their neighbours who were left alone, and presumably they can be expelled from institutions without appreciable additional risk. But for many other ex-inmates and potential inmates, the alternative to the institution has been to be herded into newly emerging "deviant ghettos", sewers of human misery and what is conventionally defined as social pathology within which (largely hidden from outside inspection or even notice) society's refuse may be repressively tolerated. Many become lost in the interstices of social life, and turn into drifting inhabitants of those traditional resorts of the down and out, Salvation Army hostels, settlement houses, and so on. Others are grist for new, privately-run, profit-orientated mills for the disposal of the unwanted - old age homes, halfway houses, and the like. And yet more exist by preying on the less agile and wary, whether these be 'ordinary' people trapped by poverty and circumstance in the inner city, or their fellow decarcerated deviants.

Busfield (1986, pp.328-9) views Scull's analysis as too reductionist and overly influenced by "the Marxist-functionalist approach he adopts" which she argues is "defective on grounds of timing". In Busfield's (1986, p.352) view a two tier mental health service emerged with a well funded "upper tier" consisting of an acute care system directed towards younger adults, women and the middle classes and a "lower tier", in which the patients are likely to be older, male and working class. In reality, the views of Scull and Busfield would seem not be mutually exclusive. Busfield has simply elaborated and refined Scull's critique suggesting a class and gender bias in the administration of mental health policy.

The development of mental health policy in Ireland during the second half of the twentieth century lends credence to Scull's critique. Community care predates the introduction of psychotropic drugs. It was anticipated by section 24 of the Mental Treatment Act 1945, which provided for an alternative to hospitalisation. The 1949 Report of the Inspector of Mental Hospitals recommended the development of out-patient clinics, sixty of which had been established in general hospitals or dispensaries by 1950 (Leane and Powell, 1991, p.11).

In 1984 a seminal report on the psychiatric services in Ireland was published entitled *Planning for the Future*. This report set out its philosophical orientation clearly in the community care mould, identifying institutionalisation as the problem:

> The range of facilities in a comprehensive psychiatric service should be developed to serve the needs of a particular community. The services should be located in the community so that they are close to where people live and work. This kind of service will provide an alternative to the centralised and largely institutional services now in existence which were planned at a time when modern treatment methods were not available. (Planning for the Future, 1984, xii).

This rhetoric would appear at first sight to be reformist in orientation. In fact as Butler (1987, p.50) has pointed out in relation to the strategic approach informing *Planning for Future* 'this view of the planning task is similar to that of the planners of the network of district lunatic asylums in the nineteenth century'. Butler (1987, p.48) attributes this continuity of thought to the overweening influence of the medical profession:

> *Planning for the Future* is above all a medical report; that is based on an implicit asumption that the planning of the psychiatric services is merely a matter of assessing the prevalence of mental illness and establishing the structures which best facilitate the delivery of modern scientific treatment methods . . . It is assumed that all these fundamental points have long been settled and that such change as is proposed is merely building and developing from a solid base. Thus a wide range of policy options are not considered, nor are the consequences of these policies which are proposed.

There have been further attempts at reform during the 1990s. A Green Paper on Mental Health was published in 1992. It was followed by a White Paper in 1995 that foreshadowed 'A New Mental Health Act'. But there is little in the proposed legislation that is new. Mental Health remains firmly under the control of the doctors.

Conclusion

In abandoning the task of planning for the future of mental health policy to the doctors, we have allowed them to negotiate on our behalf. We have also empowered the medical profession to attach social meanings to particular forms of behaviour that serves to exclude vulnerable sections of the community. In essence the medicalisation of mental health policy has empowered the doctors to disempower some of the most vulnerable members of society in a moral enterprise that has created the most amoral of consequences in the name of science. The late Peter Sedgewick (1972, p.220) in a sardonic comment on community psychiatry observed 'the future belongs to illness'. The underlying rationale of *Planning for the Future* is 'backwards into the future' - a future in which the social exclusion that has defined the treatment of the mentally disordered throughout the modern era is ensured.

References

Busfield, J.(1986), *Managing Madness,* Unwin Hyman: London.

Butler, S.(1987), 'The psychiatric services: a critique', *Administration,* 35(1).

Cohen, S.(1985), *Visions of Social Control,* Polity: Oxford.

Doerner , K.(1981), *Madmen and the Bourgeoisie,* Blackwell: Oxford.

DOH, (1992), *Mental Health,* GSO: Dublin.

DOH (1995) *A New Mental Health Act,* GSO: Dublin.

Donzelot, J.(1980), *The Policing of Families,* Hutchinson: London.

Foucault, M.(1967), *Madness and Civilisation,* Tavistock: London.

Foucault, M.(1979), *History of Sexuality,* Tavistock: London.

Foucault, M.(1980), *Power/ Knowledge,* Harvester: Sussex.

Inglis, H.(1836), *A Journey through Ireland ,*. London, Vol 11.

Leane, M. & Powell, F.(1991), *Towards Independence: Longstay Psychiatric Patients Returned to Community Living,* SPRU: Cork.

McDowell, R.(1979), *Ireland in the Age of Imperialism and Revolution,* Clarendon: Oxford.

Phelan, D.(1835), *Statistical Inquiry into the Present State of Medical Charities in Ireland,* Dublin.

Report of the Select Committee on the State of the Lunatic Poor in Ireland 1817,viii.

Report of the Select Committee on the State of the Poor in Ireland, 1830.

Report of the Royal Commission for Inquiry into the Condition of the Poorer Classes in Ireland, 1835, xxxii.

Report of the Inspector of Gaols, 1835, xxxi.

Robins, J.(1986), *Fools and Mad: A History of the Insane in Ireland*, Institute of Public Administration: Dublin.

Scull, A. (1979), *Museums of Madness*, Allen Lance: London.

Scull, A. (1984), *Decarceration*, Rutgers University Press: New Brunswick.

Sedgwick, P. (1972), Mental illness is illness, *Salmagundi*, 20.

5 Mental health social work and the law in Northern Ireland

Jim Campbell

Introduction

In this chapter the relationship between the mental health social worker and the law is examined, with a particular focus on the responsibilities of the Approved Social Worker (ASW). In the first part of the chapter the origins and development of the role of the ASW is examined critically, using literature which has emerged in Britain and Northern Ireland. This will allow for a comparison of ASW function and practice between these jurisdictions as well as providing a backdrop for the debate about Authorised Officers in the Republic of Ireland.

The second part of the chapter raises key issues in contemporary mental policy - deinstitutionalisation, community care and managing risk in the community - which influence mental health social work practice in the 1990s. In conclusion it is argued that mental health social workers must find new ways of refining their knowledge and skills base if they are to preserve the legal and professional status gained through the legislation of the 1980s.

The creation of the ASW

It is now over a decade since the ASW was created, first in Britain within the Mental Health Act (DHSS, 1983) and later in Northern Ireland, the Mental Health Order (DHSS(NI), 1986). When the statutory role and function of the ASW was defined by the 1983 Act, much was expected of this new type of mental health social worker. A contrast can be made between the relatively powerful role of the ASW and the marginalised position of the Mental Welfare Officer (MWO) which existed before 1983.

The 1960s and 1970s were decades which saw the decline of mental health specialists and an increasing trend towards generic social work training and practice. During this period , MWO practice was weakened because of gaps in skills and knowledge and ineffective legal authority (Olsen, 1984, Caul and Herron, 1992, Prior, 1993); in contrast, the 1983 legislation provided ASWs with an expanded role and increased powers.

The creation of the ASW within the new mental health legislation can best be explained by the coincidence of a number of social and policy factors which converged in the late 1970s. It can be argued that the legislation was the product of a time before UK social and health policy shifted rightwards during the 1980s and 1990s. Gostin's (1975) work on reforming the mental health legislation in England and Wales was not only influenced by the recommendations of the British Association of Social Workers, it was profoundly shaped by the ideology of the 'anti-psychiatry' movement of the 1960s and 1970s (Adams, 1996, pp140-142, Pilgrim and Rogers, 1993). The ethos which underpinned the subsequent legislation was marked by a broad concern for the rights of patients and a perception that they should be protected from a discredited psychiatric system. By strengthening legal safeguards for patients it was assumed that the worst excesses of psychiatric incarceration could be curbed. What emerged were a series of checks and balances in the patient's favour - these included much more stringent rules about compulsory admission to hospital, the protection of patients' rights and property whilst in hospital, greater access to mental health review tribunals, the establishment of a mental health commission, and a substantial role for the newly created ASW.

A crucial aspect of this role is the responsibility placed upon the ASW during the processes of 'application for assessment' and 'application for reception into guardianship'. In both cases ASWs are expected to provide an independent professional judgment about risk, to interview the patient in a suitable manner, to liaise with nearest relatives, carers and relevant professionals and, when appropriate, be the applicant. In an early attempt to contextualise these processes, Olsen (1984,pp. 41-42) described the role of the ASW as follows:

1. To investigate the patient's social situation and to identify, in consultation with others involved, the extent to which social and environmental pressures have contributed to the patient's behaviour.

2. To use his (sic) professional skills to help resolve any social, relationship, or environmental difficulties which have contributed to the crisis, and to mobilise community resources appropriately.

3. To know the legal requirements and to ensure that they are complied with.

4. To form his own opinions, following an interview with the patient, with those closest to him, and with others involved, as to whether compulsory admission is necessary having regard to any alternative methods of resolving the crisis, and of securing necessary care or treatment.

5. To ensure that care and treatment is offered in the least restrictive conditions possible

In the beginning there was considerable optimism that this role would offer increased opportunities for social workers in the mental health and learning disability fields; perhaps for the first time, they would acquire a higher status within the traditionally closed system of psychiatric power. In some ways these issues are being rehearsed, once again, albeit a decade later, in the current debate about the new mental legislation in the Republic of Ireland. Expectations were also raised by the introduction of specific training for ASWs, which in turn led to registration and employment by local authorities. Yet, at a time when more ASWs became qualified to practice (training was eventually introduced throughout Northern Ireland in the late 1980s), some doubts about the efficacy of the social work role emerged.

In an inauspicious start for the new cadre of ASWs, training was boycotted by trades unions, both in Britain and Northern Ireland. The dispute mirrored the general debate about whether social work could or should be professionalised, and the contentious issue of formal assessment of course members. This issue was resolved by the time competence-based training was introduced for all post-qualifying social work programmes. When qualified ASWs began to practice, it emerged that the service was not available evenly throughout English local authorities (Barnes et al, 1990). This problem of planning and resourcing ASW services is still commonplace. For example, Huxley and Kerfoot (1994) in their survey of eighty two local authorities found a wide variation of ratios of ASWs to areas of population. Decisions by local authorities about how many ASWs there should be appeared to be taken in haphazard ways, with very little attempt to achieve standardisation. The researchers found ASWs to be working in a variety of settings, including generic, specialist and other client-based teams.

Another problem in understanding the ASW is the paucity of research into the decision-making processes of practitioners. Sheppard (1990, 1993) has attempted to develop a methodology for making judgments about dangers, hazards and risks using his Compulsory Admissions Schedule (CASH), but there is no evidence that a common practice knowledge base exists amongst ASWs. One worrying paradox is that, despite the fact that the ASW role was created to protect the rights of clients, it is only in recent years, that service users have been included in the training of ASWs (Hastings and Crepaz-Keay, 1995, Whittaker and Cox, 1997). This suggests that ASWs and those who train them may still be harbouring prejudicial notions about the need to empower service users. Such issues are a challenge for ASWs in Britain and Northern Ireland; they also illustrate some of the dilemmas which will be faced by mental health social workers in the Republic of Ireland if and when they are given statutory powers within the impending Mental Health legislation.

The ASW in Northern Ireland

Analyses of the ASW role in Britain are helpful in understanding social work practice in Northern Ireland, and ultimately what will happen in the Republic of Ireland. Although Prior (1993) argues that there has been a post-war trend towards convergence in law making between Northern Ireland and the rest of the UK, the particular legal and administrative differences in mental health law in Northern Ireland has created some sense of difference for the ASW. Aspects of this sense of disparity in the law for Northern Ireland was reflected in the lengthy deliberations of the McDermott Committee (DHSS(NI), 1981) during the review of the 1961 Act. The committee was influenced by arguments presented by professional bodies, interest groups and local politicians. As a consequence the Order differs from the British Act in the following respects:

1 The concept of 'mental disorder' was defined for the first time.

2 The conditions of personality disorder and substance misuse were excluded from the definition of mental disorder. People who have a personality disorder are thus excluded from the legal process.

3 Increased powers were given to ASWs to enable them to override the wishes of the nearest relative in certain circumstances.

4 The application for assessment was to involve the general practitioner, ASW and/or the nearest relative.

5 The application for assessment was designed, when necessary, to allow for a quick regrading to voluntary status, helping to preserve patients' rights and dignity.

6 The Mental Health Commission for Northern Ireland was to have powers to protect the rights of voluntary as well as involuntary patients, and to have a role in the examination and monitoring of the quality of community-based services.

In the last decade some analysis of the role of the ASW in Northern Ireland has taken place; this has helped reveal the particular nuances of practice in this part of the UK. In an early attempt to understand the professional relationships between GPs and ASWs in their use of the Order, Quinn (1992) found that GPs were, at times, confused about aspects of the legislation and unclear of the role of the ASW. Prior (1992) has compared and contrasted the respective roles of ASWs in Britain and Northern Ireland. She challenges the underlying assumption that ASWs, in the process of carrying out their legal responsibilities, can be both providers of services and advocates for the client at the same time. She is also concerned that too much emphasis has been placed on the statutory function of the ASW at the expense of resources and training for everyday mental health social work. Prior does, however, acknowledge that ASWs in Northern Ireland have marginally more professional power than their British counterparts, particularly around the issue of overturning nearest relatives' wishes in the process of reception into guardianship and application for assessment. Potter's discussion of the Order helpfully outlines various aspects of the role of the ASW in Northern Ireland. He raises the very important issue of individual legal responsibility placed upon ASWs because of this professional status under the Order. The ASW should be aware of the possibility of litigation in the course of carrying their duties (Potter, 1996, pp.158-160).

There is generally a lack of data on the broad activity of ASW practice in Northern Ireland during the last decade. In a recent survey of about 150 ASW contacts over a one year period in south and east Belfast, Byrne (1997) found that over half of all applications for assessment were carried out by ASWs in psychiatric hospital settings. This should be of concern to ASWs if there is a possibility that the independent judgment of the ASW is compromised by pressure from hospital professionals to 'regrade' a patient from voluntary to involuntary status. The ASW may be less able to challenge the weight of such opinion, particularly as the assessment of risk and consideration of the least restrictive alternative may be harder to make in the context of a hospital setting. Surprisingly, in Byrne's study, only 20% of applications for assessment were carried out in the client's home;

this imbalance between the hospital and community settings is not, one assumes, what the legislators envisaged in 1986. Although there were a number of indications of good practice by ASWs during assessment and during contact with nearest relatives and other professionals, Byrne is concerned that opportunities for considering alternatives to compulsory admission to hospital continue to be hampered by the lack of community-based resources. She argues for a more preventative rather than crisis-orientated ASW service, if the needs and rights of mental health service users and their carers are to be attended to.

Government agencies who have the responsibility for the administration and monitoring of the legislation continue to shape the way ASWs practice in Northern Ireland. The production of the Code of Practice for the Order (DHSS (NI), 1992) has helped to clarify the role and duties of the ASW. The Code usefully describes, in some detail, principles of good practice in the areas of application for assessment and reception into guardianship. In doing so it makes clearer the relationship the ASW should have with the client, their nearest relative and other interested professionals. For example, it explains how the ASW should interview the client 'in an appropriate manner', transport the client to hospital, deal with nearest relatives who object to ASW decisions, and provides guidelines on how mental health professionals should liaise with each others in the course of their legal duties.

The Mental Health Commission for Northern Ireland has frequently commented on the role of the ASW and has made recommendations about the need for increased referrals to ASWs, particularly in cases of guardianship or application for assessment where nearest relatives are reluctant to become involved in the process. These recommendations may partly explain the increasing use of ASWs in these areas, and why, in recent years, ASWs have begun to outnumber nearest relatives as applicants for assessment and guardianship (Mental Health Commission for Northern Ireland, 1994; 1996). The use and availability of ASWs in Northern Ireland has been also commented upon by the Social Services Inspectorate for Northern Ireland (SSI (NI), 1995, 1997). An important issue raised in these reports is the uneven ratios of ASWs employed by health and social services trusts in Northern Ireland - echoing the points raised in the Barnes et al (1990) research. Although there may be legitimate reasons of demography and geography for these disparities, this unevenness of service delivery should be of some concern to planners. There is also disquiet that some ASWs do not continue to practice with relevant client groups after approval and that this may dilute the overall standing of the profession. The ASW Programme in Northern Ireland is about to commission research into these and other aspects of training and employment.

The review of this literature indicates a range of common practice circumstances throughout the UK, but also reveals the particular nuances of ASW practice in Northern Ireland. The decade which followed the establishment of the ASW has been marked by increasing financial retrenchment within health and social services, and a growing awareness that deinstitutionalisation and community care policy has left aspects of the legislation unwieldy or inadequate. In the second part of this chapter, key policy issues which influence and shape contemporary ASW practice will be discussed. Comparisons between Britain and Northern Ireland will be drawn, and key challenges for ASW practice discussed.

Practice in the 1990s

Northern Ireland : the organisational context

Any discussion about mental health social work practice in Northern Ireland must take into account the impact of a range of significant social, economic and political factors. Northern Ireland consists of only 1.6 million people living in a society which suffers from long-standing political conflict (Whyte, 1991). Yet this is a society which, paradoxically, contains relatively homogenous characteristics with evidence of stable social systems. For example, there is less diversity in family structure and support networks than in the rest of the UK. In Northern Ireland there are relatively small, although increasing ethnic minority populations, when compared to Britain, and less migration than is the case in the Republic of Ireland.

The centralisation of health and social services by the state following Direct Rule in 1972 led to the formation of a unique system which is commonly described as the 'integrated service'. In Northern Ireland, ASWs benefit from organisational arrangements which, on paper at least, allow for smoother working relationships between health and social work professionals (McCoy, 1993). There is an assumption that, unlike British services (Davis, 1984), health care professionals in Northern Ireland can deliver a more efficient, multi-disciplinary service for clients. This assumption seems logical given that Northern Irish ASWs have significant contact with GPs, community psychiatric nurses (CPNs), psychiatrists and other health and social care professionals, often on a daily basis. Because most of these professionals are employed by a common hospital or community health and social services trust, there is an implication that decision-making between relevant professionals in the mental health field should be more transparent than is the case when professionals work for different organisations. It can be argued that, at least in principle, the use of such multi-disciplinary teams makes the complex processes around application for assessment and guardianship easier to manage.

The integrated service in Northern Ireland, however, has also created practice dilemmas for ASWs. Despite the apparent rationality of the integrated service, social workers may not have benefited as much as other professional groups, particularly medics. There have been recent concerns expressed about how social workers in Northern Ireland may be a vulnerable professional group amidst these organisational arrangements, particularly in the adult community care and mental health fields (Caul and Herron, 1992). The predominance of the medical profession within the integrated service in Northern Ireland and the consequences for the status of social workers, suggests that a closer comparison might be made with the Board structure in the Republic of Ireland, rather than the dual system of health and social welfare which exists in Britain. There is not the same sense of professional independence and identity for social workers in the integrated service in Northern Ireland compared to that which exists for social workers employed by local authorities in Britain. With the advent of a new mixed economy of welfare which emerged in Northern Ireland, post-Griffiths, and since statutory mental health functions were delegated to hospital and community health and social services trusts (DHSS (NI), 1996), mental health social workers have been further marginalised. There now exists a proliferation of organisational units, often located in sparsely populated areas. ASWs now find themselves employed by many of these small trusts, rather than the four health and social services boards as had been the case previously.

The rationale for the creation of the integrated service can be best explained by the state's attempt to resolve political and social conflict by removing powers from local authorities and placing responsibility for health and social welfare in the hands of bureaucracies. Campbell, Pinkerton and McLaughlin (1995) have critically discussed the assumptions which underpin this 'technocratic' approach to social and health care in Northern Ireland. They argue that there tends to be too much of a focus by social workers on formal task and function, alongside a general failure to empower communities and disadvantaged clients. An additional negative factor has been the propensity of the centralised administration in Northern Ireland to 'push through' quite radical reforms in health and social care; this was made easier by the lack of a mature social and political culture which might have helped resist such change.

'The Troubles', as the political conflict of the last twenty five years have become known, have had a profound impact on life, society and mental health in Northern Ireland; it would be surprising if mental health social workers were not affected by the conflict. Over three thousand people have died as a direct result of social conflict alongside tens of thousands who have been traumatised physically, psychologically and emotionally. In a society where conflict is so pervasive, social workers, like other professional groups in Northern Ireland, practice in circumstances quite different to those experienced by their counterparts in Britain and Ireland. One example of this is how, in the course of their statutory duties, ASWs sometimes have to work alongside the security forces when carrying out their functions in areas where the conflict is at its most intense (Smyth and Campbell, 1996). A well-known, but under-researched phenomenon is the care and treatment of paramilitaries and security forces personnel by professionals in the mental health and criminal justice sectors in Northern Ireland. Psychiatrists, mental health social workers, probation officers, psychiatric nurses and psychologists have all been involved in helping these client groups, both in and out of hospital. These are abnormal circumstances which rarely occur for professionals working in Britain and the Republic of Ireland.

As a result of 'The Troubles' there are inevitable psychological consequences for the wider community. Although Lyons's early work (1974) found an unexpected absence of psychiatric morbidity amongst patients who had been truamatised, more recent evidence suggests substantial emotional and psychological damage caused by violent events (Heskin, 1980, Cairns and Wilson, 1989, Benson, 1994). Loughrey et al (1988) found evidence of post-traumatic stress disorder amongst patients who had experienced violence at first hand.

ASWs practising in Northern Ireland are undoubtedly affected by such factors, both in terms of the impact on their own personal identities and when carrying out their legal function. One of the consequences of adopting a technocratic approach to delivering social work in Northern Ireland is a tendency towards collusion in not acknowledging how the conflict has affected social work practice in a society which is sectarianised (Smyth and Campbell, 1996). These are areas which demand more attention from the profession and their employers.

From hospital to community

Much has been written about the way in which large numbers of patients, formerly residing in psychiatric institutions in the UK, have been discharged into the community. This process is both complex and contentious - explanations for the accelerated discharge include critiques of institutional living, analyses of the role which institutions play in the manufacture and control of deviance, changing social values in wider society and the discovery and use of psychotropic drugs (Tomlinson, and Carrier, (eds), 1996, Busfield, 1986, Scull, 1977). What emerged from the debates of the 1960s was a consensus that the rights of people with mental health problems are generally best preserved by having them live with other citizens in the community. Interestingly, it was not until the 1980s that this ideological consensus on deinstitutionalisation crystallised in the run-down and closure of institutions. It remains something of an irony that it was a right-of-centre government in the UK, pledged to challenge many of the assumptions of the post-war settlement, which used this consensus to carry out such a radical mental health policy. The result has been substantial shifts in the psychiatric hospital populations in Northern Ireland as well as Britain. In England and Wales, for example, psychiatric bed numbers fell from a high point of 165,000 in 1955 to 50,000 by the early 1990s (Bean and Mounser, 1993). In Northern Ireland, a similar pattern emerged. In the early 1960s over 6,000 beds were available in Northern Ireland (in Prior, 1993). Through the 1980s numbers fell from 3,500 to 2,300 (DHSS(NI), 1991). By the year 1995/6 only 1521 psychiatric beds remained in Northern Ireland (DHSS(NI), 1997). One of the current strategic goals of mental health policy in Northern Ireland is that "long-term, institutional care should no longer be provided in traditional psychiatric hospital environments" (DHSS(NI), 1997, p.90). There has been much criticism about the negative effects of such accelerated closure of psychiatric hospitals in Britain. In particular pressure groups are concerned about the well-being of former psychiatric patients living unsupported in the community; it is argued that their needs are not being adequately met because of the logistical and financial problems caused by the organisational split between health authorities and local authorities. Evidence suggests that such problems caused by unplanned or underresourced discharge are not as great in Northern Ireland - bridging finance during the early stages of deinstitutionalisation may have helped patients in this transition (Donnelly et al, 1994). Despite these benefits, a constant and prolonged transfer of resources from large institutions to community services has been difficult to achieve in Northern Ireland.

These substantial policy changes over the last decade have inevitable consequences for ASW practice. Bean and Mounser (1993) point out that there exists an inherent paradox in this process of reducing bed numbers in psychiatric hospitals - whilst bed numbers fall, admission and readmission rates climb (Rafferty, 1996). One side-effect is that it becomes increasingly difficult for practitioners to find places in hospital, not only for voluntary patients, but also those in need of compulsory treatment. For, example, in the past few years in Northern Ireland ASWs have not always been able to find beds in the nearest psychiatric hospital, with the consequence that some clients have found themselves admitted to institutions at a distance from their families and communities. Shortage of bed-space has also led to 'revolving door policies' which may at times lead to premature discharge. It seems reasonable to imply that this increases the chances of relapse and readmission, particularly if community-based resources are not available.

Managing risk in the Community

Alongside allegations of failure of systems of care and supervision in the community, a moral panic has been generated about the alleged 'dangerousness' of some psychiatric patients discharged from psychiatric hospitals. A popular discourse has emerged in Britain about the failings of mental health policy, particularly following the murder of Jonathan Zito in 1992 and the subsequent inquiry about the care and treatment of Christopher Clunis (Adams, 1996, p.145). As beds have become scarcer in psychiatric hospitals, and pressure mounts to keep and control disturbed individuals in the community, the state's response has been to seek to legislate for stronger methods of control.

The liberal ethos which underpinned both the 1983 Act and 1986 Order is increasingly being tested as a result of these changes in mental health policy during the 1980s and 1990s. It could be argued that rights seceded to patients at the expense of professional power evident in the mental health legislation of the 1980s are gradually being clawed back by the state through a range of initiatives in the 1990s. Bean and Mounser (1993), for example, have documented the history of the concept of the Community Treatment Order (CTO), from an early interest by BASW to recent espousal by Royal College of Psychiatrists. However attractive and expedient such an order might seem, substantial problems in its practical operation remain. In particular it is difficult to know how CTOs could be administered, particularly if professionals are unwilling or unsure about the use of coercion. Community Supervision Orders (CSOs) suffer from the same problem. The limited gains which might be acquired through the use of such orders would be far outweighed by the serious deterioration of clients' rights; service users groups have been quick to realise this possibility.

Existing mental health legislation provides the ASW with a role which can offer an alternative to the medical perspective on mental ill-health and risk. An increasing focus on methods of control in the community may be a signal of how patients' rights may be once again be replaced by professional judgments. For instance, it has been reported that a proposed CSO would have the psychiatrist as applicant, with the ASW in a supporting role. Not only would this imply a marginalisation of the ASW role, even worse, the proposal included an idea that ASWs could be left to enforce the order (Marchant, 1993, p.15).

Exworthy (1995) has reviewed British and international law in an effort to clarify the strengths and weaknesses of different legal methods of control in the community. The proposal that clients should be compelled to take medication, live in certain types of accommodation or attend clinics for treatment, Exworthy argues, creates substantial ethical and practice dilemmas. Although many people with chronic mental health problems are entitled to a quality of life in the community which some form of compulsion may help deliver, the downside of such arguments is that professionals may abuse the power which a CSO or CTO gives them. Drawing on examples from the USA, Exworthy argues that control in the community will only work if and when support services in the community are coherent and well-resourced:

> The proposals of supervised discharge and supervision registers from the Department of Health bring with them a reciprocity of obligations. If patients are to be obliged to be subject to compulsory orders in the community as well as in hospital, to suffer further loss of rights, of privacy or to refuse to consent to treatment, then they are entitled to expect at least a reasonable standard of care. (1995, pp.238-9)

The debate about control in the community has also taken place in Northern Ireland. Plans for supervised discharge were considered as early as 1993. To date, the administration in Northern Ireland has resisted a legislative approach to the issue of control and has, instead, focused on refining guidelines for practice when dealing with mentally disordered people at risk in the community. This has entailed the circulation of procedures on discharge, provision of services, multidisciplinary working and assessment of risk (DHSS(NI), Management Executive.1996a). In an attempt to resolve organisational and legal problems in dealing with people with mental health problems at risk of offending, it has been proposed that, for the first time, a medium secure unit be established by 2002 (DHSS(NI), 1996).

This discussion about the control of people with mental health problems living in the community has been exacerbated by local factors in Northern Ireland. In particular, the Fenton Report (WH&SSB., 1995) highlighted gaps in systems of care and protection, following the murder of a young person by a patient, recently discharged from a psychiatric hospital. A range of criticisms were made by the committee which has refuelled an earlier debate about the benefits of exclusion of personality disorder from the mental health legislation in Northern Ireland. It has often been argued that by excluding people with personality problems from the legislation, there remains a significant group of people living who are being left without access to care and treatment in psychiatric hospitals. Their position is made even more problematic because they are often rejected by their families and the wider community because of their behaviour. These circumstances are not helped by the failure of the psychiatric profession to offer viable forms of care and treatment, despite attempts to differentiate and subdivide various behaviours which may describe the broad range of personality disorder (Prins, 1995). Although the law technically excludes people with personality disorders from compulsory admission to hospital, it is the case in Northern Ireland that such people are sometimes admitted for assessment - this may not contradict the ethos of the Order because it is designed to allow community-based practitioners (ASWs and GPs) to make judgments about disturbed behaviour and harm. Making quick judgments about whether a mental disorder is evident, often in situations of crisis, is difficult and an imperfect science. It could be argued that, where there is doubt, then it may be best left to the process of assessment in hospital, carried out by multi-disciplinary specialists, to establish whether a mental disorder or personality disorder exists.

Rather than look towards compulsory methods of treatment inside or outside hospital, mental health professionals should focus on developing community-based services; if the issue of personality disorder is generally one of a problem of living then it is to the community where solutions will be found. For example, at the point of the assessment period in hospital when it is decided that someone has a personality disorder, rather than a mental disorder, a forensic team should be available to advise and plan for discharge. Mental health social workers should be viewed as an essential part of such a team. In Northern Ireland no comprehensive forensic mental health service has ever existed, and plans for the care and treatment of disturbed people living in the community are at best piecemeal and arranged in *ad hoc* ways. What does exist are a range of agencies - the probation service, agencies concerned with housing and homelessness and statutory community mental health teams - all these agencies have overlapping functions and responsibilities. For example, a recent study of homelessness and mental health in Belfast revealed high levels of need which remain unmet. McGilloway and Donnelly (1996) found that many of the clients surveyed had been in contact with the criminal justice, psychiatric and care systems. Although there were considerable levels of psychiatric morbidity in the homeless population, there was an unevenness of access to social and health services and a lack of a coordinated approach to deal with the needs of this vulnerable client group.

Mental health social workers have a role to play in addressing such problems. CCETSW (1995) have recognised the need to reappraise levels of skills of mental health social workers employed in forensic services. It seems clear that interagency collaboration is essential if the tragedies which have occurred in Britain and Northern Ireland are to be avoided. ASWs are expected to make judgments about risks in the community and to consider the 'least restrictive alternative' to institutional care; this task is only possible when community-based services exist, are known about and are accessible. ASWs should work towards developing knowledge and use of community services rather than being pushed into a marginalised role which leads to more coercion and control of clients' lives.

Conclusion

In the course of this chapter, the role of the mental health social worker in Northern Ireland has been described and analysed. It is argued that the creation of the ASW has led to greater powers and responsibilities which can be used to protect the rights of patients and their nearest relatives. In comparing the position of the ASW in Northern Ireland with their counterparts in Britain, there are a number of interesting differences, both in terms of legal responsibilities and in the context of social work in a divided society. The Order, in the operation of exclusions and a period of assessment, is arguably a more progressive piece of legislation than the 1983 Act. The organisational context in Northern Ireland, and in particular the 'integrated service', promises opportunities for sound multi-disciplinary working between professionals in the mental health field. In theory these factors should provide a positive environment for ASWs to practice in Northern Ireland. On a more critical note, this role may be increasingly compromised by trends in mental health policy which imply the need for greater control of clients living in the community.

This wider social debate affects practice in Northern Ireland, just as it does in Britain and the Republic of Ireland. ASWs and mental health social workers in Northern Ireland should resist the temptation to change and move away from the position described by the Order. Instead there should be a greater focus on developing skills in assessment and planning appropriate to this new social environment. The advances made in training ASWs in Northern Ireland, through competence-based learning, should be built-upon and resourced by employers as a way of complementing this agenda. This approach should also include a greater willingness by mental health social workers to actively engage in the organisation and development of community-based resources for mental health service users and their families. It is only by developing partnerships with communities, groups and individual service users that we can understand their needs and adjust legal and agency practice accordingly.

References

Adams, R. (1996), *The Personal Social Services*, Longman: London.

Barnes, M., Bowl, R. and Fisher, M. (1990), *Sectioned: Social Services and the 1983 Mental Health Act*, Routledge: London.

Bean, P. and Mounser, P. (1993), *Discharged from Psychiatric Hospitals*, Macmillan: London.

Benson, J. (1984), 'The secret war in the disunited kingdom: psychological aspects of the Ulster conflict' , *Group Analysis*, 28, pp.47-62.

Busfield, J. (1986), *Managing Madness: Changing Ideas and Practice*, Hutchinson: London.

Byrne, M. (1987), 'Mental Health Social work in Northern Ireland: What does the Future Hold?, in R. Manktelow, J. Campbell and J. Park (eds), *Social Work in Mental Health - Proceedings of the Third Northern Ireland Conference*, DHSS(NI)/SSI.

Cairns, E. and Wilson, R. (1989), 'Mental health aspects of political violence in Northern Ireland', *International Journal of Mental Health*, 18 (1).

Campbell, J. and Pinkerton, J. and McLaughlin, J (1995), 'Social Work Social Conflict: The Case of Northern Ireland', *International Perspectives in Social Work*, Vol I, 127-34.

Caul, B. and Herron, S. (1992), *A Service for People*, December: Belfast.Central Council for Education and Training in Social Work (1995), *Forensic Social Work: Competence and Workforce Data*, CCETSW: London.

Davis, A. (1984), 'Contemporary social policy towards the mentally disordered' in R.M. Olsen (ed) op cit.

DHSS (1983), *The Mental Health Act 1983*, HMSO: London.

DHSS(NI) (1981), *Northern Ireland Review Committee on Mental Health Legislation* (MacDermott Committee), HMSO: Belfast.

DHSS(NI) (1986), *The Mental Health (Northern Ireland) Order 1986*, HMSO: Belfast.

DHSS(NI) (1991), *Health and Personal Social Services: A Regional Strategy for Northern Ireland 1992-97*, HMSO: Belfast.

DHSS(NI) (1992), *Code of Practice for the Mental Health (NI) Order 1986*, HMSO: Belfast.

DHSS(NI) (1995), *Promoting Social Welfare, Annual Report of the Chief Inspector, Social Services Inspectorate*, DHSS: Belfast.

DHSS(NI), Management Executive (1996), *Appointment of Approved Social Workers Direction*, Belfast.

DHSS(NI), Management Executive (1996a), *Guidance on Discharge from Hospital, Continuing Care and Mentally Disordered People*, Belfast.

DHSS(NI) (1997), *Health and Wellbeing: Into the Next Millennium, Regional Strategy for Health and Wellbeing, 1997-2002*, Belfast: HMSO.

DHSS(NI) (1997a), *Promoting Social Welfare, Annual Report of the Chief Inspector, Social Services Inspectorate*, DHSS: Belfast.

Donnelly, M., McGilloway, S., May, N. and Perry, S. (1994), *Opening New Doors: An evaluation of community care for people discharged from psychiatric and mental handicap hospitals*, HMSO: Belfast.

Exworthy, T. (1995), 'Compulsory care in the community: a review of the proposals for compulsory supervision and treatment of the mentally ill in the community', *Criminal Behaviour and Mental Health*, Vol 5, No.3, pp.218- 241.

Gostin, L. (1975), *A Human Condition*, Vol 1, MIND: London.

Hastings, M. and Crepaz-Keay, D. (1995), *The Survivor's Guide to Training Approved Social Workers*, CCETSW: London.

Heskin, K. (1980), *Northern Ireland: A Psychological Analysis*, Gill and Macmillan: Dublin.

Huxley, P. and Kerfoot, M. (1994), 'A Survey of Approved Social Workers in England and Wales', *British Journal of Social Work* 24, pp.311-322.

Loughry, G.C., Bell, P., Kee, M., Roddy, R.J. and Curran, P. (1988), 'Post-Traumatic Stress Disorder and Civil Violence in Northern Ireland', *British Journal of Psychiatry*, 153, pp.554-60.

Lyons, H.A. (1974), 'Psychiatric Sequelae of the Belfast Riots', *British Journal of Psychiatry*, 118, pp.265-73.

Marchant, C. (1993), 'Taking Liberties' in *Community Care*, 4 February 1993.

Mental Health Commission for Northern Ireland (1994), *Report for the period April 1992- March 1994*, HMSO: Belfast.

Mental Health Commission for Northern Ireland (1996), *Report for the period April 1994-March 1996*, HMSO: Belfast.

McCoy, K (1993), 'Integration - A Changing Scene' in DHSS(NI), SSI *Perspectives in Integration*, Belfast.

McGillowey, S. and Donnelly, M. (1997), *Don't Look Away:Homelessness and Mental Health in Belfast*, Council for the Homeless (NI): Belfast.

Olsen, R. M. (ed) (1984), *Social Work and Mental Health: The Role of the Approved Social Worker*, Tavistock: London.

Pilgrim, D. and Rodgers, A. (1993), *A Sociology of Mental Health and Illness*, Open University Press: London.

Potter, M. (1996), 'Mental Health' in Kieran White (ed) *Law For Social Workers in Northern Ireland*, Gill and Macmillan: Dublin.

Prins, H. (1995), *Offenders, Deviants or Patients?*, Routledge: London.

Prior, P. (1992) ,'The Approved Social Worker - Reflections on Origins', *British Journal of Social Work*, 22, pp.105-19.

Prior, P. (1993), *Mental Health Politics in Northern Ireland*, Avebury: Aldershot.

Quinn, B. (1992*), Social Worker - GP Liaison in Compulsory Admissions for Assessment*, DHSS(NI) SSI, Belfast.

Rafferty, J. (1996), 'The decline of asylum or the poverty of the concept?' in D. Tomlinson and J. Carrier (eds) *Asylum in the Community*, Routledge: London.

Scull, A. (1977), *Decarceration ; Community Treatment and the Deviant*, Polity: Oxford.

Sheppard (1990), *Mental Health: The Role of the Approved Social Worker*, JUSSR: Sheffield.

Sheppard (1993), 'Theory for Approved Social Work: The Use of the Compulsory Admission Assessment Schedule', *British Journal of Social Work*, 23, pp.231-257.

Smyth, M. and Campbell, J. (1996), 'Social Work, Sectarianism and Anti-Sectarian Practice in Northern Ireland', *British Journal of Social Work*, 26, pp.77-92.

Tomlinson, D. and Carrier, J. (eds) (1996), op.cit.

Western Health & Social Services Board (1995), *The Brian Doherty Inquiry* (Fenton Report), WH&SSB.

Whittaker, A. and Cox, M. (1997), 'Approved Social Work Training: Service Users Setting the Agenda' in Roger Manktelow, Jim Campbell and John Park (eds), op. cit.

Whyte, J. (1991), *Interpreting Northern Ireland*, Clarendon: Oxford.

6 Mental health social work and the law in the Republic of Ireland

Paul Guckian

Introduction

This chapter examines the current developments in mental policy in the Republic of Ireland. Particular attention is paid to the legislative changes proposed in the White Paper for the New Mental Health Act (DOH., 1995). Major differences currently exist concerning the legislative responsibilities of mental health social workers on both sides of the Irish border although many of the Republic's proposals seem to mirror, to some degree, current policies in Northern Ireland (DHSS (N.I.), 1986). Psychiatric social work in the Republic needs to be put into an organisational context which pays particular attention to structure and the blurring of multidisciplinary roles within mental health teams and its wider relationship with community care social work. The key recommendations of the White Paper - the role of Authorised Officers, the Mental Health Review Board and Adult Care Orders - are examined. The chapter will include a critical analysis of possible dilemmas faced by social workers should these proposals be enacted. Other recent social legislation in the Republic which impinges on the psychiatric social work role is also discussed.

Current developments in Irish mental health policy

In common with developments elsewhere, there have been major changes in the mental health services in the Irish Republic in recent years. The national long stay psychiatric population has dropped from 21,000 in 1958 to 6,130 in 1992 (Guckian and Finnerty, 1997) as mental health services moved away from institutionalised hospital care to a community based multidisciplinary service. This move was greatly influenced by the Department of Health's study group report, *The Psychiatric Services –*

73

Planning For The Future (DOH, 1984). This report favoured the replacement of institutional services with a community based multidisciplinary model aimed at specific population sectors of 25-30,000 people. While the report recognized that the social worker should be part of the multidisciplinary team, it failed, however, to define thoroughly the social work role. Unfortunately the radical policy changes that have occurred in the Republic since 1984 have occurred within a legislative vacuum. Current mental health policy is still shaped by the Mental Treatment Act, 1945 (GSO, 1945) and much concern has been voiced that there is a mismatch between this old legislation and present mental health policy; much of this concern focuses on patients' civil liberties. Some attempts have been made to upgrade legislation, notably the proposed 1981 Act, which has been passed by both Houses of the Oireachtas, but concerns about how this legislation was to be implemented meant that the old law still prevails (GSO, 1981). A Green Paper (DOH, 1992) and a White Paper on Mental Health were eventually published in 1992 and 1995 respectively. As this chapter is being written, the outlook for a new Mental Health Bill combining the proposals of these papers does not appear to be anywhere near completion.

The Mental Treatment Act 1945

The 1945 Act was a major, innovative piece of legislation in its time, because it signaled a shift from the previous 'legal' attitude to mental health care in favour of a medically based model. For example, the Act allowed for the first time the admission of 'voluntary' patients to psychiatric hospitals. Furthermore it attempted to examine and define the needs of 'detained patients'. The Act currently allows the detention of Temporary patients or as patients deemed to be Persons of Unsound Mind (P.U.M.).Temporary detention orders are considered suitable for those people whose mental illness requires not more than six months inpatient treatment and who are unsuitable to obtain treatment as a voluntary patient. The status of this order may be reviewed for a maximum period of two years at six monthly intervals. P.U.M. orders cover those people whose care and treatment would take longer than six months, or who are not under proper care and control at home, or who are at risk of being neglected or cruelly treated. Issues of public safety and the safety of the persons themselves are also considerations for placing a person in hospital for treatment under this order. The 1945 Act also specifies that addicts may be detained under either order if this is deemed necessary for preventive and curative treatment.

The present criteria for detention in psychiatric hospitals are a cause of serious concern for social workers in the mental health services. The broad scope of the Act, and the way in which it defines categories considered suitable for detention in mental hospitals might explain the relatively high admission rates and numbers of the long stay population in the Republic. These categories also allow patients whose primary diagnosis is mental handicap, or with difficulties associated with old age, to be detained in a psychiatric hospital against their will. It may even be the case that even those considered 'vulnerable' within the community could be detained involuntarily. The absence of an independent review body and the fact that P.U.M. orders are not restricted by a time limit raises serious doubts about the efficacy of the 1945 Act in protecting civil liberties; these issues need to be addressed. The additional possibility that people with addiction problems can be detained conflicts with modern treatment programmes in this field and is out of line with the current legislative approach in Northern Ireland. It is not surprising that the evolution of community based addiction services in the Republic of Ireland in recent years has taken place outside the existing legislative framework.

The 1945 Act clearly legislated for mental health treatment from a medical point of view and while current approaches have expanded to include psychosocial interventions, social work involvement is limited, particularly in terms of statutory duties. The current Act would seem to encourage outdated philosophies and policies at odds with the role of the modern mental health social worker. On a more positive note, however, it may be that this lack of a statutory role may allow psychiatric social workers to develop more flexible therapeutic approaches based on interests and expertise with a minimum of bureaucratic constraint.

Mental health social work in the Republic of Ireland

The sectorization of the mental health services as proposed by Planning for the Future Report should have seen a rapid and major expansion of psychiatric social work posts in the Irish Republic. There is considerable scope for the development of specialist mental health social work services given the proposed size of the population sectors. Despite this opportunity, services are not being constructed in ways which offer mental health social workers extensive roles. According to Social Workers in Psychiatry (a special interest group of the Irish Association of Social Workers) there are only 40 adult psychiatric social work posts in the Republic and this number includes eight posts at private psychiatric hospitals in Dublin. It is of some concern that two regional health boards covering seven separate catchment areas are not, at the time of writing, employing any psychiatric social workers at all. This seems to indicate a lack of commitment to a comprehensive multidisciplinary approach in psychiatry in some geographical areas. At a more general level, relatively few areas have the recommended minimum of one social worker per sector and it is not uncommon for one social worker to cover two, three or even four sectors. Furthermore there are six health board areas whose total catchment areas are served single-handedly by lone psychiatric social workers.

There are a number of factors which may account for the lack of development of psychiatric social work in the Republic. Firstly, although Planning for the Future recommended a minimum of one social worker per sector, it did so without commenting on what the specific role of psychiatric social workers should be. This, coupled with the lack of specific legislative responsibilities, has left the profession in somewhat of a limbo. Secondly, the profession itself seems not to have adequately promoted a clear message about the value of social work intervention in mental health. This is happening despite the growing awareness of strong links between adverse socio-economic factors and poor mental health, and the fact that no other mental health profession can offer similar expertise in the areas of social policy, family law, social networking and current childcare responsibilities. What emerges from this picture is a lack of understanding by the profession of its value in the mental health field combined with clear government policy on the social work role. The result is a situation where weak policy directions feed into a profession which has found it hard to raise self-esteem. For these reasons, it is entirely understandable how psychiatric social workers, some of whom work alone, might find it hard to develop and emphasize the importance of their profession with their own health boards.

The lack of emphasis on training for mental health social work within the academic curriculum is another factor for consideration. The professional courses in the Republic's colleges tend to be at best generic; at worst, overly focused on childcare and child protection. The lack of a mental health component on some professional social work courses needs to be addressed, as newly trained social workers enter the job market with little or no knowledge or work experience in the field of psychiatric social work. The result is that many social workers feel unqualified and lacking in confidence in the field of mental health social work. However, with the advent of the National Social Workers Qualifications Board which replaced the Central Council for Education and Training in Social Work in the Republic, it is hoped that the training needs of psychiatric social workers will be addressed. Perhaps the structure of training and numbers of mental health social workers qualifying will in the future mirror the expansion that has taken place in the area of childcare in recent years.

Health boards are at present offering three programmes of service provision. These are Community Care (including childcare), Special Hospitals (including psychiatry and the institutional care of the elderly) and General Hospitals. Unfortunately the quite rigid boundaries of these programmes can sometimes render interprogramme communication difficult, a factor which can heighten feelings of isolation of some psychiatric social workers. Unusually some psychiatric social workers, while working with the Special Hospital Programme, are actually employed by the Community Care Programme (under the supervision of a child care expert). This is a less than satisfactory situation which may lead to greater isolation of the mental health social worker. Change may, however, be possible if the recommendations of the Department of Health's National Health Strategy (DOH, 1994) are carried out, but even then problems still arise. For example, the Department now suggests the abolition of the Special Hospital's Programme and in its place the development of Community Services and Acute Services under area management. Mental health services may find themselves in a 'no-mans land' straddling both areas. Yet again improved mental health services may not necessarily mean improved status and conditions for mental health social work. The obvious question which arises from these issues is whether psychiatric social workers should operate a separate service within the psychiatric system. Perhaps it may be more viable for psychiatric social workers to find a place for themselves within the larger community services programme alongside child protection services

The White Paper in mental health : key recommendations

The urgent need to update mental health services in order to comply with European Union law and United Nations conventions on civil liberty (United Nations, 1991, European Convention, 1950) has begun to be addressed with the publication of the Green Paper (DOH, 1992) and the White Paper (DOH, 1995). The eventual establishment of the Mental Health Bill will have numerous implications for psychiatric services. Aspects of social work practice will be included in the proposed changes; it remains to be seen whether there will be positive long-term outcomes for the profession. Interestingly the White Paper carries with it parallels with legislation in Northern Ireland. In particular three recommendations may directly effect the future development of social work practice: admission criteria; the Mental Health Review Board; and Adult Care Orders.

The question of who should initiate an application for the detention of a mentally ill patient is part of an ongoing debate in the Republic of Ireland. The existing 1945 Act allows application by a spouse or relative, but in certain circumstances members of the Garda Siochana or community welfare officers (formally home assistance officers) can apply for detention orders. It can be argued that these categories of applicant are quite limited and outdated. Nowadays the concept of family for example is very different to that of the past. Thus a common law spouse cannot initiate an application under current legislation. On the other hand, one must also bear in mind the central role and authority of family as defined and restated in the Irish Constitution (GSO, 1939). Such dilemmas about what constitutes the family are reflected in the considerable number of judicial reviews which have focused on the use of detention orders rising out of marital disharmony. One anomaly which arises concerns the minimum age of a person entitled to initiate an application - this is 21 years as opposed to the minimum legal age for marriage in the Republic which is 18 years. Similar discrepancies occur regarding the definition of an 'adult' requiring treatment - 16 years under the current Act, yet the definition of adult under the existing Child Care Act is 18 years. It could be argued that the clearer involvement of a social worker, who should bring a greater understanding of family life and social policy to situations of possible detention would be beneficial. These ambiguities need further clarification because, at present, some community welfare officers may be reluctant to apply for detention orders because of fear of litigation.

The Green Paper examined the role of Approved Social Worker (ASWs) as described in the Mental Health Order (N.I.) 1986. In the context of the Republic the Green Paper envisaged social workers (also some clinical psychologists and nurses) as being trained to assess the social situation and dynamics of families during this legal process. The Paper stressed that if the social worker's role was to be similar to that of the ASW then there should be clear independence of judgment which would avoid a conflict of interest with the social work role as understood within everyday mental health services. The White Paper proposals in fact recommend the creation of the post of Authorised Officer who would have the power to apply for detention orders at the request of a spouse or relative, or more importantly when a spouse or relative was unwilling, unavailable or disqualified from making such an application (DOH., 1995, p.33).

The White Paper seems to suggest that the role of the Authorised Officer would be a minimal one. This may be because, historically, there has been a very high percentage of detention applications made by relatives. However, these types of detention may not be the most appropriate if the client's civil rights are to be protected. Psychiatric social workers have considerable experiences of working with families who have been traumatised by mental illness and the need to have a family member detained against their wishes and the worry about what happens when the patient returns. It can be argued that the Authorised Officer would provide a positive, alternative route to detention for families of mentally ill people, thus avoiding the traumas which many families currently face. The experience of ASWs in Northern Ireland and Britain (Ogden, 1997) confirms the potential of this role.

The White Paper did not discuss two issues which critically affect the proposed role of Authorised Officers. Firstly, the Authorised Officer is viewed solely as an available person with the authority to sign application forms in the absence of relative family members. It is not clear if Authorised Officers would be empowered to ensure that detention orders were the least restricted alternative or indeed that Authorised Officers would provide a balance to the medical model involved in the process. It is not clarified whether a detailed social assessments of a patient's history and circumstances outlining prior conditions are required. Such crucial issues are in need of clarification prior to the enactment of the forthcoming legislation and codes of practice which may follow, if a satisfactory social work service is to be provided.

Secondly, the professional backgrounds of proposed Authorised Officers requires some examination. Clinical psychologists, public health nurses and social workers exercise very different criteria when making professional assessments and bring to the assessment different areas of expertise. Each profession focus on diverse aspects of need and treatment options when dealing with their clients. If the role of an Authorised Officer is simply one of 'rubber-stamping' forms it may be that no professional group would embrace the task in an increasingly litigatious society. There may even be an idea that Authorised Officers may not necessarily come from the mental health area. If this were the case then logistical problems arise. For example, there is not a service specifically designed for adults within health boards so it may mean that staff from Community Care programmes would have to be recruited. Clinical psychologists in that service are in short supply and consider themselves to be over-burdened, the same can be said for public health nurses. Community Care social workers are struggling to implement the Child Care Act in very difficult circumstances, not least of which is a shortage of appointments. Such problems in human resources, inter-professional rivalry and the additional spectre of legal challenge to professional judgment suggests that the White Paper lacks the degree of clarity which is required in a modern mental health service. It is clear, therefore, that the concept of Authorised Officer needs further review and the commitment of additional resources. The number of social workers with ASW qualifications gained in the United Kingdom may provide a useful resource in these early stages. For the time being, key questions of who will sign the orders and how will Authorised Officers be resourced remains. Hopefully the eventual outcome will be the most favourable to user needs and receive broad approval from all the professionals involved.

The Mental Health Review Board

At present there is no independent Mental Health Review Board in the Republic. The roles of the Inspector of Mental Hospitals and the Minister for Health are not considered to be suitably independent or legally adequate for the review of detention procedures. The result is that no independent Board or procedure exists to assess detention orders. The White Paper recommends the setting up of such a body thus bringing current legislation in line with the European Convention and the law of our nearest neighbours, the United Kingdom. This development is generally welcomed by social workers because it would allow for the re-examination of each decision to detain a person in hospital. Additionally it would help to dispel some of the concerns about the apparently arbitrary regulations used in the process of P.U.M. Orders.

The White Paper proposes that such a Board would be comprised of a lawyer of high standing, psychiatrists, a G.P. and other mental health professionals, including a social worker. Local panels would be set up to carry out the Review Board's responsibilities. It is at this level that psychiatric social workers might find considerable changes in their role. The Review Board, it can be assumed, would require detailed social and family assessments in order that the appropriateness of each detention might be decided and thus the most suitable course of treatment chosen. The social worker's expertise in this area would be highly beneficial. However, the danger exists that social workers' time would be taken up with report writing at the expense of therapeutic interventions; this would be particularly problematic in areas with limited social work resources. All these issues have clear resource implications. The appointment of a social worker to the Review Board, along with the proposal to appoint a social worker as Assistant Commissioner for Mental Health can only serve to improve the profile of social work in the specific context of the law and mental health services generally.

Adult Care Orders

The concept of supervising vulnerable adults in the community has proved to be a difficult one. The move towards care in the community has led to concern for a small group of vulnerable adults who might be at risk of abuse and/or exploitation. Indeed many voluntary groups, including the Simon Community, have expressed concern for the plight of these people when discharged from hospital (Simon, 1992). The Green Paper (DOH, 1992, p.106) examined the option of Supervision Orders as a means of dealing with the situation. This would require an application to the courts which would, it suggested, be accompanied by a medical recommendation establishing medical grounds and a welfare recommendation from a social worker outlining welfare grounds for the order. The categories of people suggested as suitable supervisors included relatives, officials of health boards and employees of mental handicap centres. The Green Paper envisaged the supervisors having such powers as to:

1 Require person to live at a specific place.

2 Require the client to attend specified places at certain times for treatment, occupation, education or training.

3 Enable the guardian to give access to the patient at the place of residence by any doctor, nurse, social worker or other professional.

The debate about the practicalities and ethical consistency of Supervision Orders is one which has caused a great deal of controversy in the Republic. Many health professionals, including social workers, have voiced some concerns about the proposals. While some social workers found the suggestions favourable, others were uncomfortable about the prospect of applying such powers to individuals living in the community. Another uncomfortable issue debated within the profession was whether the Orders should be primarily directed towards those with learning disabilities and whether in fact such powers should be dealt with in separate legislation (SWIP, 1992).

Following a review of submissions on the Green Paper the Department of Health introduced the concept of Adult Care Orders in the White Paper replacing the aforementioned Supervision Orders. This proposal was particularly significant in terms of social work practice. The aim of such Orders would be to protect mentally disordered persons who are being abused, neglected or exploited, using the least restrictive form of care possible. The Adult Care Orders were modeled on the Care Orders in the Child Care Act (GSO, 1991) aimed at protecting children from abuse. Adult Care Orders, it was proposed, could only be granted by the courts following an application by an Authorised Officer of a health board seeking the placement of the person named in the care of a relative, health board or voluntary agency. Evidence would be required when lodging an application which would include a report from a consultant psychiatrist that the person concerned suffered from a mental disorder. Evidence would also be required to demonstrate that the person had been, or might be, at risk of abuse, neglect or exploitation and as such needed a Care Order for his/her protection. The court would, if satisfied with the application, determine the duration of such an Order and an agreed supervisor would be responsible for overseeing the provision of care and protection.

It is likely that social workers, by virtue of their professional expertise, would be key persons in both applying for, and perhaps supervising any Orders. It seems apparent that the role of the social worker with regard to Adult Care Orders arose from a recognition by the legislators of the similarities between these and Child Care Orders in which social workers have a primary role to play. There are considerable ethical and practice implications for social workers in the operation of these Orders, particularly in the area of sanctions available to non-compliant patients. If a client failed to comply with an Order and continued to be at risk what options would exist for the social worker? Detention Orders in many cases would be unsuitable and a judicial sentence inappropriate. Social workers could find themselves in a vulnerable position with no available means of dealing with such a situation yet remaining open to criticism from many for not enforcing the Order. The failure to resolve such dilemmas would damage the professional and public image of social work. Another issue which needs to be considered is the importance of a definition which identifies the parameters of Adult Care Orders. Failure to do so could lead to other services, for example, learning disability and geriatric services, using what is mental health legislation for non-mental health purposes. These dilemmas are not unique to the Republic of Ireland, social worker and other mental health professionals face similar problems in the UK; this has led to recent arguments for the reform of the Mental Health (1983) Act.

Finally, legislation in the field of mental health must be viewed alongside various laws enacted recently in other areas of social care. These have already impacted on psychiatric social workers in the Republic. The Child Care Act, 1991 has created increased workloads for psychiatric social workers' caseloads largely because the Act states clearly that childcare issues must take primacy in the decision-making process. Health boards are developing a system of corporate responsibility as a way of meeting their responsibility under the legislation. It is no longer possible for psychiatric social workers to view the child care sector as an area totally separate from their own. The Act demands that social workers and other professionals make a holistic assessment which can provide a 'total picture' of the causes of and solutions to the care of children; this often involves an examination of mental health issues during this process. The developing issue of mandatory reporting of child abuse/neglect impacts directly on the legal and ethical role of adult psychiatric social workers in the Republic of Ireland. Similarly the Domestic Violence Act, 1996 (GSO, 1996) has implications for social work in mental health. The broadening of definitions of domestic violence and particularly Section 6 of the Act has implications for adult mental health services. In this Section the health board is enabled to apply for Safety Orders and Barring Orders on behalf of aggrieved parties should that party be prevented or deterred from acting on their own behalf. The family law role of psychiatric social workers makes it inevitable that they will become key workers in the area of domestic violence.

Conclusions

This chapter has discussed and analysed the future impact of recommendations from the Mental Health White Paper on psychiatric social worker practice in the Republic of Ireland. The publication of new mental health legislation is awaited with interest and it is anticipated that there will be considerable debate about its purpose and the role of a variety of professionals in its operation. There are many issues still unresolved and open to further debate - particularly in the fields of resources available for education, training and employment, if the aspirations of the legislation are to be realised. Hopefully, the role of the psychiatric social worker will develop in a positive way and be given a constructive place in the operation of the legislation rather than returning to an outdated administrative position as was the case in the 1945 Act; this is important if the rights of clients, protected by the new legislation, are to be enhanced. Whatever the future holds one thing seems certain, social work in the Republic of Ireland is at a crossroads; debate, openness and consideration of the professional/client relationship is an essential prerequisite on the best possible path to a better future in mental health.

References

Bunreacht na hEireann (1939), GSO: Dublin.
DHSS(NI) (1986), *The Mental Health (NI) Order, 1986*, HMSO: Belfast.
DOH (1945), *Mental Treatment Act,1945*, GSO: Dublin.
DOH (1981), *Health (Mental Services) Act, 1981*, GSO: Dublin.
DOH (1984), *The Psychiatric Services – Planning For The Future*, GSO: Dublin.
DOH (1991), *Child Care Act, 1991*, GSO: Dublin.

DOH (1992), *Green Paper on Mental Health*, GSO: Dublin 1992.

DOH (1994), *Shaping a Healthier Future*, GSO: Dublin.

DOH (1995), *White Paper A New Mental Health Act*, GSO: Dublin.

DOH (1996), *Domestic Violence Act, 1996*, GSO: Dublin.

DOH (annual publication) *Report of the Inspector of Mental Hospitals*, GSO: Dublin.

EU (1950), *European Convention for the Protection of Human Rights and Fundamental Freedoms*, EU: Strassbourg.

Guckian, P. and Finnerty, S (1997), 'Deinstitutionalisation – A Pathway to Homelessness? - The Experience of the Clare Psychiatric Services' in DHSS(NI) *Personal Social Services in Northern Ireland*, No. 55, 1997, 101-107.

Ogden, J. (1997), 'Revolving Doors', *Community Care*, 10-16 April, 1997.

Simon Community Dublin (1992), *Still Waiting for the Future*, Simon: Dublin.

Social Workers in Psychiatry(S.W.I.P.) (1992), *Submission to the Department of Health on the Green Paper in Mental Health*.

United Nations (1991), *Principles for the Protection of Persons with Mental Illness and the Improvement of Mental Health Care*, UN: New York.

7 Community care and the social inclusion of individuals with psychiatric disabilities in Northern Ireland

Roger Manktelow

Introduction

This chapter addresses the question of how best to assist the social integration in the community of former long-stay psychiatric patients. De-institutionalisation and the development of community care projects have dramatically changed the relationship between people with mental illness and the wider public. No longer are sufferers removed from public scrutiny in psychiatric hospitals, rather they are returned to live in the midst of small local communities. However those who suffer severe mental illness, even if they have benefited from rehabilitation, are likely to have retained residual psychiatric disabilities, particularly in respect of undertaking social interaction. As appropriate sheltered accommodation and day-care has developed for such disabled individuals it has become apparent that those disabled also require a social infrastructure to be sponsored on their behalf. Criticisms of institutional regimes have tended to undervalue the communal aspects of hospital life. On discharge, life in the community can often be a lonely and isolating experience. In response to these concerns, ten years ago, in a small town in Northern Ireland, Rehability was established as a voluntary group to help meet the social and recreational needs of people who are psychiatrically disabled and who live outside hospital.

In this chapter, the implementation of the policy of community care within the local context is first described. This is followed by an evaluation, based on research findings, of the effectiveness of the resettlement programme for former psychiatric patients in terms of social inclusion. The interactional difficulties which former patients encounter in the community are then analysed in a symbolic interactionist framework. Finally, the service response to these concerns is described - the voluntary group, Rehability, together with a number of case vignettes to illustrate the practical difficulties of life outside hospital.. A theoretical analysis is combined with a description of a community development project to promote social inclusion.

Community care

From a study of the history of the county psychiatric hospital, it can be seen that at certain times there has been a movement away from the model of isolation and custodial care for people with mental illness. This movement occurred firstly in 1948 - when the Northern Ireland Hospital Authority took over hospital management from the County Councils, secondly in 1961 - with the new Mental Health Act and its commitment to developing alternatives to hospitalisation, and finally from the mid-1980s with the policy of community care. The resettlement of long stay patients is now a social policy of considerable significance. The number of discharges is so substantial that the question of the long-term survival of psychiatric hospitals, certainly in their present form, is now raised. Nevertheless, the policy of community care is not something new; rather, in a historical perspective, ideas about community care and treatment have come full circle over the past 150 years (Busfield 1986). Public policy developed from one of the care of the mentally ill by their local community, to one of housing them in state mental hospitals, only to return to a re-emphasis on moving individuals back into the community.

The ideology of community care

The movement of people with mental illness out of hospital to community settlement, known as community care, has three ideological justifications. The first ideology is that of deinstitutionalisation, a sociological perspective. This term is used to describe the critique of psychiatric hospitals as total institutions, which aggravate residents' disabilities, and reinforce their dependence (Goffman, 1961). The effects of institutionalisation can only be countered by the experience of normalisation (Wolfensburger, 1972). Living in the community in domestic situations amongst ordinary people enables the behaviour of the sufferer to become normalised. The second ideological justification is destigmatisation, the perspective of the social psychologist (Rabkin 1974). People with mental illness warehoused in institutions away from society are seen by the public as a stigmatised group on whom the public projects all its fears and prejudices (Barham, 1992). When public attitudes have been investigated, it has been found that the public see 'the mentally ill' as having a 'negative halo' (Nunnally, 1961). A negative image of the mentally ill is reinforced by their portrayal in the mass media (Matas et al, 1986). However, as the public begins to experience people with mental illness living in local neighbourhoods their prejudices are challenged (Link and Cullen 1986). Decentralisation, the perspective of the social geographer (Smith & Giggs 1988), is the third ideological justification for the movement out of hospital. No longer are huge Victorian institutions seen as an acceptable way for devalued groups to be cared for (Scull, 1986). Rather, popular sociology has idealised the community as 'an urban village', characterised by a system of mutual aid and close ties of friendship and kinship (Young and Willmot, 1967). However, today individuals usually live in one world, work in another, and have limited contact with their extended family who live elsewhere. The concept of social worlds is used to describe this modern form of social organisation (Unruh, 1983). Despite the breakdown of communities as single spatial entities, the policy of community care has been promoted on the basis of this outmoded idealisation of life in traditional communities.

Rehabilitation and resettlement

The great era of Victorian institutional provision bequeathed some 36 psychiatric hospitals located in the counties of Ireland. This Victorian legacy has resulted in the Republic of Ireland having the highest ratio of psychiatric beds to population in Europe, and in Northern Ireland a bed/population ratio higher than in England, Scotland and Wales (Orbell, Trew and McWhirter 1990).

From the six psychiatric hospitals in Northern Ireland, 509 long-stay patients were discharged between 1987 and 1992 (Donnelly et al, 1994). This total discharged met the DHSS five year target of a 20% reduction in the hospital patient population (DHSS, 1987). A further 30% reduction in the long-stay hospital population was demanded by the Regional Strategy Plan for the period 1992 to 1997 (DHSS, 1991). When the destinations of the first group of 509 dischargees were investigated, it was found that the group had changed substantially over the five years. During the first two years, 1987-89, almost half of those discharged went into independent living, as compared to only 5% in this category in 1992. At the same time, the proportion of those discharged to highly staffed accommodation, such as residential and nursing homes, jumped from 25% of discharges in 1987 to 83% in 1992 (Donnelly et al, 1994). There are three possible explanations for this change in discharge destinations. First, the 'creaming off' hypothesis argues that those early dischargees possessed better self care abilities and were therefore better able to live independently without support. Against this explanation, the Care in the Community Study revealed that similar skill levels were found for all groups discharged to the community throughout this period (op cit). Secondly, skills may have declined in the community over time and the study does report a marked decline in self-care in the discharged group between 1990-1992. Finally, a third possibility may be that rehabilitation staff became less optimistic about the potential of former patients to live independently in the community.

My own professional experience was as a social worker throughout this period, working as a key member in the rehabilitation and resettlement program in a Northern Ireland psychiatric hospital. Certainly, the early years from the mid-80's were characterised by staff enthusiasm which created high expectations of the potential of dischargees. However, some early 'failures' who were quickly re-admitted to hospital from independent accommodation taught caution in the form of a more realistic assessment of individual ability and a recognition of the limitations of the community to care. As a result, opposite the hospital multi-disciplinary rehabilitation team, a community multi-disciplinary rehabilitation team was established with an exclusive remit to follow up, long-term, those discharged from the hospital rehabilitation and resettlement programme. It was recognised that those discharged were individuals with substantial disabilities who would require long-term monitoring and service support.

One of the particular problems reported by ex-patients was an experience of loneliness in the community. This is not entirely unexpected; after all, the social milieu of the psychiatric hospital catered for both the physical and social needs of its inmates. There was both an 'official' programme of social and recreational activities and a network of informal social contacts amongst patients and between patients and staff. Within the patient world, cigarettes and small loans of money had great significance as the 'currency' of social interaction. Life outside hospital could be very different: in sheltered accommodation there were only limited opportunities for social contact with a restricted group of other residents. Some individuals continued to pay frequent social visits to the hospital. It quickly became clear that people who had spent lengthy periods in hospital were not in a position to create a new social life on discharge and a service response was urgently needed to meet this need for a sponsored social infra-structure.

It has been observed that the stigma attached to the condition of being mentally ill is as much a stigma of place.(Johanson, 1969), that it is the fact of being a patient in a mental hospital which is stigmatising (Sarbin & Mancuso, 1970). Green et al (1987) found that the status of ex-patient, although still stigmatised, carried a number of positive ratings as compared to the persistently negative stereotype of the mental patient. Discharge marks a transition from the role of psychiatric patient to the role of ex-patient, and rehabilitation represents a rite of passage between hospital and community. More often than not, individuals remain attached to their previous status through the ex-patient label so that their social identity is still determined by the time they spent in institutional care. In this sense, being an ex-patient is a transitional status made meaningful by past hospitalisation, although although the individual is now located in the community. How can the ex-patient begin to assert a new positive social identity whilst still defined by a predominantly negative and stigmatising label?

The social networks of people with psychiatric disabilities

There is a significant body of research into the social lives of former long-stay patients outside hospital. Much of this research is part of larger follow-up studies in a variety of settings which include Northern Ireland (Donnolly et al, 1994), the Republic of Ireland (Leane & Powell, 1992), and England.(TAPS, 1991) Smaller studies have been conducted in Belfast (Prior, 1991) and Antrim (Doherty et al, 1991; Rauch, 1994) A different theme has been followed by this author in investigating the community's response to the resettlement of discharged patients in County Antrim.(Manktelow, 1993a, 1993b, 1994)

The concept of social networks has been utilised to measure, objectively, social isolation and, subjectively, the experience of loneliness amongst former patients. The investigation of social networks takes place on several dimensions: in terms of size - the number of acquaintances; of density - the frequency of contact; and of composition - the nature and quality of these contacts. Firstly, as regards to the size of the social networks, it was found in Belfast that 'the friendship networks of the ex-patient group were no different in size from those of the in-patients, and it proved just as easy to be isolated in the community as it had been in hospital (Prior, 1991). This picture has been substantiated in other areas such as Antrim where Rauch (1994) reported that the size of networks remained small although the density and interconnectedness increased, in County Waterford (Leane & Powell, 1992) and in London (TAPS, 1991). Moreover, in Antrim it was found that 39 per cent of a group of 60 patients reported significant and prolonged periods of loneliness, and that this experience of loneliness proved to be the single best predictor of readmission to hospital (Rauch, 1994). In Northen Ireland as a whole, three-quarters of the studied group had no close friendships in hospital or after twelve months in the community (Donnolly et al, 1994).

When the composition of the social worlds of former patients is examined it is found that they are divided between the psychiatric world of fellow sufferers and mental health workers and the outside world of the wider community. The social worlds of ex-patients are based upon accommodation (hostel, group home and sheltered flats), work (workshop and day-centre) and leisure (hospital coffee bar, recreational programme and resource centre). All the research studies found that former patients had impoverished networks with the main social contacts being with fellow sufferers and with mental health professionals (Donnolly, 1994). Moreover their points of contact with mainstream society were 'few and fleeting' (Prior, 1991). In Waterford, attending Mass constituted the only source of community involvement for many individuals(Leane and Powell, 1992) and in Antrim, an increasing proportion of contacts were with mental health professionals (Rauch, 1994). When social activities in the community were compared with those previously experienced in hospital, 40 per cent of the Northern Ireland group of former patients, and 50 per cent of the Republic of Ireland group, found fewer activities outside hospital than in (Donnolly et al, 1994; Leane & Powell, 1992).

The social life of the former patient

An investigation of the nature of social interaction between former patients and others revealed important differences in the interaction of former patients with each of the three groups which comprised their social worlds. (Manktelow, 1994). Former patients interacted with neighbours in their social world of the neighbourhood based around their accommodation; they interacted with a matched befriender in leisure and social activities; and they interacted with their families in those cases where family contact had been maintained.

With neighbours, interaction occurred chiefly in public places, at the shops, the bus stop and the post office; meetings were casual and consisted of a nod and a greeting. Former patients who attended sheltered employment followed a routine which was similar to others in regular employment and this helped acceptance. In such meetings, neighbours often did not perceive the individual as a former patient although the extent of their 'passing' was partly determined by the degree of anonymity and the regime of the sheltered-care facility in which the ex-patient resided. Situations in which the status of the ex-patient was revealed occurred because of particular behaviours which were different from the expected norm. These behaviours were both positive and negative. Examples of positive behaviours were quiet, reliable neighbours who would, for example, keep a weather eye on a neighbour's washing, or who would bring in the empty dustbins after collection. Regular, supportive visits by Health Board staff was also seen in a positive light. Negative behaviours included over-friendliness or the reverse behaviour of walking with head lowered avoiding eye contact..

A second more intensive form of socialising was with individuals who had volunteered to be befrienders whose purpose was to integrate the ex-patient by introducing him or her to the volunteer's own social network. There were difficulties around these relationships caused, firstly, by the residual disabilities of chronic mental illness and, secondly, by misunderstandings about the limits of befriending. One of the disabilities of severe mental illness is an inability to sustain close emotional involvement. As a friendship develops there is usually a sharing of emotions, confidences and a growth of understanding in how the other thinks and acts. However, it was reported that in these befriending relationships this 'getting to know you' process often did not occur. Befrienders had to be prepared for an unpredictable response from the ex-patient from a bubbly and warm welcome one week to a withdrawn and monosyllabic response the next. This all added up to a frustrating experience particularly for befrienders with high expectations of change and, as a result, befriending relationships were often not sustained over time.

Finally, families provided the most valued form of social contact for former patients. The level of social contact which families provided was influenced by two important factors. These were, firstly, the extent and degree of disruptive behaviour which had been experienced within the family prior to hospitalisation, and, secondly, following admission, the length of hospitalisation, during which time, there was often an unravelling of family ties.(Fisher & Tessler, 1986) As a result of these past experiences, the relationship between the former patient and his family was a complex one which could be brittle and strained. Following discharge, these difficulties were further compounded by the family's preoccupation with potentially contentious management issues such as medication maintenance, day-time activity and supervision of income.

It can be seen that when the interaction of former patients with the wider community was investigated, it was found that opportunities for social integration were restricted. These findings underline the need for the development of a service response to meet the social needs of individuals with psychiatric disabilities if they are to survive outside hospital.

Social strategies and social dilemmas

What are the determinants of the potential for non-stigmatising social interaction for the individual ex-patient? Goffman (1968) has written eloquently of the management of spoiled identity by handicapped individuals. The present analysis of the individual dilemmas and strategies available to ex-patients in their interaction with the wider community utilises this symbolic interactionist framework. If the ex-patient chooses to 'own up' to his past psychiatric patient status, community attitudes towards people with mental illness will determine the level of tolerance displayed by local residents to former patients resettled in their neighbourhoods. The author's study (Manktelow, 1994) found that there were positive attitudes overall towards resettled former patients in a small town in Northern Ireland. Specifically, as measured by the Community Attitudes to Mental Illness (CAMI) Scale, respondents were strongest in their expression of benevolence but expressed reservations about bringing people with mental illness into their personal and family life. Although attitudes expressed were positive there is a real possibility that these are socially desirable responses given to present the respondent as liberal and tolerant (Rothbar 1973). Given this caveat, these findings suggest that, whilst ex-patients might be acceptable into casual social interaction between acquaintances, there exists a real problem in relation to meaningful personal integration.

An extreme and risky strategy for former patients might be to 'ham it up' in order to make a positive identity of their psychiatric condition. However, there was no evidence of any individual acting in this way. Alternatively, in order for the ex-patient to become accepted as a member of the community, it may well be best for the individual to 'cover' his past biography of hospitalisation. The extent to which this 'passing' strategy will be successful will be determined, firstly, by the ability to perform normal social role behaviour and, secondly, by the active control of information about past biography. In respect to role performance, people with mental illness have difficulties in performing socially in several areas. Firstly, the sufferer of severe mental illness is limited in the ability to sustain prolonged social interaction and close emotional involvement. Secondly, there is an unpredictability in mood, response and behaviour which further restricts the growth of friendship. Social interaction is marred by psychiatric symptomatology with the sufferer being preoccupied by delusions and lacking concentration. Finally, although the medication used to treat symptoms might improve the sufferer's grasp on reality, its side-effects can produce noticeable behaviours, either lethargy or pronounced tremors and restlessness, which are in themselves noticeably stigmatising. It can be seen that, taken together, these difficulties amount to substantial handicaps to be overcome for the performance of acceptable social interaction.

The extent to which individuals might 'cover' their previous identity is also determined by the anonymity of the community care schemes in which they reside. If neighbours view the facility as a 'place apart' then they are likely to avoid contact with its residents (Dear and Taylor 1982). The facilities studied in Northern Ireland included mental health hostels, group homes and sheltered flatlets. Policy has dictated that residential schemes should be housed in small-scale, outwardly inconspicuous, domestic accommodation integrated into ordinary housing (Manktelow, 1992). This policy seems to have been effective judging by the fact that one respondent who lived alongside a hostel only became aware of its existence after five years when visitors asked directions to a mental health facility. Furthermore, if the facility regime offers opportunities for everyday activities such as paying bills, shopping and using public transport then these provide instances for social interaction which is in itself normalising and integrating (Segal and Averim 1976).

Partial asylum in the community

In his definitive sociological analysis of being mentally ill, Scheff (1966) viewed being mentally ill as a master status in the light of which all subsequent actions were viewed and from which exit was fraught with difficulties. We have reviewed these interactional difficulties in the previous section. In the European policy context, there has been enthusiastic promotion of the policy of social inclusion for people with disabilities, physical, learning and, to a lesser extent, psychiatric (Helios 1995). However, a realistic appraisal of the situation of sufferers of severe mental illness has indicated limits on their social integration and their consequent need for 'partial asylum' within the community (Tomlinson and Carrier 1997). What such partial asylum can offer is an escape from the pressures and anxieties of everyday life. But this haven is not contained in a single geographical location with the danger of creating a 'service-dependent ghetto (Dear and Wolch 1987). It is, rather, an integral element of each of the social worlds of the former patient - accommodation, work and leisure. As Barron and Haldane (1992) emphasise, it does no service to individuals with disabilities to ignore their realities in the push for normalisation, rather it is important to recognise and respect difference.

Rehability - a group response

At an early stage of the resettlement programme of long-stay patients from hospital to community, the paucity of their social networks, which was later confirmed in research studies, became glaringly evident to members of the rehabilitation team in which the author worked as a social worker. It was clear that it was a totally unrealistic expectation to assume that individuals, having completed a rehabilitation programme, were now sufficiently socially skilled to achieve their social integration into the wider community on their own. If there was to be a real and sustained improvement in the quality of life for people now living outside of hospital and if rapid relapse and readmission was to be prevented then it was necessary to sponsor a social infra-structure for the community of discharged individuals. Acting pro-actively, three core members of the rehabilitation team - social worker, community psychiatric nurse and occupational therapist - and a small group of former patients came together with a local clergyman, a family relative of an ex-patient and a local teacher to address the problem of social isolation. As a result, the voluntary group REHABILITY was formed in 1987 with the expressed aim of helping to meet the social and recreational needs of people with severe mental illness living outside hospital in the local area. Its formation was founded on the following basic principles:

1. User empowerment - that ex-patients owned and managed the organisation and its resources
2. Partnership - that key members of the wider community were involved in the project
3. Bottom-up planning - that this initiative was driven by grassroots experience of life outside hospital
4. Action research - that founder members shared knowledge with users, relatives and key community members to achieve change
5. Targetting those with long-term difficulties - that because much innovation is directed towards the short-term user of psychiatric services at the expense of the long-term sufferer the needs of people with severe mental illness were to be an exclusive priority
6. Availability outside normal hours - that a social club would be established which would open when other services closed, given that evenings, weekends and holidays were times of greatest loneliness
7. Accessibility - that a service should be located in a local neighbourhood in close proximity to people's homes

Over the last ten years, Rehability has put in place the following structure and services:

Membership Model. Rehability is open to all individuals who have had prolonged contact with the mental health services. Members pay a small membership fee per annum which entitles them to membership of the social club, to partake in the holiday programme and to receive a membership identification card which may be used for general I.D purposes such as cashing state benefits. Membership in 1996 totalled 130 members, 63 per cent male, and 36 per cent in the age group 31-45 years.

94

The Social Club Model. Rehability functions as a social club along similar lines to the local golf club or a gentlemen's club in Pall Mall (apart from the strict ban on alcohol). Members operate a stewarding system (with the support of the co-ordinator) being responsible for the opening and closing of the club on their duty night. It is the principle aim to engender in members a sense of ownership of the centre.

Management. Members compose a club committee which meets monthly to discuss future activities and club management. There is also a management committee of members and interested others which is responsible for staffing, planning and fund-raising.

Accommodation Rehability has rennovated two adjoining houses given rent-free by the public housing body into a clubhouse. These houses are located in a public housing estate, an area of social need, within walking distance of the local mental health hostel, a sheltered housing scheme and two group homes. The centre consists of a coffee bar, T.V room, games room, catering kitchen, craft room and office. An extensive programme of events is offered on a monthly basis both inside and outside the centre, and publicised by a monthly newsletter sent to all members. The centre is open seven nights a week, every day of the year including bank holidays.

Attendance Attendances for the year 1996 totalled 7,458, an increase of 32 per cent over the last three years.

Holiday scheme In 1987, Rehability began with a summer holiday for a group of ex-patients and has held an annual holiday every year since. These holiday experiences provide a number of therapeutic benefits: individuals practice and develop new social skills in new social situations; they learn to save through a holiday savings scheme; they learn how to get along with each other in a living group and they gain experiences beyond their everyday social world.

The philosophy behind Rehabilty is based on the three core principles:

1. Small is beautiful. Rehability does not intend building a management structure and is staffed only by a co-ordinator and a relief co-ordinator. By keeping small members interests stay paramount
2. Self-help. Rehability raises a considerable portion of its income by fundraising involving members. Jumble sales, flag days, and sponsored walks. All these activities provide members with further opportunities to interact with the public and promote a sense of ownership of Rehability.
3. Building bridgeheads. Rehability aims to provide opportunities for members to build their self-confidence by individual contacts with the wider community. This is a social process which cannot be forced but which must be allowed to evolve naturally.

Case vignettes

Individuals discharged from long-term psychiatric care differ widely in relation to social background, age and psychiatric diagnosis. In order to illustrate the range of behaviours encountered when working with people with psychiatric disabilities, the following case vignettes are described. These accounts also highlight the common handicaps which people with long-term mental illness suffer and illustrate the way in which Rehability has helped to improve individual well-being.

- Peter came from a working class background and has spent eight years in hospital since his mid-twenties. Contact with his family had ended and hostel placements had also broken down. However, in a hospital rehabilitation programme and on long- term medication Peter was a willing and agreeable participant although having an inflated view of his own abilities. Outside hospital, he was placed in a group living situation where his poor self-care and insistence on his control of his weekly income created day-to-day problems for community support staff. After two years, Peter was readmitted to hospital and subsequently discharged to a staffed hostel as a long-term resident. He is an active member of Rehability joining the annual holidays, the day outings, acting as Steward and a frequent competitor in Rehability tournaments..

- Although Sheila has never been cared for on a long-term hospital ward, she has had numerous hospital admissions since her husband left her many years ago. She is frequently overwhelmed by her own feelings of inadequacy in her relationships with her children, her friends, and her fellow workers at a sheltered workshop. To cope with such low self-esteem she depended on tranquillisers and alcohol. However, being a member of the Centre has for Sheila restored a more positive sense of self-worth and substantially reduced her readmissions to hospital.. Sheila attends the Centre frequently and participates in the events and holidays. With her restored self-confidence she is able to deal with new situations without being overwhelmed.

- George spent more than twenty years in hospital and was a reluctant referral to the hospital rehabilitation programme. He had sufficient understanding and experience of the hardships of life outside hospital to be very wary of resettlement. However, being able to claim full benefits was a major incentive to return to community living first in a hostel and later in group living. At first, most days George walked the couple of miles up and down to hospital to see old friends but as time passed he became more involved in the Centre and dropped in as a regular, enjoying a smoke and a chat about the local news.

- Psychiatric illness was very hard to accept for Ann and her family. High hopes of good A-levels and a successful career were abandoned as the reality of chronic mental illness became clear. Ann's medication required frequent adjustments to maintain a fragile stability and produced side effects which seemed as debilitating as the illness. Her years as a young woman were spent in hospital but throughout Ann's spirit remained undaunted and her family loyal. Community care enabled the development of sheltered accommodation schemes where Anne could live with privacy but with help close at hand. Outside hospital with enthusiasm she recreated her social life with the Centre forming one part of a social network of Church, College and family.

- Sam had always lived at home with his mother who looked after him and his wages. Seldom in hospital, his mother ensured Sam's regular attendance at a sheltered workshop. After her death, Sam continued to live in their home and kept up his work. But there were frequent days off, home quickly became rundown and his behaviour when drunk was a real nuisance. A tolerant neighbourhood in memory of his mother made allowances but Sam was an isolated and lonely man. With community support his living standards improved dramatically and when the Centre was opened Sam became a nightly attender.

- Ray was a child in care, abandoned by his parents. At eighteen years of age he was hopelessly unprepared for life beyond the care system. Impulsive without being able to protect himself, through a series of incidents he entered the psychiatric services. Only a hostel placement prevented a slide into delinquency and self-mutilation. The hostel supervisor acted as a surrogate father and the hostel as a substitute family. Whilst Ray presented a 'street-wise' image to the outside world, his reality was a life of insecurity and self-doubt. The Centre offered Ray a safe haven to enjoy and to grow, to partake and to begin to assume responsibilities.

These individuals are drawn from a large group of former patients who share a commonality of intractable problems . In the not so recent past such people would have been written off as 'beyond hope and treatment' to be relegated to the back-wards of the asylum. Today, they enjoy a markedly better quality of life and through Rehability are all taking an active involvement in local community life.

Conclusion

People with severe mental illness remain a socially excluded group who require positive action on their behalf if they are not to experience life outside hospital as lonely and isolated. Whilst community care packages have been developed to include appropriate supportive accommodation and productive day-time activity less attention has been paid to the need for socially integrating activity. It has been seen that former long-stay psychiatric patients are a disabled group with special needs. One of their major disabilities is in the area of social interaction. Because of this social deficit they are not able to perform to a socially adequate level for acceptance in the activities of the wider community. In order to avoid a deterioration in mental wellbeing and consequent hospital readmission, it is necessary to provide a sponsored social infra-structure and Rehability is an example of the social club model approach to social integration. Within such protected settings individual can build self confidence, repair self esteem and begin their integration into wider society.

References

Barham, P.(1991), *Closing the Asylum- The Mental Patient in Modern Society*, Penguin: Harmondsworth.

Barron, S. and Haldane, J.(1992), *Community, Normality and Difference*, Aberdeen University Press: Aberdeen.

Doherty, H., Graham, C., McCrum, B., Manktelow, R. and Rauch, R.(1992), *One Year On: An Evaluation of the First Year of Operation of the Flat Cluster Accommodation and Support Scheme in Antrim*, Praxis: Belfast.

Dear,M. and Taylor,S.(1982) *Not on Our Streets: Community Attitudes to Mental Health Care.* Pion: London.

DHSS (1986), *A Regional Strategy for the Northern Ireland Health and Social Services 1987-1992*, DHSS (NI): Belfast.

DHSSS(1991), *A Regional Strategy for the Northern Ireland Health and Social Services 1992-1997.*DHSS (NI): Belfast.

Donnellly, M., McGilloway, S., Mays, N., and Perry, S.,(1994), *Opening New Doors: An Evaluation of Community Care for People Discharged from Psychiatric and Mentally Handicapped Hospitals*, HMSO: Belfast.

Fisher,G. and Tessler,R.(1986) 'Family bonding of the mentally ill: an analysis of family visits with residents of Board care homes'' *Journal of Health and Social Behaviour*,27,236-49.

Finnane, M.(1981), *Insanity and the Insane in Ireland*, Croom Helm: London.

Goffman, E. (1961), *Asylums: Essays on the Social Situations of Mental Patients and Other Inmates.* Penguin: Harmondsworth.

Goffman, E.(1968), *Stigma. Notes on the management of spoiled identity,* Penguin: Harmondsworth.

Green, D.,McCormack, I.,Walkey, F., and Taylor,J. (1987), 'Community Attitudes Towards Mental Illness, Twenty Two Years On', *Social Science and Medicine,* 24,417-22.

Helios (1995), *Community Action programme to assist disabled people,* European Commission: Brussels.

Johansen,W.(1969), 'Attitudes Towards Mental Patients: A Review of the Research', *Mental Hygiene,* 53, 218-228.

Link,B. and Cullen,F.(1986) 'Contact with the mentally ill and perceptions of how dangerous they are', *Journal of Health and Social Behaviour,*27,289-303.

Knapp, M., Cambridge, P.,Corinne, C.,Thomasen, J., Beechan, C. and Darton, R. (1990), *Care in the Community: Lessons from a Demonstration Programme,* University of Kent: Personal Social Services Research Unit.

Leane, M. amd Powell, F.(1992), *Towards Independence - A Quality of Life Study of Longstay Psychiatric Patients Returned to Community Living in Waterford,* University College Cork: Cork.

Manktelow, R.(1992) *Stepping-stone or Long-term home: A Study of Three Mental Health Hostels.* DHSS(NI)/ SSI: Belfast.

Manktelow, R.(1993a) 'A report on the study of the views and attitudes of people in contact with former longstay patients'. In D.Trent and C. Reed (eds) *Promotion of Mental Health Conference Proceedings vol 2.* Avebury: Aldershot.

Manktelow, R.(1993b), *Does the Community Care? A Study of the Views and Attitudes of People in Contact with Former Long-stay Psychiatric Patients Discharged from a Northern Ireland Hospital,* Health and Health Care Research Unit: Belfast.

Manktelow, R.(1994) *My Brother's Keeper? The Community Response to the Resettlement of Ex-psychiatric patients in a Small Town in Northern Ireland.* Social Work Monographs, no 124: University of East Anglia.

Matas, M., el-Guebelay, N., Harper, D.,Green, M. and Peterkin, A.(1986), 'Mental Illness and the Media', *Canadian Journal of Psychiatry,* 31, pp.431-3.

Nunnally, J.(1981), *Public Conceptions of the Mentally Ill.* New York.

Orbell,S., Trew,K. and McWhirter,L.(1990) 'Mental illness in Northern Ireland; a comparison with England and Scotland' *Social Psychiatry and Psychiatric Epidemiology,* 25, 165-69.

Prior, L.(1991), *The Social Worlds of Ex-psychiatric Patients in Belfast* Health and Health Care Research Unit: Belfast.

Rabkin,J.(1974) 'Public attitudes towards mental illness: a review of the literature', *Schizophrenia Bulletin,* 10 (Fall),9-33.

Rauch, R.(1994), *Social Networks of Ex-psychiatric Patients,* Queen's University of Belfast: Unpublished doctoral thesis.

Sarbin,T., and Mancuso, J.(1970), 'Failure of a Moral Enterprise: Attitudes of the Public Towards Mental Illness', *Journal of Consulting and Clinical Psychology,* 35, 159-75.

Scheff, T.(1966), *Being Mentally Ill.* Weidenfeld & Nicholson: London.

Scull, A. (1986), *Decarceration: Community Treatment and the Deviant,* Polity: Cambridge.

Segal,S. and Averim,U.(1976) *The Mentally Ill in Community Based Sheltered Care.* Wiley: New York.

TAPS (1990), *Better Out than In? Report from Fifth Annual Conference of the Team for the Assessment of Psychiatric Services,* TAPS: London.

Tomlinson, D. and Carrier, J. (1997), *Asylum in the Community,* Routledge: London.

Smith, C. and Giggs, J (1988), *Location and Stigma.* Allen Unwin: London.

Unruh, D.(1983), *Invisible Lives: The Social World of the Aged,* Sage: London.

Wolfensberger, W.(1972), *The Principles of Normalisation in Human Services,* National Institute of Mental Retardation, Leonard Crainfield: Toronto.

8 Deinstitutionalisation in the Republic of Ireland: a case for re-definition?

Máire Leane and Lydia Sapouna

Introduction

De-constructing deinstitutionalisation

This chapter seeks to investigate the extent to which the concepts of participation and empowerment have been realised in the practice of deinstitutionalisation in Ireland. Relevant findings from two pieces of research on Irish psychiatric practice, will be discussed. This discussion will be informed by the theoretical approaches of interactional communication and quality of life.

The concept of deinstitutionalisation has dominated the field of mental health care for the past three decades. Community care has become the official term for describing the change in contemporary psychiatric policies, which demonstrates a desire for the social inclusion of people with mental illness. These ideas are reflected in *Planning For The Future* (1984) the Irish policy document on psychiatric services. *Planning For The Future*, advocated the provision of a comprehensive, easily accessible and community based psychiatric system. The replacement of psychiatric institutions with psychiatric units in general hospitals and the development of community based, out-patient services, were also identified as key policy aims.

There is a consensus between social scientists, mental health professionals and policy makers that institutional care does not provide the only, or the best, response to mental illness. However, community mental health cannot be assumed to translate into practices which provide the client with the opportunities denied in custodial settings, opportunities such as self-determination and inclusion. It is necessary therefore to subject both the theory and the practice of deinstitutionalisation to investigation. To define deinstitutionalisation, one must begin with an analysis of what institutionalisation means. Goffman's (1961) classic analysis of institutions alleges that they lead to *"depersonalisation"*, *"civil death"* and *"alienation"* from life outside, while Foucault (1967) and Basaglia (1968) identify the structural nature of institutions as contributing to the oppression of residents and staff. Central to this oppression is the patient's learned response to professional definitions of mental illness and institutional rules. Through this process, exclusion becomes a self-fulfilling prophesy with patients adopting a role characterised by powerlessness and lack of control. Psychiatric institutionalisation is an action that isolates the person who suffers, from the rest of the society. The deinstitutionalisation of people with mental illness must therefore, be seen as a process of social change, encompassing a shift from practices of exclusion to practices of participation.

The concept of empowerment is central to this discourse of social change, having roots in feminism, education, social work and mental health reform (Labonte, 1996). Labonte (1996) suggests that empowerment developed as *"a stance against professional "others" defining the experience of the self in objectified terms. ...[and] emphasized a latent power-from-within that we all possess and, in most uses, sought to locate that self-experience within larger social structures and belief systems."* (p.134). Jones and Meleis (1993) cited in Anderson (1996), define empowerment as both process and outcome, which, "encompasses people's rights, strengths, and abilities, implying competence or the development of potential" (p.698). They advocate Gibson's (undated) definition of empowerment as:

a social process of recognizing, promoting, and enhancing people's abilities to meet their own needs, solve their own problems, and mobilize necessary resources to take control of their own lives. More simply a process of helping people assert control over factors that affect their health.

Implicit in this understanding of empowerment is the notion of participation. Such a view of empowerment in the area of mental health, implies participation in both the process and outcome of deinstitutionalisation.

De-institutionalisation as process

The theory of interactional communication

The interactional view of communication, initially developed in the field of family therapy, is a theoretical frame focusing on the process of human interaction. This approach conceptualised interpersonal and psychotherapeutic events by considering the individual within the framework of a social situation. Focusing upon the larger societal system, of which both psychiatrist and patient are an integral part, necessitated the development of concepts which would encompass large scale events as well as happenings of an individual nature. The larger system, however, is not of immediate concern to the psychiatrist or to the patient at the time of interaction. Nonetheless, the particular problem is a part of a larger system; and conclusions drawn within this smaller system may become inaccurate or even invalid in the framework of the wider system (Ruesch, 1968a). This phenomenon has been related to the general problem of *"part and whole"*.

The interactional view challenges the *linear* cause-effect etiology, which ultimately leads to unanswerable questions or simplistic assumptions about problem solving. Since institutional "events" seldom occur only once, but rather persist and overlap, the *circular* model produced by the interactional view, is often more appropriate than the linear one which abstracts such events from the intricate time sequence in which they occur.

Every message has both a content (*report*) and a context (*command*) aspect. The former conveys information about facts, opinions, feelings, experiences etc. and the latter defines the nature of the relationship between the communicants (Bateson, 1968a). With the mutual awareness of the context in which communication occurs, an entirely new order of communication emerges. This new order was introduced as *"meta-communication"*, and defined as communication about communication. This form of communication must be present if an exchange of messages is to take place, however it is difficult to recognise because it is usually implicit rather than explicit (Ruesch, 1968b). Moreover, the qualities and characteristics of meta-communication between persons will depend upon the qualities and the degree of their mutual awareness of each other's perception.

This mutual awareness of perception is closely related to the contexts of human interaction in which learning occurs. It is also crucial in our intervention to change character structures of individuals and institutions, as familiar patterns of meeting the world are reinforced by learning. In order to challenge these familiar patterns, Bateson (1968b) introduced *"deutero-learning"*, an insight into the learning process, which concisely governs the wider range of what is learned. According to Bateson, we limit solution finding by our own standards, in other words, by what we take for granted. In order to change a structure the terms we have learned to relate to it, should be under continuous negotiation.

An interactional approach to deinstitutionalisation

In institutional practices, phenomena like dependency and powerlessness can be sharply defined in terms of the deutero-learning premise, acquired in the learning contexts of human interaction. To illustrate this it is convenient to consider the interaction between a patient and a staff member in a mental hospital. If the patient learns that the right response to the staff is to be dependent on her/him, the patient views that this is the most appropriate way to relate to staff. This response will eventually evolve into a set of rules for dealing with hospital staff, and possibly with the world outside. The patient becomes powerless by learning to accommodate to people making decisions for her/him and gradually loses the ability to decide for herself/himself.

The interactional communication approach, is considered very helpful for the understanding of the changing process of a system, such as the psychiatric care system, because:

(a) the treatment -in this case the process of deinstitutionalisation- is concerned not only with the individual patient but with each member of the system (context) of which s/he is a part;

(b) reluctance to change forms of care is not viewed as a sum of the resistance of each single member, but as a resistance of the system as a whole; and

(c) change of psychiatric care involves a new learning of how to work with mental illness, and not a mere change of definitions.

Psychiatric institutionalisation is an action of alienation and exclusion, that isolates the part from the whole. The interactional view of communication is not introduced here as one more "correct" explanatory model of institutionalisation. On the contrary, it offers a wider systemic framework where more than one explanatory factor for institutionalisation can be accommodated and interrelated. The principle governing the relations of those factors to each other is that *the whole is more that the sum of its parts*.

Within professional and administrative circles, there is a strong tendency to view institutionalisation in terms of the individual behaviour of patients and staff. This view leads to a contradiction, because while institutionalisation is always subsequent to and partially dependent on some kind of gross disturbance in the relationships of the patient to other people (Goffman, 1961), the inability to practice a social behaviour is conceived as purely individual in nature.

Some common arguments used by mental health staff during the empirical research of this study, to explain the inefficiency of psychiatric care in Ireland illustrate the consequences of this form of thought. These arguments stressed difficulties caused by the high degree of staff institutionalisation, the lack of qualified carers, and above all the lack of financial resources.

The above factors sound reasonable and form a reality for carers and planners. As such they should not be ignored or underestimated. However, it should be stressed that they can mislead and limit our criteria by:

(a) locating all problems in the pathology of individuals or in a particular sub-system. For instance this approach has little understanding of mental health staff or financial resources as parts of a wider system within which they interact. By defining a pathological object as a scapegoat organisational and political reluctance for change are overshadowed (Hawkins & Sholet, 1990). Consequently, de-institutionalisation is handled as a practical-technical problem within selected established frameworks of thought, and not through the clarification and understanding of relationships that govern the institution; (b) turning the process of alternative psychiatric care into a financial matter on the one hand, implying that "if we had the money we could provide good services", as if quality services are linearly related to financial resources; and on the other justifying "no-change" when resources are considered to be unavailable or inaccessible. This thinking indicates a detachment from the decision-making process, which ultimately leads to a situation of powerlessness where mental health professionals exclude themselves from participating in the development of forms of care.

This is just a sample of the consequences of a linear etiology which does not take into account that those who do not appear as powerful participants in the psychiatric debate, **do** actually determine the way things run and are perpetuated. It is important to remember that the act of exclusion is created and perpetuated from all sides and not merely from the sides of administrative or professional power. It seems like a *"game without end"*, as it is called in communication theory (Watzlawick, Beavin & Jackson, 1967), which appears when a system is trapped into its own rigid rules and cannot create by itself, a rule which brings about a change in these rules, i.e. a *meta-rule*. In family therapy the game usually appears such: here is our sick member, correct him/her and relieve us but do not make us change in any way (Hoffman, 1981). A psychiatric system can be viewed similarly as a "pathological factor" which cannot break out of the circle which continuously produces pathology.

De-institutionalisation is a re-negotiation of the position of the mentally ill in society. Learning to make one's own bed, cooking one's own tea, budgeting, going out shopping or living in a group house are actual renegotiations for new patterns of interaction. These are more than just acts, they are communications within a wider context in which it is determined how the small acts of doing things for oneself are to be valued.

In community psychiatry, the interaction between the person and the environment became a subject for deeper understanding. As such, community psychiatry could provide that wider context in which the dysfunctional communication patterns between the person, the institution, the staff, the family and the community, could be re- evaluated and changed. The community provides a context in which these relations can be looked at and interrelated, because they all contribute to institutionalisation.

The understanding of these interdependent relations provides the context for a new learning. The conditions of learning in institutions were patterns through which exclusion had been internalised and enacted, by patients, staff, professionals, administrators and politicians. The question is whether community psychiatry as an explanatory system can offer a different pattern of learning. In other words, how can these communications, that community psychiatry diagnoses as dysfunctional, be corrected?

Institutionalisation is not the sum of patients' learned dependence on the institution, plus nurses' dependence on patients, plus governments' dependence on institutions to exercise social control. Such summing-up excludes the interaction between these different parts, yet it is exactly what institutionalisation is based on. *Institutionalisation* happens when channels of communication are blocked between different levels: policy level, interdisciplinary level, interpersonal level. All those are a part of a whole and as such they should be considered in order to bring about change. Consequently, the reluctance for change is not merely a sum of the resistance of each single member of the caring system, plus the resistance of the dysfunctional governmental policies. The problem lies in the caring system as a whole.

Community psychiatry, as an explanatory system or a change system, or both, is also a part of that whole. When community psychiatry as an explanatory system deals with individual behaviours in isolation, it applies the same conditions of learning as in the institution (i.e. to exclude and to be excluded). Furthermore, when community psychiatry as a change system operates as a mere sum of measures that re-organise the psychiatric ward into community settings, it internalises these rules of the institutions that are the object of change, thus it manipulates methods of exclusion and masquerades them as change.

This section has attempted to show that empowerment and real change in psychiatric care do not happen in isolation. Studying interaction and systems, focuses on inclusion rather than exclusion. So, in the application of community psychiatry do "changes" happen in isolation? To what extent have the policies of community psychiatry broadened the participation in the discourse on mental illness? Is communication between the parts and the whole more open? Is the community more than the sum of its services? Is de-institutionalisation more than a sum of technical measures? Some of these questions will be addressed in the discussion of findings provided in the following section.

Methodology and research design

The following discussion forms part of a larger piece of research conducted for a Masters in Social Science at University College Cork. The research explored patterns of participation or exclusion in the process of psychiatric reform in Ireland. These patterns were analysed at the *macro-level* of policy making and at the *micro-level* of practice. The findings presented here are based on fieldwork carried out in two service areas of the North Lee catchment of the Southern Health Board, namely St. Kevin's Resocialisation/ Activation Unit and St. Mary's Day Hospital. Both services are located in hospital grounds in Cork City and are attached to Our Lady's Psychiatric Hospital. The field data was gathered within a period of seven months between December 1991 and February 1993. A qualitative approach was employed and two main research methods were used. Open ended interviews were conducted with a psychiatric social worker, five psychiatric nurses, two occupational therapists and four administrative staff. The researcher was a participant observer of group sessions and informal interactions between mental health staff and clients. To inform the contextual framework of the research, extensive documentary analysis of relevant literature and statutory documents was undertaken.

The macro-level of policy-making

Psychiatric reform in Ireland did not originate from a social demand for a more democratic psychiatry. The hospital monopolised the debate on mental illness for many years (Robins, 1986) and no other elements of society appear to have participated in any form of debate that could formulate a political alternative to confinement.

The debate on the psychiatric reform, appears to have been confined to selected groups of professionals and administrators and to negotiations between central and local government (Butler, 1987). The policies themselves have been developed through a linear top-down decision making process. Within these policies community care developed in an instrumental manner as a collection of services, rather than as a form of participatory practice. At the same time, a centralised and highly technical system of re-organising Irish health services (Barrington, 1987) appears to have limited the understanding of and access to health care structures, reflecting another expression of exclusion.

Therefore it seems that at a policy level, the pattern of psychiatric reform has been characterised by a linear application of decisions, formulated by particular interest groups. This linear model of communication has been defined as a pattern of institutionalisation. What forms of practice does this linear policy-making pattern produce? How do people involved in care relate to the changing processes described in these policies? Analysis of some aspects of the de-institutionalisation process may answer these questions.

The micro-level of practising deinstitutionalisation

The areas of practice examined included: staff reactions to *Planning for the Future*; staff relations in the multidisciplinary team; staff views on resource constrains; the physical location and condition of community psychiatric facilities, and patterns of client participation in community psychiatric settings. The findings presented here are based on the first three areas of investigation outlined above.

These areas were selected because the way people talk about a policy document, illustrates how they will relate to the change it proposes. Patterns of staff participation in the de-institutionalisation process, affect client-staff interaction and in turn, determine the possibilities of client empowerment and participation in the change process.

Staff views on Planning for the Future The staff identified *Planning for the Future* as their primary guide for developing new services and forms of practice. However, they identified their frustration with a situation in which, what appeared easy at the policy level, proved in daily practice, to be fraught with problems that were neither predicted nor appreciated, by senior staff and management. Notwithstanding the common sense appearance of the above statement, it provides information on how people experience their work, and the boundaries they are confined within, be it through the resistance of "the system" or their own resistance to change. Most of the mental health workers identified a discrepancy between the theory and the practice of *Planning for the Future*. The nurses and the occupational therapist of a Resocialisation Unit speaking about their work to promote interaction, or teach life skills, commented that "the documents say what to do but not how to do it". It would appear that the staff were making an instrumental response to the recommendations of *Planning for the Future*. The continued practice of wearing nursing uniforms signified the maintenance of a dichotomy between staff and clients. This was further evidenced by the lack of staff-client interaction outside activities with an explicit therapeutic purpose. For instance, staff and clients took their coffee breaks and lunches in separate venues. Such practice is comparable to the lack of interaction experienced in the wards of the traditional psychiatric hospital. Referring to a similar phenomenon in the day hospital where she worked, a psychiatric social worker commented that "the staff are socially isolated. They usually stick together in their office and drink tea. They are very dependent upon each other, this dependence is not solidarity, they just cannot be integrated with the patients". This quote indicates not only low staff morale but an inability to relate to the policy and philosophy under which they are expected to practice.

Staff views on the multidisciplinary team The multidisciplinary team is heralded in *Planning for the Future* as facilitating a participatory style of management, which provides an alternative to the top-down communication style of the traditional institution. Deinstitutionalisation is based on participation. Therefore it is vital that interaction between staff is participatory in nature. Respondents in the re-socialisation unit identified limited staff interaction within the hospital. Lack of communication between staff in relation to planning was specifically mentioned. Staff felt that meetings only occurred when an issue of change had to be discussed. As things were changing slowly in the unit, meetings were infrequent. Due to this style of management/communication staff experienced change as something which was imposed on them rather than something in which they participated. This suggests that a linear and exclusionary model of management/communication was still being practised.

The dis-empowering nature of this model is manifested in the belief expressed by nurses, that senior medical staff and management do not listen to them. The interactional view of communication offers an approach which highlights the potential for this situation to be re-assessed. Staff at all levels contribute to the construction of management/communication patterns and because silence can easily be interpreted as agreement, new avenues of communication need to be negotiated. Failure to do this leads to a belief amongst staff, that what they require to become active participants in the change process is inaccessible. For example access to the resources which will improve the quality of their work is not seen as feasible.

Staff views on resource constraints When mapping the channels of communication between policy makers, practitioners and users in psychiatric care, the relation of staff to resource allocation, is crucial. Staff participation in decision making regarding financial resources reflects a break from exclusionary institutional practice. A senior member of the nursing staff in the resocialisation unit highlighted the complexity of the funding process which she experienced as exclusionary and dis-empowering. On the establishment of the unit, staff were unclear about who was responsible for allocating their funding. The respondent commented that "for the first two years we could not work out who was dealing with the fund". At the time of the interview, the Nursing Officer of the Hospital applied annually, to the Health Board Special Hospital Services Manager, for funding. This application demanded detailed description of the unit's activities. However, the interviewee pointed out that, activities described as "recreational", or "social", for example client outings, were considered by the fund administrators to be non-specific and undeserving of funding. Such activities are central to the work of a resocialisation unit as they bridge the gap between hospital and community and facilitate the interaction of staff and clients in a "normal" setting. Herein lies a paradox, because these same terms are integral to the "community" approach advocated in *Planning for the Future*. Furthermore, given the limited nature of inter-staff communication previously identified, it is unlikely that those applying for funding are familiar with the particular needs of the unit. These findings provide a different perspective on the problem of resource allocation in psychiatric services. Limited resources are not the only issue. The funding procedures and criteria described above, demonstrate exclusionary and dis-empowering management practice and imply an instrumental response to *Planning for the Future*.

It was argued that participation in the distribution of financial resources is a break from institutionalisation patterns. Multidisciplinary teams offer the potential for participation in decision-making. Such potential may however be obscured, by the persistence of institutional patterns of communication/management. It is essential that mental health staff recognise and avail of this potential to re-negotiate their position within the process of de-institutionalisation. This re-negotiation can be the meta-rule that changes the rules of dependency and marginalisation, learned and adopted in the psychiatric institution. If mental health staff do not take up this challenge, how will patients be enabled to re-negotiate their position within the de-institutionalisation process and within society?

De-institutionalisation as outcome

Quality of life

Quality of life has been described as the theme for the nineties, with commentators referring to the existence of a "quality revolution" (Brown et al, 1996). A review of the literature suggests that the meaning of the term quality of life continues to evolve and that it has not achieved definitional consistency. Brown et al (1996) offer an explanation for this situation when they suggest that "Quality of life is a social construct and, as such, has no inherent substance but, rather has only the meaning that it is accorded" (p.6). Perceiving quality of life in this way, implies that any effort to operationalise the concept must be based on an investigation of what people believe quality to be comprised of in their own lives. The participation of the research subjects is integral to this approach. The task for the researcher who employs the quality of life concept, is to discover what factors constitutes quality in the lives of those being researched, and why they accord these factors such importance.

That there are many ways of conceptualizing how good life is, has not always been made explicit in the design of research tools to measure quality of life. Historically the literature appeared to bifurcate into those favouring objective or subjective quality of life definitions. Some research has defined quality of life in terms of the availability of societal resources (McCall, 1975). Such conceptualisations focus on the objective conditions of life resulting in research which employs statistical indices such as per capita income, crime rates, unemployment rates etc. as measurement criteria. Other authors emphasise the subjective aspects of life experience, viewing quality of life in terms of the individual's sense of well-being, his/her satisfaction or dissatisfaction with life etc. (Bradburn, 1965; Andrews and Withey, 1976). Research based on such definitions of quality of life, utilise psychological indicators which measure either global well being, or alternatively, satisfaction with specific life areas. More recently the importance of considering both objective and subjective variables in quality of life research, has been recognised (Campbell, Converse and Rodgers, 1976; Zautra & Goodhart, 1979; Lehman 1988). Proponents of this definitional approach, claim that the quality or goodness of life resides in the quality of the life experience, both as subjectively evaluated and as objectively determined by an assessment of external conditions. The evolution of the quality of life concept as outlined above, is further elucidated by consideration of the social trends and movements which shaped it.

The term gained currency in sociological literature in the late sixties and early seventies (Szalai & Andrews, 1980), and Brown et al (1996) identify the emergence of a number of interrelated social and cultural trends as being influential in its formation. These include the development of social welfare, the espousal of equal and human rights and their underpinning in legislation, the growth of a more holistic view of human and environmental functioning, the emergence in the field of social care of the philosophy of normalisation and the recognition of the limitation of economic expansion in the promotion of improved life conditions. Referring to the area of social care, Labonte (1996) argues that increasing interest in the concept of quality of life, emerged in part, as a consequence of patient or client challenges to the invasive nature of certain medical interventions and the condescending treatment experienced by some older people and people with disabilities. The philosophies of normalisation and deinstitutionalisation, and the independent living and consumer movements, have emphasised the role social structures play in creating barriers to the full participation of the disabled (Leach, 1996, Zola, 1994, Oliver, 1990). The psychiatric institution and the pathologising of those with mental illness are classic examples of such barriers.

Quality of life and empowerment are concepts which, as Renwick et al (1996) point out, share a common commitment to changing power relations. Researchers employing the concept of quality of life, must be conscious of the way the technical/rational knowledge underpinning professional training and legitimacy, can dis-empower people. This occurs through the use of objective measures of quality of life, the prioritising of criteria not considered as important by the research subjects and the interpretation of research findings in a way that does not reflect the views of informants (Rabinow, 1984). Labonte (1996) captures the essence of empowering research and practice, when he describes them as being based on "a dialogue for shared meaning in which life-world (lay, subjective, traditional) knowledge is seen as complementary with, rather than subordinate to, 'technical-rational' (professional, objective, scientific) knowledge" (p.145). The research approach and methods employed in the quality of life study detailed below were designed to reflect this type of empowering research.

Research design and methodology

The research findings which will be examined here are drawn from a study undertaken between 1990 and 1991 in Waterford City, Ireland. The work which was commissioned by the South Eastern Health Board in conjunction with the EU Helios programme, examined the quality of life of 38 former long-stay psychiatric patients, who had transferred from institutions to community residences between 1985 and 1990. Two control groups were also interviewed. The first (*Hospital Group*) consisted of a group of 38 long-stay psychiatric patients resident in St. Otteran's hospital, Waterford at the time of the study. The second (*Community Group*) control group was comprised of 38 members of the public living in Waterford, who had no history of mental illness or institutionalisation and were in receipt of a state benefit similar to that of the ex-patient group. These control groups were matched as closely as possible in terms of age, sex, marital status and where appropriate, length of hospital stay.

A semi-structured interview was selected as the data gathering tool. The interview schedule reflected the conceptual model used by Campbell et al (1976). This model, views the experience of general well-being as a subjective matter, dependent on the following variables; personal characteristics, for example, age, sex.; objective quality of life in various life domains, for example, income; and subjective quality of life in those same life domains, for example, satisfaction with income. Abraham Maslow's (1943) hierarchy of human needs was used to identify the life domains which should be included in the study. The appropriateness of the life domains selected was investigated and validated, in a pilot run of the interview schedule. The final draft of the schedule which contained 208 questions, was divided into sections on; physical surroundings/conditions, finance, safety/security, social contact, leisure activities, occupation, autonomy, role and self-actualisation, religion and general life satisfaction. The decision to participate in the research was a voluntary one for all respondents and the interviews which had an average duration of 55 minutes, took place in the interviewees' place of residence or work. All of the interviews were conducted by the researcher.

The aim of this chapter is to consider the extent to which deinstitutionalisation as both process and outcome, has facilitated the increased participation and empowerment of users of psychiatric services. Selected findings from the Waterford study, relating to recreation, social contact and autonomy, will be presented as a means of examining some outcomes of deinstitutionalisation.

Recreation

The range of activities which the ex-patient group participated in and their frequency of participation in these activities was considered in the interview. Data was also collected regarding the location of activities and the company in which the activities were undertaken. The most common "in-house" leisure activities of the ex-patient group were watching TV, listening to radio, entertaining visitors and reading. These activities were also the most common among the control groups. However discrepancies in the frequency of the three groups' engagement in these activities were identified. The community group reported a greater frequency of engagement in most activities. The greatest discrepancy was in relation to entertaining visitors. Twenty three percent of the community group reported having a daily visitor and a further thirty two percent reported having a visit every few days. In contrast none of the ex-patient group reported having a daily visitor. Five percent reported having a visitor every few days, with the most common frequency for visitors being every few months. The frequency of visits received by the hospital group was also low. Only three percent received a daily visit, while a further three percent received a visit every few days. The most common interval for receiving visits was every few years. It should also be noted that the visits reported by the ex-patient group, were in many cases visits by voluntary groups and were made to the residents of the house as a whole and not to any one individual.

In relation to "out of house" leisure activities, the hospital group had the highest level of participation, with the ex-patient group having the second highest level of participation. The reason for this however, was that many of the activities were arranged by the hospital and were participated in on a group basis by the ex-patients and hospital residents. In contrast, the community group took part in activities which were open to the general public and did so primarily on their own. The overall level of ex-patient participation in non arranged activities was very low and while the group did make regular use of local shops and cafes, very few were involved in community activities. Those that were, tended to be the younger members of the ex-patient group. These findings suggest that since leaving hospital, the ex-patient group have had limited participation in the community and that their social circle is limited to other ex patients, relatives and health board staff. This indicates a continuation of the limited range of social contact experienced in the institution.

The ex-patients' most commonly cited reasons for limited involvement in social activities were transport difficulties and a desire not to be seen publicly in the company of other ex- patients. In contrast the majority of the community group identified lack of money as the key factor which prevented them participating in other activities. It is significant however, that despite these findings which suggest the ex-patient group have limited recreational activities, this group reported very high rates of satisfaction with their leisure time. Furthermore their satisfaction rates were higher than those of both the hospital and community groups, with the latter, being least satisfied. A possible explanation for the ex-patients' satisfaction, is that being used to minimal social interaction in the hospital setting, they have internalised institutinal rules of communication which translate into low aspirations for social contact in the community. Such findings highlight the need for evaluations of outcome, to be sensitive to the extent to which institutional attitudes are reproduced in community settings and condition expectations for quality of life.

Social contact

To elicit information regarding the social networks of the three groups, a number of questions were asked regarding the frequency and extent of contact with family and friends. The findings reveal that the majority (73%) of the ex-patient group sat and chatted, with their house-mates every evening. In contrast only twenty seven percent of the community group reported having someone to chat with in the evenings. It is significant however, that a minority (16%) of the ex-patient group reported engaging in very little verbal contact with their fellow residents. They claimed that they refrained as much as possible from joining in the general social and, in cases, domestic routine of the household. These individuals appeared to share a common desire to return to their family homes or to find a place of their own to live in. Of the three groups, the hospital group reported the lowest level of social interaction with their living companions. Only eleven percent reported that they chatted with another patient on a daily basis, while fifty five percent claimed that they never chatted with anyone in the hospital. The community group appeared to have a much greater level of contact with their neighbours than did the ex-patient group. While both groups were on good terms with neighbours, the community group visited and exchanged favours with neighbours on a much more frequent basis than did the ex-patient group. Hence it appears that physical location in a community is not synonymous with community interaction.

As with the findings in the section on recreation, the ex-patient group again proved to be very satisfied with the degree of social contact they were experiencing. Eighty seven percent per cent of them reported being satisfied with the amount of time they spent with people, while only fifty one and forty two percent respectively, of the community and hospital groups did so.

Autonomy

Of the three groups interviewed, the community group described themselves as having the greatest amount of personal autonomy, with the lowest rates of same being reported by the hospital group. Both the ex-patient and hospital group, identified nurses as the people who had the greatest decision making power over their lives. When asked directly if they felt that nursing staff has a lot of control over them, the majority (76%) of the hospital group answered in the affirmative, with only thirty percent of the ex-patient group doing likewise. Some of the hospital group appeared to resent the hospital nursing staff, viewing them as figures of authority who had to be obeyed. Other members of this group considered the authority of the hospital staff as helpful and necessary. In contrast, the ex-patient group were almost unanimous in their view, that the nursing staff from the resocialisation unit who worked with them, were a source of support rather than agents of supervision. They seemed to draw comfort from the knowledge that they could call on the staff for aid or advice, at any time. This was experienced as enabling by the majority of the clients.

The different reactions of the hospital and ex-patient groups, to their dealing with nursing staff, may be explained by the very limited decision making power which the hospital group were found to have, even in relation to basic activities such as choosing meals and clothes. Indeed the freedom to make decisions relating to such issues was highly valued by the ex-patient group. The majority of the ex-patients reported that they were making more decisions for themselves since they left hospital and eighty four percent of them claimed that since moving to the group homes, they felt more in control of their lives. The ability to make such decisions was experienced as empowering by the group, sixty eight percent of whom expressed themselves as satisfied, pleased or delighted with the control they had over their lives. The corresponding figures for the hospital and community groups respectively, were forty two and eighty three percent. Overall the ex-patients appear to have greater personal liberty and autonomy than the hospital residents, however they would appear to be subject to greater control than the community group. This implies that community living does not preclude the potential for institutional control.

Conclusion

The findings of this chapter indicate that those involved in the Irish psychiatric system, have internalised patterns of institutionalisation. This is evident in the analysis of the process and outcome of deinstitutionalisation, which reveals that neither service providers nor service users, are full participants in the changes required by *Planning for the Future*. Mental health staff, user and community groups, were in the main, excluded by the linear model of decision making adopted in the development of Irish psychiatric policy. In consequence front-line service providers, appear to be detached from the values underpinning *Planning for the Future*. Their responses to policy recommendations were instrumental, characterised by the application of discrete technical measures as distinct from the espousal of a holistic approach. This is evident, for example, in the location of the Cork resocialisation unit within the hospital, the wearing of uniforms by staff, and the lack of staff client interaction outside of formal time-tabled, social skills sessions. These practices reflect the problem of the *sum and the whole* discussed previously. Exclusion was also manifested in the interaction between mental health staff and administrators, in relation to service development and resource allocation. The outcome of such exclusionary patterns of policy making and practice, had implications for the experiences of service users who returned to community living. They had limited involvement in community activities and their social networks were largely confined to other ex-patients and staff. Furthermore, their neighbourhood integration was more superficial than that of local people who had not been institutionalised.

Deinstitutionalisation was thus characterised by non-participative interaction between clients, staff, administrators and policy makers, reflecting a failure to transcend institutional practices and resulting in the dis-empowerment of all participants. Such dis-empowerment was experienced by staff, in terms of the absence of a dialogue on deinstitutionalisation as it related to their own practice. Dis-empowerment was also experienced by community based ex-patients, in terms of their being subjected to continued regulation by mental health staff. Despite the continuation of institutional control, the move to community living was perceived by most of them as an empowering experience and a source of improved quality of life. This evaluation of deinstitutionalisation practice highlights the potential for positive change in Irish psychiatric services.

Positive change can only occur when it is recognised, that all actors in the psychiatric service are integral to the change process and must be enabled to participate in developing new responses to mental illness. Re-conceptualising deinstitutionalisation as inclusion and empowerment rather than as a series of re-location measures, offers a new paradigm for practice. This paradigm highlights the need for participation and empowerment to be the core principles underpinning the planning, implementation and evaluation of deinstitutionalisation. The essence of adhering to these principles resides in fostering a dialogue in which all participants (managers, professionals, clients and communities) seek a shared meaning of what constitutes deinstitutionalisation. Axiomatic in this sharing relationship is an attempt "to transform structured forms of power-over to collective forms of power-with" (Labonte, 1996 p.145). Re-defining deinstitutionalisation as a re-negotiation of power, presents opportunities for policy makers, professionals, researchers and service users seeking to challenge the reproduction of exclusionary patterns of psychiatric care.

Notes

1. Sapouna, L. (1993), *Community Psychiatry; Confined within the politics of a progressive language*, Department of Applied Social Studies: University College Cork.
2. Leane, M. (1992), *Towards independence: A quality of life study of long-stay psychiatric patients returned to community living in Waterford, Eire*, Helios/Social Policy Research Unit: University College Cork.

References

Anderson, J.M. (1996), 'Empowering Patients: Issues and Strategies', *Soc. Sci. Med., 43(5)*: 697-705.

Andrews, F.R. and Withey, S.B. (1976), *Social Indicators of Well-being: American's Perceptions of Life Quality*, Plenum Press: New York.

Barrington, R. (1987), *Health, Medicine and Politics in Ireland 1900-1970*, IPA: Dublin.

Basaglia, F. (1968), *L'instituzione Negata*, in Ramon, S. (1991) *Beyond Community Care: Normalisation and Integration Work*, Macmillan: London.

Bateson, G. (1968a), 'Information and Codification: A Philosophical Approach', pp 168:211 in J. Ruech and G. Bateson (ed) *Communication- The Social Matrix of Psychiatry*, The Norton Library: New York.

Bateson, G. (1968b), 'Conventions of Communication: Where Validity Depends upon Belief' pp 212:227 in J. Ruech and G. Bateson (ed), *Communication- The Social Matrix of Psychiatry*, The Norton Library: New York.

Bradburn, N.M. (1965), *The Structure of Psychological Well-being*, Aldine: Chicago.

Brown, I; Renwick, R. and Nagler, M. (1996), 'The Centrality of Quality of Life in Health Promotion and Rehabilitation' pp 3:13 in Renwick; I. Brown and M. Nagler (eds), *Quality of Life in Health Promotion and Rehabilitation: Conceptual Approaches, Issues and Applications*, Sage: London.

Butler, S. (1987), 'The Psychiatric Services: Planning for the Future. A Critique'. *Administration*, Vol 35: 47-68

Campbell, A; Converse, P and Rodgers, W.L. (1976), *The Quality of American Life*, Russell Sage Foundation: New York.

Department of Health, *Planning for the Future: Report of a Study Group on the Development of the Psychiatric Service 1984*, Stationery Office: Dublin.

Emener, W.G. (1993), 'Empowerment in Rehabilitation: An Empowerment Philosophy for Rehabilitation in the Twentieth Century' pp. 297:305, in M. Nagler (ed), *Perspectives on Disability* (2nd ed), Health Markets Research: Palo Alto: CA.

Foucault, M. (1967), *Madness and Civilisation: a History of Insanity in the Age of Reason,* Tavistock: London.

Gibson (undated), In J.M. Anderson (1996), op. cit..

Goffman, E (1961), *Asylums: Essays on the Situation of Mental Patients and other Inmates,* Penguin Books: London.

Hawkings, P. & Sholet. R (1990), *Supervision in Helping Professions,* Open University Press: Milton Keynes.

Hoffmann, L. (1981), *Foundations of Family Therapy,* Basic Books: New York.

Israel, B. Checkoway, B. Schulz, A. and Zimmerman, M. (1994), 'Health Education and Community Empowerment: Conceptualizing and Measuring Perceptions of Individual, Organizational and Community Control', *Health Education Quarterly 21*: 149-170.

Jones, P.S. & Meleis, A.I. (1993), 'Health is Empowerment', *Adv. Nurs. Sci. 15(3)*: pp.1-14.

Labonte, R. (1996), 'Measurement and Practice: Power Issues in Quality of Life, Health Promotion and Empowerment' pp 132:145 in R. Renwick; I. Brown & M. Nagler (eds), *Quality of Life in Health Promotion and Rehabilitation: Conceptual Approaches, Issues and Applications,* Sage: London.

Leach, B. (1996), 'Disabled People and the Equal Opportunities Movement' pp.88-95, in G. Hales (ed) *Beyond Disability: Towards an Enabling Society,* Sage: London.

Leane, M. (1992), *Towards Independence: A Quality of Life Study of Ex-Psychiatric Patients Returned to Community Living in Waterford Eire,* University College Cork: Helios/ Social Policy Research Unit.

Lehman, A.F. (1988), 'The Quality of Life Interview for the Chronically Mentally Ill', *Evaluation and Programme Planning* 11:51.

Maslow, A. (1943), 'A Theory of Human Motivation' *Psychological Review, 50.*

McCall, S. (1975), 'Quality of Life' *Social Indicators Research 2*: pp.229-248.

Oliver, M (1990), *The Politics of Disablement,* Macmillan: London.

Rabinow, P. (ed) (1984), *The Foucault Reader,* Pantheon: New York.

Ramon, S (ed) (1991), *Beyond Community Care: Normalisation and Integration Work,* Mind and Macmillan: London.

Renwick, R., Brown, I, and Nagler, M. (eds) (1996), *Quality of Life in Health Promotion and Rehabilitation: Conceptual Approaches, Issues and Applications,* Sage: London.

Renwick, R. & Friefeld, S. (1996), 'Quality of Life and Rehabilitation' pp26:35 in R. Renwick; I. Brown and M. Nagler (eds) *Quality of Life in Health Promotion and Rehabilitation: Conceptual Approaches, Issues and Applications,* Sage: London.

Robins, J. (1986), *Fools and Mad: A History of the Insane in Ireland,* IPA: Dublin.

Ruesch, J. (1968a), 'Values, Communication and Culture: An Introduction' pp 3:20, in J. Ruech and G. Bateson (eds) *Communication- The Social Matrix of Psychiatry,* The Norton Library: New York.

Ruesch, J. (1968b), 'Communication and Human Relations: an Interdisciplinary Approach' pp. 21-49 in J. Ruech and G. Bateson (eds) *Communication- The Social Matrix of Psychiatry,* The Norton Library: New York.

Ruesch, J. and Bateson, G (1968), *Communication- The Social Matrix of Psychiatry,* The Norton Library: New York.

Sapouna, L. (1993), *Community Psychiatry: Confined within the Politics of Progressive Language,* M.Soc.Sc Thesis: University College (Un-published).

Szalai, A. and Andrews, F. (1980), *The Quality of Life: Comparative Studies,* Sage Studies in International Sociology, Sage: Sage.

Turner, R.R. (1990), 'Rehabilitation' pp. 247-267 in B. Spilker (ed) *Quality of Life Assessments in Clinical Trials,* Raven: New York.

Watzlawick, P. Beavin, J. and Jackson, D (1967), *Pragmatics of Human Communication,* Norton Library: New York.

Watzlawick, P. and Weakland, J. (eds) (1977), *The Interactional View,* Norton Library: New York.

World Health Organisation (1986), *Ottawa Charter for Health Promotion 1986,* Public Health Association, Ottowa: Ontario.

Zautra, A. and Goohart, D. (1979), 'Quality of Life Indicators: A Review of the Literature', *Community Mental Health Review 4(1):* pp. 3-10.

Zola, I.K. (1994), 'Towards inclusion: The role of people with disabilities in policy and research issues in the United States: A historical and political analysis' pp. 49-66 in M. H. Rioux and M. Bach (eds) *Disability is not measles: New research paradigms in disability,* Roeher Institute: New York.

9 Mental health social work and addictions in Northern Ireland

Barbara Ward

Introduction

There has always been a significant problem of alcohol consumption in Northern Ireland, even though the population as a whole has a higher proportion of abstainers than many other countries. In *The Handbook of Alcohol in Northern Ireland* (Health Promotion Agency, 1992), a number of significant factors about problem drinking in Northern Ireland were identified. Northern Ireland has a very high percentage of total abstainers from alcohol, and although there are fewer drinkers, those who do drink are identified as having high levels of 'abnormal', 'problem', or 'heavy' drinking. In addition, Northern Irish drinkers have a distinctive style of drinking where their drinking is concentrated in fewer drinking occasions, usually on Friday and Saturday nights, with therefore much higher amounts being consumed on those occasions. As a result, heavy drinking has become the norm and there is not an established pattern of moderate drinking. This type of heavy drinking can bring about many short-term problems in its own right, on top of the well known alcohol-related problems which develop over many years of heavy drinking. It has also been noted in the Handbook that recently there has been a significant increase in the number of women drinking, as well as the number of young people drinking, who have begun to drink at a younger age. It has also been recognised that drinking is heaviest among the younger age groups.

Along with the problems of high levels of alcohol consumption, which society in Northern Ireland has faced for many years, since the early 1990's there has also been an increase in problems related to the use of drugs, both legal and illicit. In Northern Ireland, there is not yet a significant problem with heroin, cocaine or the other 'hard' drugs. However, there have been significant increases in the use and misuse of the four main illegal drugs of misuse: cannabis, amphetamines, LSD, and ecstasy. There are also significant problems from the misuse of prescribed medications such as benzodiazepines, better known as tranquillisers and sleeping tablets. Finally, there are problems of misuse/abuse of over-the-counter medications such as codeine linctus and kaolin morphine to name but a few. This then sets the scene for the realisation that there are significant numbers of people who are experiencing problems - physical, social, psychological, financial, and familial - which stem from substance misuse. As a result, it is incumbent on those in the helping professions, such as social workers, to be trained and be competent to deal with problems of addiction.

In this chapter we shall look at the growth of the specialist addiction services in Northern Ireland, and in particular the changing role within addictions treatment for the social worker. We shall also examine addictions problems in the light of the relevant legal framework, the Mental Health Order (Northern Ireland) 1986 and investigate how the legislation impinges on social workers, particularly in relation to their function as Approved Social Workers as stipulated under the Order. Finally, we shall examine the importance of all social workers having knowledge and specific training in assessment of and intervention with clients with substance misuse problems.

Developments in addictions treatment and social work in Northern Ireland

In examining social work with addictions in Northern Ireland one must first trace the history of the Addiction Services. In the late 1960's and early 1970's, there was a growth of in-patient treatment for problem drinkers within the psychiatric hospitals in Northern Ireland. For example, Shaftesbury Square Hospital in Belfast opened an alcohol unit in the late 1960's, while the Tyrone and Fermanagh Psychiatric Hospital in Omagh established their alcohol unit in the early 1970's. Special wards were set aside to expressly treat people with alcohol problems. At that time people with drinking problems were labelled with the title of alcoholic and they were treated under the disease model of alcoholism. There were many proponents of the disease model which originated in America. The main elements of the disease model are as follows: that the condition of alcoholism is lifelong and irreversible; that it therefore follows that one can only arrest its development; that the condition affects a distinct group of people who can be clearly identified and diagnosed; that these individuals have lost control over their substance use; and that when they stop using the substance they will experience cravings which leave them always in danger of relapsing. (Shephard, 1990, p.28). The goal for treatment is total abstinence. At the time of the adoption of the disease model, the vast majority of social workers were generic social workers who carried cases both in the community and from hospital settings drawn from all the client groups. However, with the introduction of wards for the treatment of people with alcohol problems, there was usually a social work attachment to these units. In essence, therefore, in the early seventies we actually saw within the alcohol units, a return to the development of a first specialism amongst generic social workers.

Initially, the specialist social worker's input incorporated a very specific social work role which included responsibility for the in-patients' benefits and financial difficulties and assistance with housing difficulties. Specialist social workers were also responsible for supplying the medical team with a complete social history in respect of the patient's background, and would visit the patient's home to support the family in the community. The social worker would also be responsible, in particular, for child care issues and other difficulties which may be identified in the home. During the 70's and 80's, addiction units continued to develop their treatment programmes. Such programmes were generally based on what would be loosely defined as a 'modified Minnesota Model' of treatment in which confrontational group therapy techniques were usually employed as the main foundation of treatment. Through this development, social workers attached to treatment units participated as part of the multi-disciplinary treatment team within the group treatment setting. Again, specialist social workers in addictions were ahead of the times in working within a multi-disciplinary setting.

By the mid-eighties, many treatment units, as part of their programme, included joint interviews between the in-patient and a significant member of their family. This gave the family member the chance, in a protected environment, to tell the drinker exactly what problems their drinking had caused for themselves and other members of the family. It was often the social worker's role, firstly, to contact the family member and help them to prepare for this interview. Secondly, the social worker, along with another member of staff, would also participate in the joint interview. This also helped to identify for the social worker other problems which may be occurring in the home.

Throughout the decade, the Treatment Units became more structured and alongside groupwork, one-to-one counselling was offered. The goal of treatment remained total abstinence, based on the disease model. However, the social work role was modified away from traditional social work tasks into a more facilitating role. Although within the disease model, it was recognised that the drinker may not have caused his disease, once in treatment, personal responsibility was emphasised as part of the treatment. Therefore, instead of 'doing' for the patient in areas such as benefits and housing, the social worker would explain the systems but then the patient had to do for him/herself. This process also opened the door for other behavioural-type techniques to be incorporated into the treatment regime, including the development of Relapse Prevention measures.

The rationale of the 'personal responsibility' approach within treatment was as follows: that alcoholism is a disease, which is similar to diabetes, for example; that there are various reasons and pathways which had an influence on the disease development; and that the bottom line is that once one has been 'diagnosed' as suffering from the disease of alcoholism, the individual can determine the route which the disease takes. Just as the diabetic has the choice to follow his/her prescribed diet, to monitor their blood sugar levels and to take responsibility for their treatment, so too the alcoholic also has choices to make and to follow the path of abstinence from alcohol so that the disease does not progress further. Along with the abstinence goal, the social worker has also to assist the drinker in taking personal responsibility for other areas of his/her life which were most likely neglected during the years of heavy drinking. This often involved developing skills in dealing with income management, reintegration into family life and problem-solving in relation to other difficulties resulting from past drinking.

Furthermore, in tandem with the drinker having responsibility for their own actions, the social worker's role also centred on working with the family on these issues. The social worker had to help the family understand that their actions did not contribute to their partner's or family member's drinking. The family member often suffered low self esteem and required space to begin self-development. The social worker would try to educate the family about the disease of alcoholism and work for better understanding within the family. Social workers would encourage the family members to attend Al-Anon, the self help group for family members of alcoholics which would be viewed as very beneficial for the family member's recovery. At times, if there were severe financial problems, the social worker would advocate for the family to have their own claim to benefits separate from the drinker's so the spouse would at least have some money coming in with which to run the home. Again, the social worker had to be cognisant of any possible child care issues. Occasionally, social workers would be involved with direct work with the children who may have been experiencing difficulties as a result of a parent's drinking. This was often identified as an area that most specialist social workers within the Addictions field would like to have developed more fully, but never had the time or space to do so competently.

The late eighties saw a major change in the treatments offered within the addictions field with the development of Community Alcohol Teams (CATs) in Northern Ireland. These were later renamed, with the increased usage of drugs, Community Addictions Teams. The theoretical shift changed from the disease model of alcoholism to treatment based on the social learning model. The basic principle of the social learning model is that humans act the way they do because they have been rewarded for acting in a particular way which is, in this case, maladaptive.(Heather and Robertson, 1989, p. 195). Therefore, the determinants of their substance misuse behaviour include their personal situation and other environmental factors, such as family history, peer behaviour, and what they have learned to see as acceptable behaviour. In relation to substance misuse, then, we can see that a person's substance misuse behaviour can be learned through his/her interactions with the environment; it is influenced by behaviour modelled on childhood experience and affected by peer pressure and behaviour. But, if one has learned these problematic behaviours, one can also unlearn them and replace them by new patterns of behaviour, skills and coping mechanisms. (Miller & Hester, 1989, p.7).

This shift in, or addition to, the theoretical model changed not only the treatments on offer, but also the goals of treatment. No longer was abstinence the only goal of treatment, but controlled drinking was also advocated. As treatment was offered in the community, it centred around one-to-one counselling, usually on a contractual basis. The advantages of treatment in the community included the idea that there was less stigma attached to receiving professional help at premises often located away from other statutory services, which were more accessible, and encouraged people to seek help at an earlier stage in their substance misuse careers. Community Addiction Teams (CATs) provided a more rapid response to referrals. Counselling was performed by multidisciplinary staff, most often either a social worker or a Community Psychiatric Nurse. Because it was a counselling role, it was often difficult to differentiate between the role of the nurse and the role of the social worker. However, it can be argued that the social learning model came much easier to social workers, than the medicalised disease model approach, because of the generic nature of social work training

This counselling centred on behavioural techniques by which the client was helped to develop specific 'rules' to follow in order to change their behaviour in relation to their substance misuse. Motivational interviewing techniques were used specifically to increase motivation to make changes in relation to substance misuse behaviours. Along with work with clients in the community, social workers also continued to work with relatives; this work sometimes involved relatives whose substance misusing partner would never seek help for their problem. The focus was to help relatives look at their own behaviours and attitudes to their partner's substance use based on the rationale that, if the relative can have different reactions to the problems and behaviours, they can make life more acceptable or less traumatic and chaotic at home.

In addition to the counselling role, an area of difficulty for social workers in addiction related to the question of client self-determination. Because there must be some degree of motivation and 'wanting help' for counselling to be successful, clients were only seen who wanted to address their substance misuse problem. However, there is always a core of chronic drinkers and substance misusers, some of whom may be described as the down and outs, whom society believes must be cared for and helped. These chronic drinkers often do not wish to have any help or intervention. In a traditional social work role, there would be input to these vulnerable clients within the community, but because of the afore-stated nature of addictions counselling, this was not a role taken on by a social worker in the specialist addiction services.

In summary, because of the advances in the addictions field, social work with clients with addictions problems in Northern Ireland now involves a more individualised package of care, formulated to meet the specific needs being presented by the individual client. It is also important to note that more women are coming forward for help with addiction problems, who require treatment packages in interventions that are person identified and problem specific.

Addictions and the Mental Health Order

The Mental Health Order (Northern Ireland) 1986 presented new challenges to social workers with the introduction of Approved Social Workers, required to have special training. The main functions of Approved Social Workers include making an application for assessment (Articles 5 & 40), application for Guardianship (Article 18(4,2) & 40(1)), as well as specifically stated functions such as interviewing in a suitable manner (Article 40(2) & 5(2)), consulting with the patient's nearest relative (Article 5(3) & 19(3)),and, if the applicant, arranging conveyance of the patient to hospital (Article 8), among other functions. In particular, there have been difficulties in relation to the Admission for Assessment procedures. Article 4(2) of the Mental Health Order (NI) 1986, states

An application for assessment may be made in respect of a person on the grounds that:
(a) he is suffering from mental disorder of a nature or degree which warrants his detention in a hospital for assessment (or for assessment followed by medical treatment); and (b) failure to so detain him would create a substantial likelihood of serious physical harm to himself or other persons. (Mental Health (NI) Order 1986).

Under previous legislation (Mental Health Act (NI) 1961), prevailing practice was often to make a 'formal admission' on persons whose behaviour was proving unacceptable in the community , which included people who were intoxicated or who had addiction related problems. Under the new legislation this is no longer possible. Article 3:2 of the Mental Health Order (NI) 1986 states:

> No person shall be treated under this Order as suffering from mental disorder, or from any form of mental disorder, by reason only of personality disorder, promiscuity or other immoral conduct, sexual deviancy or <u>dependence on alcohol or drugs.</u> (author's emphasis).

This clause does not negate against the above persons receiving treatment on a voluntary basis, but it is made perfectly clear that a person cannot be admitted for assessment and treated for addiction-related problems against their will. In the first instance, this also implies that if a person is under the influence of alcohol or drugs that an assessment should not even be undertaken until the person is substance-free, at which time a proper assessment of the person's mental health status may be more appropriately conducted. This new procedure has caused difficulties because of the fact that, in the past, formal admission had taken place in such circumstances under the old legislation.

There are exceptions where a patient can be admitted for assessment under the legislation who has addiction-related problems. Firstly, alcohol-related mental illnesses such as Wernicke's encephalopathy, Korsakoff's psychosis and alcoholic hallucinosis are legitimate grounds for action under the Mental Health Order. Secondly, patients could be suffering from a co-morbid mental illness, which in the majority of cases is depression; the major decision then to be made is whether the person meets the other criteria for Admission for Assessment, that there is a substantial likelihood of serious physical harm to themselves or to other persons, and that their illness is of a degree which warrants their detention in hospital (Mental Health (NI) Order, 1986). Thirdly, the second most common mental illness with a co-morbidity with alcohol problems is schizophrenia; patients may use alcohol to help mask or alleviate the symptoms of schizophrenia, such as hearing voices.

A second area which presents great difficulties for an ASW involved in an Assessment for Admission is the situation when a person who is obviously under the influence of alcohol and who is threatening deliberate self-harm or is threatening violence towards another person. Such a person is excluded under Article 3(2) from compulsory admission but is certainly at serious physical risk to himself or to others. In this instance, the best alternative is for the person to be 'made safe' by talking him/her to bed or to a safe place. However, if an assessment seems appropiate, the medical recommendation, if made, must be considered, and the possibility of other alternatives discussed. In the event of a crisis situation, it can be extremely difficult for a proper assessment and investigation of alternatives to take place. In practice, this person may often be Admitted for Assessment by virtue of erring on the side of caution to prevent physical self-harm, or harm to another person. If the person is found not to be actively suicidal once the effects of the alcohol or drugs wears off, then he or she is discharged from hospital or regraded to voluntary status.

The challenge of addictions work within generic social work

It has been estimated that at least 25% of all social work cases and up to 40% of family and child care cases include an element of addictions related problems. Many people can experience addiction or alcohol-related problems without being dependent on a substance or without needing intensive specialist input for the problem. For example, a person who is convicted of a drink driving offence may lose his or her job resulting in marital strain and severe financial difficulties which may be the consequence of a one-off error in judgement. All social workers need to be able to recognise when addiction problems may be a contributing factor to current difficulties and all social workers need to have a basic knowledge and competence to feel confident in discussing possible alcohol/addiction-related difficulties.

Individuals seldom present to social services with addiction-related problems identified as being their chief concern. Rather, diverse problems such as child care difficulties, financial and debt-related problems, homelessness and depression are more commonly reported. Spouses may complain of a whole range of problems from the stress experienced living with a problem drinker or person with substance misuse problems. Such presenting problems may include inability to cope, physical health problems and mental health problems. Children may also be referred with behavioural difficulties or poor school attendance which are later revealed to be symptoms of underlying family problems caused by substance misuse. Therefore, it is imperative for social workers to always consider these possibilities as they begin to gather information and make initial assessments as well as on-going assessments within their caseloads.

Social workers often do not attempt to identify and work with substance misuse for three main reasons. (Cartwright et al, 1980) Firstly, role adequacy; social workers feel that they do not have the information and skills necessary to recognise and respond to people with substance misuse problems. Secondly, role legitimacy; social workers are uncertain whether raising the subject of substance misuse is within their sphere of responsibility. And thirdly, role support; social workers feel they have nowhere to turn for help and advice when unsure of how to respond to substance misuse problems. These three reasons together lead to what is described as role insecurity. This, in turn, leads to a low therapeutic commitment to tackle substance misuse problems. However, the consequences of low therapeutic commitment are that hours of client contact/work will not produce improvement if underlying substance misuse problems are not tackled.

In this scenario, the specialist social worker in addictions, as part of the Community Addictions Team, has an important role. Through expertise and training, the specialist worker can help other social workers develop a high therapeutic commitment. Social workers with high therapeutic commitment usually have four positive characteristics. Firstly, they often have some experience in working with substance misuse problems; secondly, they work or have worked in a situation of good role support and encouragement/help from their supervisor and/or peers; thirdly, they have had adequate training in counselling skills; and, finally, they have sufficient clinical knowledge about substance misuse problems to enable them to recognise the likely physical, psychological and social consequences of substance misuse problems. (Cartwright, A. et al, 1980).

The role of the specialist social worker in addictions is therefore twofold. Firstly, it is to help run training courses, particularly in-service training courses for primary care workers in order to raise their recognition, knowledge and skills in relation to clients with substance misuse problems. Secondly, it is to provide a Consultation Service to primary care workers who may be working with substance misusers within their own caseloads. It is often to the client's disadvantage to be referred on to specialist addiction services. Referral can increase the client's defences regarding their problem and their anxiety about talking about the possible difficulties which their substance use is causing them or their families. Another consideration is that the social worker already involved with the family has established a therapeutic relationship with the client and, therefore, valuable time can be saved by not introducing a new worker. By offering consultation, the social worker or other primary care worker can benefit from the expertise of the specialist worker who can discuss the case and suggest various methods of helping the client work through their difficulties. The social worker can then use the suggested interventions with the client in consultation with the specialist worker. At times, social workers experience that, although they have raised the issue of a possible substance misuse problem, their client has either denied the problem or refused to talk. An important aspect to remember is that by raising the issue, the social worker has at least put substance misuse on the agenda.

This makes the subject easier to come back to again in the future and has given the client food for thought which may provide the impetus to deal with the problem or acknowledge it in the future. It is clear that asking the question of substance use within an assessment interview is never a wasted effort.

In educating and helping a social worker to increase his/her therapeutic commitment and ability to work with clients with substance misuse problems, it is important to recognise all the social work skills which social workers already possess and which can be used in counselling or working with substance misuse problems. Firstly, in initial contacts interviewing skills can be utilised. The social worker's ability to establish a therapeutic relationship is an essential prerequisite; in particular, the ability to empathise and be non-judgmental can be the key to unlocking the problem. All social workers have assessment skills and these are particularly relevant for gathering information and following up relevant issues. The ability to question, to actively listen, to impart knowledge and to help the client understand the links between their substance use and their immediate problems are all important social work skills.

The specific theoretical models and approaches which social workers are familiar with are also particularly relevant when working with a client with possible substance misuse problems, such as systems theory. By applying this model, the social worker can help the client see the overlapping and inter-relationships in their social systems and how the one problem, substance misuse, can effect other areas in their lives. Crisis intervention theory explains how a crisis situation is an important time of potential growth and change for the client. Another theory is the task-centred approach which many social workers employ in specific situations. This approach can be used to define a specific problem, set manageable tasks for the client to achieve and formulate clear methods of achieving these goals. This approach is similar to setting rules regarding drinking levels and, by attempting to bring about small achievable changes which can happen quickly, enhances the client's confidence to continue to work on specific tasks.

When social workers have the confidence and knowledge to begin to raise the issue of substance misuse with their clients, it is important that they realise that they will not, nor do they have to, tackle the issue in the same way as the specialist worker within the Addiction services might deal with the problem. For example, rather than pursuing the line of quantifying a person's drinking or other substance misuse and attempting to 'label' the person, such as saying they are an alcoholic, it can be more helpful to look at the substance misuse from a functional standpoint. Substance use may serve a particular function. It may be a social function in order to gain acceptance within a particular group, or because it gives the user self-confidence and reduces feelings of inhibition. The user may also believe they benefit from the altered perceptions which result from substance use and which lessens the worry of current problem. Alternatively, substance misuse may serve the function of helping to escape responsibilities, receive attention and avoid particular situations. Another function of substance misuse may be to satisfy emotional needs. It may help to reduce anxieties or depression or to cope with particular negative feelings. Physiological difficulties may also be dealt with by drinking which creates a tranquillising effect and improves sleep patterns. If a social worker can help the client to identify the situations in which substance misuse occurs, this can help to identify the function that the substance use is serving. It is also important to remember that the function may be the product or the result of the other problems the client is experiencing, or it may be the cause of the other problems. Once the function of substance use is identified it is then incumbent to find alternative ways to achieve the identified functions without recourse to substance use or misuse.

In relation to older people, it is important to identify the function of drinking or substance misuse for older people which may be very different for each individual. Although one may encounter chronic substance misusers who have managed to survive to old age, it is more likely that the elderly clients have only started to experience problems from recent substance misuse. The reasons may be very varied. For example, the elderly person may have suffered a recent bereavement or be very lonely so they drink or use other substances to combat their distress. Other elderly people may use substances to help sleep at night, or on the mistaken assumption that they can use less heat and that alcohol will help to keep them warm. Some elderly people find it easier to take a drink than to prepare a meal for themselves, and others may use alcohol or other substances for their pain-relieving effects. The effects of alcohol and other substances can impair an elderly person's co-ordination and lead to an increased risk of accidents. Because many elderly people are in poor health and do not eat as much as they should, the effects of alcohol and other substances may also be much greater. Other difficulties substance use may cause arise from the interactions substances may have with other prescribed medications. If an elderly person is misusing substances they may present with symptoms of confusion or memory loss which are actually caused by their substance misuse.

Conclusion

The case has been presented for the importance of all social workers to have training, to be confident and competent in raising the issue of substance misuse with their clients and to be able to incorporate within their casework work on substance misuse issues. In Northern Ireland this approach needs to be supported by social workers' line managers and by the consultation process with staff from Community Addictions Teams. At present, within social work training courses, there is only lip service paid to teaching about substance misuse problems. One or two teaching sessions on the topic is not nearly sufficient to develop the knowledge and skill base and to increase the therapeutic commitment to work with their clients' substance misuse problems. It is imperative, therefore, there is further training incorporated within the post qualifying curriculum and also addressed within in-service training within all social work organisations. In addition to working with their client's substance misuse problems, it is also crucial that social workers know when it is appropriate to refer the clients on to the specialist addiction services. This knowledge would include where to refer clients, what specialist services are on offer, and the appropriate procedures for referral. By not dealing with alcohol and substance misuse problems a social worker may be wasting considerable time and effort . Because these problems permeate so many of the client's other problems, clients are not able to move forward with many other problems like financial problems, violence, child neglect and accidents without addressing the impact of misuse. If social workers address the substance misuse problems and the client even makes small changes in their substance using behaviours, then the client is more likely to cope better and interventions for other problems become more effective.

References

Cartwright, A. Shaw, S., Sprately,T., and Harwin, J. (1980), 'The Attitudes of Helping Agents toward the Alcohol Client, The Influence of Experience, Support, Training and Self-Esteem', *British Journal of Addiction*, 75, 413-431.

Health Promotion Agency for Northern Ireland (1992), *Handbook on Alcohol in Northern Ireland*, HMSO: Belfast.

Heather, N., and Robertson, I., (1989), *Problem Drinking*, (2nd Edition), Oxford University Press: Oxford.

Miller, W.R. and Hester, R.K. (1989), 'Treating Alcohol Problems: Toward an Informed Eclecticism' in R. Hester and W. Miller, (eds.), *Handbook of Alcoholism Treatment Approaches, Effective Alternatives*, Pergamon Press: New York.

Shephard, A. (1990), *Substance Dependency, A Professional Guide*, Venture Press Limited: Birmingham.

10 Mental health social work and addictions in the Republic of Ireland

Shane Butler

Introduction

The role of social work in the mental health services of the Republic of Ireland has generally been a limited one, its specific contribution to services for problem drinkers and drug users has been even more modest. This is not to say that social work has had no impact on addiction services, neither is it to imply that social work has no distinctive and worthwhile perspective on these problems, but the bulk of this chapter will be concerned with tracing the evolution of alcohol and drug treatment and rehabilitation services in the Republic of Ireland and attempting to understand how social work remained largely marginal to this process.

The period to be considered here is the post-war period, commencing in 1945 as the Oireachtas (the Republic's bicameral legislature) prepared to enact its first mental health legislation since self-government in 1922, and continuing up to 1997 when, unbelievably perhaps, the Mental Treatment Act 1945 is still operative, despite a protracted period of consultation and preparation for new legislation. Over the course of the intervening half-century major changes have taken place in Irish drinking habits, involving a decline in temperance sentiment, a general increase in the proportion of the population which drinks (with a particularly notable increase in drinking amongst women) and an overall trend towards increased *per capita* consumption (Walsh, 1983, Corrigan and Butler, 1991, National Alcohol Policy Ireland, 1996). The other important change to have occurred which is relevant to this chapter, is the growth in the use of illicit psychoactive substances; this phenomenon began in the mid 1960s and, despite a range of anti-drug policy measures, has continued more or less unabated ever since (Butler, 1991). Epidemiological evidence suggests that the more problematic forms of illicit drug use - intravenous use and, in particular, intravenous opiate use - are largely confined to the Greater

Dublin Area, although the use of 'softer' drugs, such as cannabis and ecstasy, appears to be widespread (O'Higgins and Duff, 1997).

It seems important, therefore, to explore treatment and rehabilitation responses in terms of the conceptualisations which, either implicitly or explicitly, underpin these therapeutic practices; specifically, what will be considered here is whether the dominant models of alcohol and drug treatment either incorporate, ignore or are antipathetic to social work perspectives. What is also important, of course, is to examine whether, or how, social work as a profession negotiated a role for itself in this expanding treatment arena. While there were some psychiatric social workers in the country's mental health system prior to the Health Act 1970, it was only following the enactment of this legislation that a major expansion took place in social work posts in the reorganised public health and social service system. Regardless of how alcohol and drug problems were conceptualised, however, it would be naive to expect that social workers would play an important role in treatment services unless they clearly and consistently staked their claim in this multi-disciplinary arena.

The Mental Treatment Act 1945 and the disease concept of alcoholism

It would be impossible to review health service responses to problem drinking in the Republic of Ireland during the second half of the twentieth century without acknowledging the centrality of what is commonly known as the 'disease concept of alcoholism'. There has always been some ambiguity about this term but, broadly speaking, it refers to the tendency to conceptualise persistent problem drinkers - whether their problems consist of alcohol dependence, physical or mental disorders, behavioural problems or some mix of all of these - in terms of a putative underlying disease, *alcoholism,* rather than in moral or criminal justice terms. Conceptualisations of this kind, which emphasise loss of control, or at least diminished control, over alcohol as a key diagnostic feature, have existed for at least a couple of centuries; however, it was only following the repeal of Prohibition in America in 1933 that the disease concept gained popular and official acceptance there and subsequently, through American influences on the World Health Organisation (WHO), that it · was disseminated internationally (Beauchamp, 1980; Jellinek, 1960).

Historical studies of the network of district lunatic asylums established in Ireland from 1817 onwards (Finnane, 1981, Robins, 1986) confirm that alcohol-related admissions were always relatively common in these institutions, and problem drinkers were also a distinctive group within the general prison population. In 1900 the General Prisons Board of Ireland established at Ennis, Co. Clare, a state inebriates' reformatory; this was intended to provide a rehabilitative regime which would end the pattern of recidivism amongst problem drinkers in the general prison system. The inebriates' asylum, which may validly be regarded as the first specialist alcoholism treatment facility in Ireland, never flourished, however, and survived for less than twenty years. There were legal, financial and administrative difficulties associated with the Ennis asylum, but, as Smith (1989) points out in her detailed study of this late Victorian experiment in social reform, it was not without significance that: "Quite bluntly no-one knew how to cure a drunk" (p.64).

In general, it appears as though there was little sympathy at public policy level for the therapeutic approach to problem drinkers in Ireland during the first half of the twentieth century. Perhaps the best illustration of this is to be found in the report of the Intoxicating Liquor Commission 1925, which had looked *inter alia* at the possibility of reviving the inebriates' asylum:

> [We] recommend that where a person is convicted of drunkenness three times in one year, he should on the third and every subsequent conviction within the year, be sent to gaol without the option of a fine...
>
> Inebriate homes are at best degrading institutions, and we have not sufficient evidence to justify us in the revival of the State home for inebriates. We think that the only effective home for such people is gaol and the only suitable occupation plenty of hard labour (Commission on Intoxicating Liquor, 1925, Final Report, paragraph 16(a)).

This harsh recommendation was not literally accepted or acted upon by the legislature, but the very fact that it was made in such uncompromising language clearly demonstrates that the disease concept of alcoholism had little credence in policy terms in the Ireland of the 1920s.

The first indication that an explicitly therapeutic approach to drinking problems might be incorporated into public policy is to be found in the Mental Treatment Act 1945. Viewed in the context of the era in which it was enacted, this was an important and progressive statute which provided for the first time for voluntary admissions to the country's mental hospitals, established a rudimentary set of safeguards against wrongful or unnecessary detention, and laid down a statutory basis for the creation of outpatient services and facilities. From the perspective of addiction treatment, the Mental Treatment Act was important because it made specific provision for both the voluntary and compulsory admission of 'addicts', defined in Section Three of the legislation in the following way:

In this Act - the word addict means a person who -

(a) by reason of his addiction to drugs or intoxicants is either dangerous to himself or others or incapable of managing himself or his affairs or of ordinary proper conduct, or

(b) by reason of his addiction to drugs, intoxicants or perverted conduct is in serious danger of mental disorder.

It was argued by opposition deputies in Dáil Eireann (the lower house) that these definitions, particularly the references to 'ordinary proper conduct', were excessively vague and subjective (Dáil Debates, Vol. 96, Columns 1009-1012) and would put unreasonable pressure on admitting psychiatrists - especially where relatives were eager to have troublesome drinkers compulsorily detained. With the wisdom of hindsight, it appears that there may have been some substance to these arguments, but there is reason to believe that this section of the legislation was not fully thought through, being an amendment introduced at the committee stage of the legislative process. The Parliamentary Secretary (the equivalent of a Junior Minister in modern political terminology) who introduced the Mental Treatment Bill explained this eleventh hour decision to include references to addiction in Section Three in the following way:

I should tell the House that, at this stage, we can only provide the necessary [legal] machinery, and that until such time as suitable institutions are available we cannot deal adequately with the problem that this amendment is intended to deal with. It will only be in case of urgency, or particular emergency, that addicts will be received in the ordinary institutions. In the course of time it is hoped that we may be able to provide special institutions. (Dáil Debates, Vol. 96, Column 1009)

It can be concluded, therefore, that the addiction provision in the Mental Treatment Act 1945 represented a policy shift - albeit a policy shift which was not fully thought through or intended to take immediate effect - towards the disease concept of alcoholism.

Table 10.1

Alcohol-related admissions as a proportion of all admissions to Irish psychiatric hospitals and units for selected years*

Year	All Admission	Alcohol Admissions	Alcohol Admissions as % of all Admissions
1958	11,231	644	5.7%
1965	15,350	1,638	10.7%
1972	22,964	4,143	18.0%
1979	27,358	7,158	26.2%
1986	29,392	7,132	24.3%
1993	27,005	5,718	21.2%

Sources: *Report of the Inspector of Mental Hospitals for 1958,* and *Annual Activities Reports* of the Medico-Social Research Board and Health Research Board.

Detailed statistical information on annual admissions to the psychiatric inpatient system in the Republic of Ireland were not routinely gathered and published until 1965, the breakdown by diagnostic category of admissions for 1958 contained in the *Report of the Inspector of Mental Hospitals* for that year being an exception. It is clear from Table 10.1, however, that the major increase in alcohol-related admissions to the inpatient system, which was to become a contentious policy issue in the 1980s, did not really commence until the mid 1960s, twenty years after the enactment of the Mental Treatment Act 1945. While Section Three of the Mental Treatment Act may have been necessary in terms of providing a statutory basis for this growth in the treated prevalence of alcohol-related problems, it certainly is not sufficient in itself to explain the growth in popularity of the disease concept of alcoholism which occurred some twenty years later. It is important, therefore, to examine the other influences which were at play in this process, and this will be done in the following section.

The Commission of Inquiry on Mental Illness 1966 and the treatment of alcoholism

If the enactment of the Mental Treatment Act 1945 is regarded as a 'defining moment' in mental health policy for the immediate post-war period, then the *Report of the Commission of Inquiry on Mental Illness*

1966 provides a useful analytic focus for a later period, the 1960s and 1970s during which the rhetoric, if not always the practice, of community mental health services was high on the health service agenda. With the exception of the recent 'Celtic Tiger' experience - the popular description of the economic growth which has occurred in the Republic of Ireland since the early 1990s - the 1960s stands out in modern Irish history as a period uniquely characterised by belief in economic growth, allied to cultural and social progress (see Lee, 1989, ch.5). The Commission of Inquiry on Mental Illness which reported in 1966 generally reflects these modernistic and upbeat characteristics, and nowhere is this more in evidence than in its consideration of alcoholism and alcoholism treatment.

The section on this topic begins with the following unequivocal statements:

> Alcoholism is a disease and is regarded by the World Health Organisation as a major health problem. The concept of alcoholism as a disease is not new, or even recent, but its general acceptance has been hampered and confused by the diversity of the causes of alcoholism and the variety of alcoholic behaviour and because some people regard alcoholism merely as a moral problem. (*Report of the Commission of Inquiry on Mental Illness, 1966,* p. 77)

It is clear from a reading of the Commission's discussion of this topic that, twenty years after its initial and rather implicit inclusion in the Mental Treatment Act, the disease concept of alcoholism had now been fully and explicitly incorporated into Irish mental health policy. Some of the influences which had contributed to this may also be discerned from a reading of the Commission's thoughts on alcoholism and its treatment. There is, for example, a very positive reference to the work of Alcoholics Anonymous (AA) and to the close collaboration which had grown up between AA and Irish mental health services since the Fellowship's inaugural Irish meeting in 1946. There is also a welcome for the more recently established Irish National Council on Alcoholism (INCA), a voluntary body 'specially formed to spread a more enlightened attitude towards alcoholism' (*Report on the Commission of Inquiry on Mental Illness,* p.82). The implicit suggestion that those who questioned the validity of the disease concept were unenlightened or moralistic was a feature of this period, when it was part of the conventional wisdom that the medicalisation of drinking problems was based on scientific research rather than being primarily a policy shift based on value judgement. It was acknowledged that most inpatient treatment of alcoholism took place in private psychiatric hospitals, although no reference was made to the Voluntary Health Insurance (VHI) funding which had contributed significantly to the growth of private alcoholism treatment since the establishment of VHI in 1957. It was concluded that specialist alcoholism treatment units offered the best prospect for service development in the public mental health services, and that three or four such inpatient units, dispersed regionally, would be sufficient for the country as a whole.

The Commission was generally well disposed towards psychiatric social work and recommended that training opportunities for specialist PSWs should be extended, since it believed that: 'At present there are about ten fully qualified psychiatric social workers in Ireland' (*Report of the Commission of Inquiry on Mental Illness,* p.122). This general acceptance of the role of social work in mental health was also reflected in the Commission's recommendations on alcoholism, where it was specifically argued that:

> The problem of alcoholism is a social as well as a medical one and the Commission recommends that health authority social workers should be made available to provide the necessary follow-up support in the community. Social workers should also participate in the study of environmental factors contributing to alcoholism. (*Report of the Commission of Inquiry on Mental Illness,* p.81)

There was, however, to be no major expansion of social work's role in the psychiatric service response to alcohol-related problems from the late 1960s onwards, despite the fact that, as may be seen from Table 10.1, the burden of these admissions to the inpatient system rose dramatically from the mid 1960s. By the late 1970s, alcohol-related admissions tended to account for a quarter of all admissions to psychiatric hospitals and units in the Republic of Ireland; in 1979, for example, alcohol-related admissions accounted for 26 per cent of all admissions, but they accounted for 38% of male admissions, and for some of the private psychiatric hospitals - such as St John of God's Hospital in Stillorgan which had a 52 per cent alcohol-related admission for that year - they were also unusually high (O'Hare and Walsh, 1981). Clearly, the belief expressed in the *Report of the Commission of Inquiry on Mental Illness* that three or four specialist inpatient units could cater for all the country's alcoholism treatment needs had proved to be very wide of the mark.

While it would be presumptuous to attempt a definitive explanation as to why social workers did not carve out a larger role for themselves in the alcoholism treatment field, there are a few factors which, in explanatory terms, at least have a high degree of plausibility. The most important of these involves the reorganisation of the Republic of Ireland's health system which took place following the Health Act 1970 and the implications of this reorganisation for the development of professional social work in

Ireland. Eight regional health boards were established and within these boards services were delivered through three administrative programmes: the *Hospital Programme* which delivered general hospital care; the *Special Hospital Programme* which provided mental health and mental handicap services; and the *Community Care Programme* which administered the General Medical Service (or family doctor scheme) for those eligible, as well as a range of other community health and social services.

As these Community Care Programmes came to be established in the years following the enactment of the Health Act, they offered employment opportunities on an unprecedented scale and in relatively congenial settings for professional social workers. While the rhetoric of Community Care suggested that social work would be generic in nature, comparable to the post-Seebohm system in the UK, the reality was that Irish Community Care social workers quickly became preoccupied with child care, ultimately to become 'child protection'. There are obvious stresses associated with child protection social work but, at least during the 1970s, it appeared to be an area which was uncontested, in the sense that no other profession was questioning the legitimacy of social work's ownership of this particular area. It also had the advantage for social workers that it allowed them to work together in teams, which was a different and welcome experience for social workers frequently accustomed to being the only social worker in multidisciplinary teams dominated by doctors and nurses.

It is difficult to estimate the number of qualified psychiatric social workers employed in the Republic of Ireland during the early 1970s, but it was probably at least double the figure of ten estimated in 1966 by the Commission of Inquiry on Mental Illness. What appears to have happened, however, is that some of the more senior and influential practitioners left the mental health services to avail themselves of the enhanced career prospects which beckoned in Community Care and to a lesser extent in academic posts. This outflow of senior practitioners from the psychiatric service undoubtedly deprived the specialism of some of its most vocal and able advocates and, as a consequence, social work's influence in the mental health services has remained small ever since.

There were two other developments, which will be discussed more fully in the next section, which further contributed to keeping mental health social work with addictions in a position of relative unimportance: the first of these involves the broadening and enhancement of the role of the psychiatric nurse which started at around this time, and the second involves the gradual popularisation and official acceptance of the concept of counselling, and of addiction counselling in particular.

Community alcohol services and social work

The disease concept of alcoholism had not been long institutionalised within Irish mental health policy when it began to come under critical scrutiny internationally. The WHO, which had been one of its most influential proponents for the previous twenty years, became increasingly unhappy with this concept, and it is fair to say that by 1980 the WHO had done a complete *volte face* on this subject. This critique and rejection of the disease concept was exemplified in the publication (Bruun et al, 1975) of a collaborative international study *Alcohol Control Policies in Public Health Perspective,* which argued for the conceptualisation of drinking problems in multi-dimensional terms, and as constituting a spectrum or continuum rather than a discrete disease entity. Equally importantly, this new public health approach insisted that alcohol was an inherently risky commodity and that the incidence and prevalence of related problems was largely explicable in terms of societal patterns of consumption. The logic of this public health perspective suggested that prevention of alcohol-related problems was more likely to be successful if it consisted of control policies: these would include fiscal measures; restriction of opening hours in retail outlets; curbs on alcohol advertising and promotion; and strict enforcement of existing legislation, such as the drink-driving code and the minimum age for legal purchase of alcohol.

In tandem with this emergence of a public health perspective on alcohol and its associated problems came a gradual realisation that conventional alcoholism treatment conferred disappointingly few therapeutic benefits on its patients. Evaluative research (for example: Orford and Edwards, 1977, Vaillant, 1983) generally revealed that the maxim 'alcoholism is a treatable illness' was rather facile, and that the enormous growth of intensive alcoholism treatment services which had taken place internationally was not justified by the outcomes. In many ways, the research suggested that little progress of a technical nature had been made since the original experiment with the inebriates' reformatory at Ennis; Smith's contention that 'no-one knew how to cure a drunk' still had some validity.

In the Republic of Ireland all of these policy issues were addressed explicitly in *The Psychiatric Services: Planning for the Future* (1984), a report on the development of the public mental health services which was drawn up by a study group appointed by the Minister for Health. This report, which is usually referred to simply as *Planning for the Future,* was comparable to the *Report of the Commission of Inquiry on Mental Illness* in its broad insistence that the dominance of the hospital, or inpatient system, in mental health services should be broken through the establishment of comprehensive, community oriented services and facilities. *Planning for the Future*, however, was a good deal clearer and more specific as to how this should be done, and its central recommendation was that services should be reorganised so as to be delivered on a sectorised basis; essentially this meant that a comprehensive mental health team, headed by a consultant psychiatrist and with access to a range of facilities, would deliver an integrated service to the residents of a clearly-defined geographic area or sector.

In its discussion of alcohol-related problems, *Planning for the Future* reflected the wider debate then current on prevention and health promotion, and provided an outline of a national alcohol policy which, in many ways, resembled the document *National Alcohol Policy Ireland* (1996) produced by the Department of Health's Health Promotion Unit some twelve years later. In relation to the management of drinking problems by the mental health services, *Planning for the Future* reflected the evidence then available from evaluative research, arguing that:

> The effectiveness of specialised alcohol treatment programmes has been seriously questioned. There is no evidence that intensive, high-cost in-patient treatment is in any way superior to simple, inexpensive community-based intervention. Compared with the latter form of management, the intensive approach is not considered to be cost effective. *(The Psychiatric Services: Planning for the Future,* p.107).

Given the popularity of the disease concept and the widespread acceptance of the psychiatric hospital as the preferred locale for the management of drinking problems, it is understandable that *Planning for the Future* did not argue for a total abandonment of alcoholism treatment. Instead, in line with its general approach to service provision, it recommended that alcohol-related problems should be managed, as far as possible, in community rather than in hospital services. It did, however, recommend the establishment of a specialist alcoholism service as part of each sector service and, without elaborating on this theme, referred to the participation in this specialist service of 'alcoholic counsellors' (p.110).

There is, of course, a certain degree of ambiguity in relation to the concept of counselling; it could be argued that counselling is a general function of all mental health professionals, whether they be doctors, nurses, social workers, clinical psychologists, occupational therapists, or whatever their specific background. In the Republic of Ireland, however, the popular use of the term 'alcoholism counsellor' (not the idiosyncratic 'alcoholic counsellor' which appeared in *Planning for the Future* !) had become gradually more commonplace in the six or seven years preceding *Planning for the Future,* and it appeared to refer to the emergence of a new mental health professional rather than to the development or fine-tuning of existing knowledge or skills by traditional mental health professionals. The initial impetus for the acceptance of the notion of alcoholism counselling in this style came, it would appear, through the establishment of specialist alcoholism treatment services based on what is known as the *Minnesota Model*. These services were in the voluntary sector, usually established by priests or nuns, and their philosophy - which draws heavily on the programme of Alcoholics Anonymous - can fairly be characterised as a new and particularly evangelical form of the disease concept (Anderson, 1981; Johnson, 1973). The Minnesota Model saw alcoholics as people who were cognitively impaired, in the sense that they were alleged to consistently misconstrue reality and in doing so fail to realise the gravity of their alcohol-related problems or the necessity for accepting personal responsibility for change. Alcoholics were described, in one of the most commonly used terms of this model, as being in 'denial', and consequently it was believed that counselling must include a heavy degree of 'constructive confrontation'.

In America, where this model originated, alcoholism counsellors tended to be recovering alcoholics, but in the Republic of Ireland the development of alcoholism counselling from the late 1970s onwards involved a more mixed group of people, amongst whom psychiatric nurses were especially prominent (O'Hagan and McGovern, 1987). The Irish National Council on Alcoholism (INCA), with the approval of the Department of Health, played an important role in this process through its counsellor training programmes which began in 1979. Mrs Mary O'Hagan, who was originally an education officer with INCA and later its executive director, was herself a social science graduate, but as she developed this aspect of her organisation's work it was clear that she saw alcoholism counselling not as a form of social work, but as 'a new health care profession' (O'Hagan and McGovern, 1987, p.1987). A further important step in the institutionalisation of alcoholism counselling in the Republic of Ireland took place in 1990 with the establishment of the Irish Association of Alcohol and Addiction Counsellors (IAAAC), a professional body for counsellors specialising in alcohol and drug problems.

As already stated, *Planning for the Future* did not contain a detailed proposal for the development of alcoholism counselling, nor indeed was any such proposal produced at Department of Health level over the subsequent decade. The 1992 *Green Paper on Mental Health*, which reviewed progress in implementing the recommendations of *Planning for the Future* , was largely positive in its assessment of the creation of local alcoholism treatment services but did not contain any critical analysis of this area. The reasons why psychiatric nurses were so successful in colonising this new area of professional specialism have already been suggested. The energies of social work within the health board system were almost completely tied up with child protection within the Community Care Programmes, and *Planning for the Future* reported that in 1984 there were only 36 social workers employed within the psychiatric system. By contrast, there were more than 6,000 psychiatric nurses employed within the health service at this time, of whom 169 were community psychiatric nurses. Although a case could have been made that social work education and training was highly appropriate for the new alcoholism services, no such case was in fact made and psychiatric nurses dominated these services.

When these developments in community services for problem drinkers in the Republic of Ireland are compared with developments in the United Kingdom at around this same period in the 1980s a number of significant differences emerge. Following the pioneering work of the Maudsley Alcohol Pilot Project (Shaw et al, 1978), the major policy shift in the UK was towards the creation of Community Alcohol Teams (CATs); the role envisaged for these CATs was not so much as a direct service provider to problem drinkers, but as a source of consultancy and advice to primary care providers who would be encouraged to develop their own therapeutic commitment in this area. While the implementation of the CATs scheme was not without its difficulties (Stockwell and Clement, 1987; Harrison, 1996), it did at least preserve intact the notion of *teamwork* in the alcohol problems field, with teams being made up of different professionals. This, for instance, is still the position in Northern Ireland where community addiction services typically involve psychiatrists, nurses, clinical psychologists *and* social workers. In the Republic of Ireland, however, there continues to be no real involvement of social workers in community alcohol services, and these new services are exclusively the preserve of 'counsellors', most of whom trained originally as psychiatric nurses. This failure of social workers to secure a role for themselves in community alcohol services is, it would appear, attributable to their own failure to stake a claim for themselves in this area as much as to any discernible antipathy towards social workers on the part of policy makers and administrators. Any claim which social workers might now make for an increased role in these new services could well be compromised by the fact that a small number of social workers, those in fact with a particular interest in alcohol problems, have become active in the Irish Association of Alcohol and Addiction Counsellors and in so doing appear to have abandoned their original professional identity.

Mental health social work and illicit drugs

Problems associated with the use of illicit drugs in the Republic of Ireland have, as already stated, been largely confined to the Greater Dublin Area, and treatment and rehabilitation services have accordingly been developed in this area to a much greater extent than elsewhere. Historically, the first evidence of concern at policy-making level with this phenomenon is to be found in the *Report of the Commission of Inquiry on Mental Illness* (1966) which reviewed this subject and warned that 'drug addiction could reach serious proportions in this country unless a constant effort is maintained to prevent the abuse of habit-forming drugs' (p.84). Two years later, in 1968, the Minister for Health appointed the Working Party on Drug Abuse, the first official policy-making body to look at this area. Of the 14 members of this committee, two were social workers, and the *Report of the Working Party on Drug Abuse* (1971) was generally sympathetic to social work and its perspectives. In 1969 a drugs clinic, which was soon to be designated the National Drug Advisory and Treatment Centre, was set up at Jervis Street Hospital in central Dublin and this clinic remained in existence until, following the closure of this hospital, its functions were transferred to the newly-established National Drug Treatment Centre at Pearse Street in 1988. This centralised clinic has always had a social work department, and currently four social workers (including one Head Social Worker) are employed in the Pearse Street centre.

The fear that 'drug addiction could reach serious proportions' was, unfortunately, well founded, although it was not until 1979/80 that the first wave of heroin use in Dublin occurred (Butler, 1991). While there have been periodic increases and decreases in prevalence of opiate use over the intervening years, there is by now an acceptance at policy level that this problem is more or less endemic in Dublin. Perhaps this is best illustrated by contrasting the scene with which the Working Party on Drug Abuse was concerned with the current scene: in 1970, according to the *Report of the Working Party on Drug Abuse* (p.14), the Gardai (the police force) were aware of 940 people who used drugs - mainly, it appears, cannabis and LSD; in 1995, however, 3,566 drug users (for 87 per cent of whom opiates were their primary drug of use) were in touch with treatment and rehabilitation services in Dublin (O'Higgins and Duff, 1997). This latter figure refers to treated prevalence and it is difficult to estimate the real prevalence of heroin use in Dublin. The *First Report of the Ministerial Task Force on Measures to Reduce the Demand for Drugs* (1996) suggested, however, that there might be up to 8,000 heroin addicts in Dublin and reviewed in detail the range of problems - from criminal activity, such as shop-lifting, burglary and mugging, to public health concerns with HIV and Hepatitis C - associated with this phenomenon.

Throughout the 1980s, but particularly since the *Government Strategy to Prevent Drug Misuse* (1991), a good deal of progress has been made in decentralising treatment and rehabilitation services in the Dublin area. The Eastern Health Board has recently created a new administrative programme in response to the perceived seriousness of the drugs problem, and is currently in the process of expanding its work force. In terms of its treatment philosophy, the overall health response has changed from an abstinence model to a more pragmatic harm reduction model, with methadone maintenance now playing a central role in the Dublin services. As with the alcohol services, however, the new jobs are designated as counsellor posts, and once again it appears that nurses are occupying the bulk of these posts. In opting to establish addiction counselling as the mainstay of its drug treatment system, the Eastern Health Board has effectively excluded social workers and clinical psychologists since members of these two professions would, should they be employed as counsellors, take a considerable drop in salary.

Conclusion

Over the past half-century, since the enactment of the Mental Treatment Act 1945, alcohol problems have been a major source of concern for and consumer of resources within the mental health services of the Republic of Ireland. Over a somewhat shorter period, and largely within the Greater Dublin Area, problems associated with the use of illicit drugs have also been of concern to the health services generally but have not been treated to any great extent within the inpatient mental health system. The disease concept of alcoholism was introduced into the Republic of Ireland from the 1940s onwards, gaining great popularity and official policy status in the 1960s. Attempts to replace the disease concept with a public health or health promotional approach have, at best, been only partially successful, and, impressionistically at least, the public still appears to be more concerned with the provision of treatment services than with prevention.

The role of social work, and of psychiatric social work in particular, in this evolving health care scene has been a relatively minor one. To some extent this is attributable to the fact that mental health social work in the Republic of Ireland has had no clear statutory basis; there has been no equivalent of the *Approved Social Worker* in the Republic, and the *White Paper - A New Mental Health Act (1995)* does not propose to give social workers any such role in new mental health legislation. On the other hand, the Child Care Act 1991 has imposed clear statutory duties on health boards in relation to child welfare and protection, and while these are not duties which are statutorily the responsibility of any single profession, in practice health boards have given social work the key role in carrying out these new functions. It is perhaps understandable, therefore, that social work as a profession has not attempted to negotiate a definite role for itself in the mental health service, addiction area, but has been largely content to develop and consolidate its position within the Community Care Programmes. On a critical note, it is ironic that a profession which claims to be competent in advocacy and in 'networking' has made no effort to negotiate a role for itself in the addictions services scene, preferring to concentrate on an arena where it has a clearer statutory role and where it does not have to, as it were, start from scratch to establish a legitimate function for itself.

This author (Butler, 1996) has argued elsewhere that social work has a valuable contribution to make to society's management of alcohol and drug problems, and this contribution was presented in terms of the critical sociological and social policy perspectives which social workers acquire during the course of their professional socialisation, rather than in terms of specific therapeutic competencies. Critics of addiction treatment in America, such as Peele (1995), have argued that the 'treatment industry' has itself become out of control, and this is an argument which is not entirely without validity in the Republic of Ireland also. A greater involvement of social work, bringing with it a broad critical view, might well make a valuable contribution to this scene.

References

Anderson, D. (1981), *Perspectives on Treatment: The Minnesota Experience,* Hazelden Center City: Minnesota.

Beauchamp, D. (1980), *Beyond Alcoholism: Alcohol and Public Health Policy,* Temple University Press: Philadelphia.

Bruun, K. et al (1975), *Alcohol Control Policies in Public Health Perspective,* Finnish Foundation for Alcohol Studies: Helsinki.

Butler, S (1991), 'Drug Problems and Drug Policies in Ireland: A Quarter of a Century Reviewed'. *Administration,* 39(3), 210-233.

Butler, S (1996), 'Substance Misuse and the Social Work Ethos'. *Journal of Substance Misuse* 1(3), 149-154.

Corrigan, E and Butler, S (1991), 'Irish Alcoholic Women in Treatment: Early Findings', *International Journal of the Addictions,* 26 (3), 281-292.

Department of Health (1925), *Report of the Intoxicating Liquor Commission,* Stationery Office: Dublin.

Department of Health (1958), *Report of the Inspector of Mental Hospitals 1958,* Stationery Office: Dublin.

Department of Health (1966), *Report of the Commission of Inquiry on Mental Illness*, Stationery Office: Dublin.

Department of Health (1971), *Report of the Working Party on Drug Abuse*, Stationery Office: Dublin.

Department of Health(1984), *The Psychiatric Services: Planning for the Future*, Stationery Office: Dublin.

Department of Health (1991), *Government Strategy to Prevent Drug Misuse*, Stationery Office: Dublin.

Department of Health (1992), *Green Paper on Mental Health*, Stationery Office: Dublin.

Department of Health (1996), *First Report of the Ministerial Task Force on Measures to Reduce the Demand for Drugs*, Stationery Office: Dublin.

Department of Health (1996), *National Alcohol Policy Ireland*, Stationery Office: Dublin.

Finnane, M (1981), *Insanity and the Insane in Post-Famine Ireland*, Croom Helm: London.

Harrison, L (ed.) (1996), *Alcohol Problems in the Community*, Routledge: London.

Jellink,E.(1960), *The Disease Concept of Alcoholism*, Hillhouse Press: New Haven.

Johnson, V (1973), *I'll Quit Tomorrow*, Harper and Row: London.

Lee, J (1989), *Ireland 1912-1985: Politics and Society*, Cambridge University Press: Cambridge.

O'Hagan, M and McGovern, T. (1987), 'The Alcoholism/Drug Dependency Counsellor, Health Care Professional in the U.S. and Ireland', pp 987-988 in *Proceedings of the 12th Conference on Health Education (Dublin, September 1985)*, Health Education Bureau: Dublin.

O'Hare, A. and Walsh, D. (1981), *Activities of Irish Psychiatric Hospitals and Units 1979*, Medico-Social Research Board: Dublin.

O'Higgins, K. and Duff, P. (1997), *Treated Drug Misuse in Ireland: First National Report 1995*, Health Research Board: Dublin.

Orford, J. and Edwards, G. (1997), *Alcoholism*, Oxford University Press: Oxford.

Peele, S. (1995), *The Diseasing of America: How We Allowed Recovery Zealots and the Treatment Industry to Convince Us We Are Out of Control*, Lexington Books: New York.

Robins,J. (1986) *Fools and Mad: A History of the Insane in Ireland*, Institute of Public Administration: Dublin.

Shaw, S. et al (1978), *Responding to Drinking Problems*, Croom Helm: London.

Smith, B. (1989), 'Ireland's Ennis Inebriates' Reformatory: A 19th Century Example of Failed Institutional Reform', *Federal Probation* (March), 53-64.

Stockwell, T. and Clement, S. (1987), *Helping the Problem Drinker: New Initiatives in Community Care*, Croom Helm: London.

Vaillant, G. (1983), *The Natural History of Alcoholism*, Harvard University Press: Massachusetts.

Walsh, D. (1983), 'Alcohol Problems and Alcohol Control in Ireland' in Davies, P. and Walsh, D. (eds), *Alcohol Problems and Alcohol Controls in Europe*, 90-105, Croom Helm: London.

11 Mental health social work with older people in Northern Ireland

Faith Gibson

Introduction

The increasing number of people living into advanced old age raises profound questions about how society may achieve inter-generational equity, the nature of relationships between older people with lifelong mental health problems or more recently acquired age-related conditions and their carers, and the quality and availability of health and social care provision. This chapter primarily concerns dementia with some attention to functional mental illness in later life, most especially depression. It examines the policy framework, nature, prevalence and incidence, good care practice, service provision, and the role and contribution of professional social workers. It seeks to locate the discussion within the wider United Kingdom context but in particular draws on relevant Northern Ireland literature and research.

Policy framework

The dramatic policy shifts foreshadowed in the Griffiths' Report, *Community Care: Agenda for Action* (1988) and enshrined in *People First: Community Care in Northern Ireland for the 1990s* (1991) introduced far reaching reforms which set the policy framework within which mental health social work with older people must be located. The reforms aimed to maintain people in their own homes for as long as possible; introduced new arrangements for financing residential and nursing homes; care management; comprehensive assessment and care planning; targeting of resources on persons in greatest need; separation of purchaser and provider functions; and support for the mixed economy of welfare.

More detailed mental health policy for older people has been set by the *Regional Strategy for Health and Social Wellbeing into the Next Millennium* (DHSS, 1997) and specifically for dementia in the *Dementia Policy Scrutiny Report* (DHSS, 1994). In keeping with the policy thrust which emphasises care in the community for people of all ages, considerable stress is laid on the contribution of primary care and after that on community mental health services. Many long-stay psychiatric patients with functional illness have been relocated in residential and nursing homes as hospitals have contracted. Depending on the continued retraction of psychiatric hospitals, some people presently in hospital may eventually be relocated to nursing homes specialising in psychogeriatric care.

Over time with increasing emphasis placed on preventing new hospital admissions, it is assumed that the psychiatric hospital population will be an ever ageing one and hence will risk the double jeopardy of both long existing functional mental illness and possibly more recent physical and/or cognitive deterioration. The continuing reduction of long stay beds and the provision of psychiatric beds in general hospitals should mean that people over sixty five who newly develop a functional mental illness will be treated either in the community without hospital admission or in local psychiatric units offering short admissions and community follow-up. This view is consistent with the target of having 88% of people aged 75 years and over supported in their own homes and is reinforced by the intention to establish a regional working group to develop a strategy and an action plan for the promotion of mental health, including implementation targets (DHSS, 1997). Another relevant strategic requirement concerning older people with mental illness is the intention to shift resources from institutional care to community based services and also to improve the availability and flexibility of community based respite services.

Policy concerning dementia is both more explicit and more comprehensive. It is the outcome of detailed considerations undertaken by an inter-professional scrutiny group whose recommendations have been adopted as Departmental policy (DHSS, 1994). These recommendations have been further reinforced by the *Regional Strategy* (1997) which enjoins Boards to continue implementation of all the Report's recommendations and in the first year of the strategy period to conduct a detailed audit of the needs of people with dementia and the services available to meet those needs. The Scrutiny document charts clear directions and unequivocally focuses attention on the growing demands for health and social care provision which will be required to meet the needs of people with dementia and their carers well into the twenty first century.

It was undertaken because of increasing awareness that dementia was a growing problem which makes excessive demands upon carers and requires a complex mix of care needs which can only be met by a multi-professional response. Furthermore, as services had developed historically in Northern Ireland there was ambiguity and uncertainty about whether responsibility was best located within mental health services or within services for older people. Both arrangements existed but nowhere did comprehensive provision exist and care in the community was both patchy, spasmodic and inadequate. Provision was largely institutionally focused, concentrated in hospitals and generic residential care and nursing homes. Availability and quality was immensely variable both within and between Boards.

The Policy Scrutiny Action Team worked within a tightly defined remit and a four month reporting time scale, thus pioneering a new approach to the formulation of departmental policy. It reviewed health and social services needs by means of visits; considered written and oral evidence; identified components of an appropriate and effective dementia policy; and made recommendations to guide the cost-effective development of services over the next decade. The work of the team was supported by an extensive literature review undertaken by the Dementia Services Development Centre in the University of Stirling (1994).

The Report identified the components of a good service designed to maintain quality of life for people with dementia and their carers as follows:-

- early diagnosis
- early and timely support in line with assessed need
- support for carers
- specific provision for younger people with dementia
- a continuum of care provision
- coordinated cooperative multi-professional response

The strategic plans of the Boards for 1997-2002 indicate that the obligatory dementia audits are underway. Some short term Scrutiny requirements have been implemented. For example multi-disciplinary planning teams have been established by Boards with responsibility for developing coherent plans and purchasing strategies but until the current audits are complete, purchasing plans remain very general, commonly couched in terms of more respite and attention to carers, more day care and more domicilary provision. Provider Trusts have mostly developed multi-professional teams with both planning and operational functions. Dementia has become the responsibility of elderly programmes of care, who have established either multi-disciplinary dementia specific teams or alternatively, or exceptionally, psychiatry of old age teams. Generally Boards' purchasing plans pay little attention to mental illness in later life. There is little evidence to suggest that the urgency required to address the growing problems posed by an ageing population prone to develop either depression or dementia, or both are receiving the attention and resources required. Most of the inadequacies identified by the extensive enquiries of the Scrutiny Group appear from a recent enquiry (Alzheimer's Disease Society, 1997) to persist but it was always envisaged that progress would be phased over a number of years. Delays in assessment and transfers from hospital abound. Where progress is evident it emanates from committed individuals who are creatively using the Scrutiny Report to move developments forward rather than resulting from energetic strategic service planning at senior levels. Some Trusts have reported actual deterioration in dementia services and contraction in the amount and quality of service provision because of financial constraints imposed upon community programmes and the failure to transfer monies from the hospital to the community sector.

With *People First* monies care managers from various professional backgrounds, many from social work, were appointed to develop and manage domiciliary care packages which have proved extremely successful. Older people, given genuine choice are increasingly preferring to remain at home, supported by tailor-made care. Funds to support residential and nursing home placements are insufficient to meet the demand and family carers, most commonly old themselves are increasingly burdened. Discussions about rationalising the charging anomalies between institutional and in-home care are on-going. Present arrangements create perverse financial incentives which do not always serve the assessed needs of the older person. At present domicilary care is largely free whereas residential and nursing home care is means tested once a relatively small capital sum (£16,000) is disregarded. This means that some families, for financial reasons continue to care for people at home when the needs of the older person and themselves may be better served by admission to care.

As early as 1995 the Social Services Inspectorate (DHSS, 1995) noted that although relatively early after the implementation of the 1993 community care reforms, financial constraints were already inhibiting development of new domiciliary services required to enable people to remain at home. Additionally they expressed concern over how financial constraints might also reduce conventional services upon which many older people, not subject to care management relied.

Boards have recently identified an impending crisis in the funding available to support all older people, including those with dementia whose needs assessment indicates they require nursing care. Unless alternative arrangements are introduced once the preserved funding for people already in care on 1 April 1993 reverts on death to the Treasury, a substantial number of places in the private sector will remain unfunded. This is likely to result in over-provision in the sense of available but unfunded beds which are still likely to be required for use by new people with assessed complex needs. This funding problem could mean that some nursing homes will close and that some Boards may shift to block contracts with a smaller number of high quality providers. This impending crisis in funded bed availability, linked to an identified shortfall in elderly mentally infirm or EMI beds (DHSS, 1995, McLaughlin et al, 1997) may well place inordinate demands upon hard pressed families and their financial resources.

Functional mental illness

Depression has been described as the pervasive epidemic of old age but accurate statistics about its prevalence and incidence are not available. There is great concern that it frequently goes unrecognised or if recognised, remains untreated in people living either in their own homes or in residential homes and nursing homes. Depression may co-exist with dementia or may be mistakenly assumed to be dementia as some of the symptoms appear similar. Bipolar depression is very rare in older people but life long recurring depressive episodes or reactive depression linked to repeated loss of various kinds is very common. Many older people may not be clinically depressed but may more accurately be described as demoralised as they struggle with ill health, low income, loss of significant others and increasing isolation. Old people are also at most risk of suicide with the highest rates occurring in those who are elderly, male, divorced, widowed or single (HMSO, 1994).

The Northern Ireland psychiatric hospital population is an ageing one. Well over half (544) or 54.6% of the 995 long-stay patients in psychiatric hospital on 31 March 1995 were over 65. The most common primary diagnoses of this age group were identified as schizophrenic/paranoid states (233); dementia (173); affective psychoses (42); neurotic/depressive states (19); personality disorders (16) and alcohol/drug related states (11) and others (50). Women outnumbered men in each category except for equal numbers with personality disorders and more men than women having alcohol/drug related disorders (DHSS, 1994).

The nature, incidence and prevalence of dementia

Dementia is a general term applied to a group of conditions marked by progressive decline in intellectual, physical and memory functions, usually accompanied by changes in personality, behaviour and social functioning. It is variable in its onset, difficult to diagnose, traditionally regarded as irreversible in its progression and is not a normal part of ageing. Alzheimer's type with a slow and insidious onset and gradual decline accounts for approximately 50% of cases. It has no known cause or cure. Vascular dementia, including multi-infarct dementia accounts for approximately a further 25% of cases and is potentially preventable. Onset is usually abrupt and decline continues in a step like pattern as subsequent small strokes impair cerebral tissue. A number of different dementias accounts for the remainder. These include Lewy Body type dementia characterised by rapid onset, mood disturbance, hallucinations and delusions, Pick's disease, Creutzfeldt-Jacob disease, Parkinson's disease, Huntingdon's Chorea and dementias associated with excessive alcohol, Aids and various other conditions. In planning services, rather than classify dementia by stages defined as early, moderate and severe, it is more useful to assess the ability of people to perform certain crucial functions of daily living, their physical condition and their emotional state. Acute onset confusional states are caused by various infections, most commonly of the chest or urinary tract or by medication. Once the underlying condition responds to treatment, the associated confusion usually gradually improves. A person may simultaneously have more than one type of dementia and a confusional state may be superimposed on existing dementia.

Dementia is predominantly a disease of later life. It is estimated that in Northern Ireland there are approximately 12,500 people presently with dementia. An increase of about one fifth or 2,800 is expected by 2001 as the population ages. Of people living beyond 65, one in twenty will likely have dementia and the prevalence doubles for every five year increase in age (Jorm et al, 1987), (See tables 11.1 and 11.2). Most general practitioners in Northern Ireland probably have around 13 known patients with dementia and they may expect to see one or two new patients each year.

Table 11.1
Percentage prevalence of dementia in population by age

Age (yrs)	% Prevalence
45-59	0.1
60-64	0.7
65-69	1.4
70-74	2.8
75-79	5.6
80-84	10.5
85-89	20.8
90+	38.6

Using provisional 1992 mid-year population estimates for each Board the following estimates have been calculated by the Regional Information Branch of the DHSS. These estimates should be used with some caution.

Table 11.2
Estimate of the number of people in Northern Ireland with dementia
1992

Age	Total population	% with dementia	Number of people with dementia
60-64	69,198	0.7	484
65-69	65,132	1.4	912
70-74	54,851	2.8	1,536
75-79	40,275	5.6	2,255
80-84	26,420	10.5	2,774
85-90	12,716	20.8	2,645
90+	4,138	38.6	1,597
Total	517,287	-	12,448

Source of tables 11.1 and 11.2: DHSS (1994) Dementia in Northern Ireland Report of the Dementia Policy Scrutiny (p59)

Boards and Trusts are being guided by rule of thumb prevalence estimations in beginning to plan service developments. Comprehensive case finding procedures have not yet been introduced and some understandable apprehension exists, given financial constraints, which will prevent them responding appropriately to growing need. The obligatory annual medical check of people over 75 years of age has potential for screening and case finding. However, until an agreed standardised screening and assessment tool is available province-wide and primary care teams become more aware of dementia and more skilled in its recognition, accurate information and consequential access to assistance will remain patchy.

Probably only approximately half the estimated number of people likely to have dementia are actually known to medical consultants, general practitioners or social services and some estimates suggest that less than 15% of these known people are receiving social services. Under-diagnosis is commonplace and many people remain unassessed and without assistance until late on when either a serious medical problem, carer's death or other acute crisis demands attention.

Younger people with dementia

It is not known how many people under 65 in Northern Ireland actually have dementia. The number, however, is likely to be relatively small and geographic dispersal makes the provision of age-related specialist services unlikely, unless perhaps in the greater Belfast area. Elderly care services are seldom appropriate for this group which includes a small but increasing number of people with Aids-related dementia. The employment of people with early onset dementia will be disrupted and prematurely terminated, family life threatened and anxieties about possible hereditary implications and rapid deterioration all indicate the need for early and continuing social work and care management involvement. Domicilary care packages need to be highly idiosyncratic, well focused and responsive to changing needs and circumstances. Respite of various kinds, particularly in-home relief is very important in order to sustain carers who are likely to have multiple family responsibilities.

People with learning difficulties

Some 55% of people with Down's syndrome aged 50-59 are likely to develop an Alzheimer's-type dementia. This number increases to 75% in the over 60 age group. With 725 births of Downs syndrome babies recorded in the eighteen years up to 1991, the potential size of this emergent condition can be foreseen. Care is likely to be best provided within learning disability services but will need to be augmented by involvement of psychogeriatricians and social services staff with dual understanding of both learning disability and dementia.

Good practice in dementia care

Knowledge about the nature of dementia and hence ideas about how best to respond have radically changed in the relatively recent past. A consensus about good practice is emerging internationally but it would be misleading to suggest that all health and social care professionals, including social workers, necessarily know about and accept the new culture and apply its principles in service planning and daily practice. Fortunately more are beginning to do so and rewarding advances in care practice can now be seen (Kitwood, 1997).

Early diagnosis is the foundation of good practice. It is essential, notwithstanding the inherent difficulties in making a definitive diagnosis, if reversible conditions which may be mistaken for dementia are to be treated. Preventative treatment for high blood pressure which is often implicated in multi-infarct dementia may significantly reduce or curtail further brain damage. As new effective drug treatments for dementia are developed it will be essential to identify the onset of dementia early if benefits are to be derived from medication.

Downs (1996) citing Drinckamer and Lachs (1992) identifies the difficulties associated with early diagnosis and sharing information. They acknowledge that early diagnosis is surrounded by some controversy. Sharing the diagnosis permits maximising autonomy; arranging of personal and financial affairs; and writing advanced directives. These advantages must be weighed against diagnostic uncertainty; emotional vulnerability; lack of effective treatment; the person's lack of cognitive capacity to comprehend; and the family's wishes.

Treatment for dementia, in the conventional medical sense, is presently extremely limited. In April 1997 the first drug for use by people in the early to middle phases of Alzheimer's disease, Aricept (donepezil hydrochloride) was licensed in the United Kingdom. Aricept is only available on prescription and is administered daily in 5mg or 10 mg tablets. It is not a cure but achieves temporary improvement in memory functioning for six months to a year in some people in the early stages of dementia. Several side-effects, usually temporary, may occur. General practitioners will face increasing demands for this and subsequent drugs and many appear to be ill prepared and ill equipped for this development (DHSS, 1994). Despite the acknowledged limitations of the present generation of dementia drugs, early contact with primary care practices could, if health care professionals are alert, mean that information, advice and referral to supportive services could be made. Early referral to social services could be a means of offering timely information, advice, counselling and reassurance that services will be available, when and if they should be required.

Carers universally say they wish to be told the diagnosis but many still complain that their experience is otherwise. Obviously sharing a diagnosis which has such catastrophic import requires great sensitivity, skill, continuing support and reassurance about present and future care provision. Old fashioned paternalism, professional arrogance and a genuine desire to protect are increasingly giving way to a willingness to talk more frankly, albeit guided by the needs and circumstances of each individual.

People with challenging behaviour

Behavioural problems have been customarily and not always appropriately treated with tranquillisers and sedatives. There is increasing interest in seeking to understand and imaginatively respond to the underlying causes of troubled and troubling behaviour. Past life experience, poorly designed environments and stressors in present social interactions and living arrangements may all have been implicated.

The care of people with challenging behaviours including incessant wandering, shouting, aggression, disinhibition, inappropriate sexual behaviour and extreme solitariness is becoming more sophisticated. A number of authors suggest in Hunt et al (1997) that the origins of much disturbed behaviour are just as likely to lie in past trauma which resurfaces in late life or mismanagement in the present in poorly designed environments as in actual brain cell loss. Kitwood (1992; 1997) has argued persuasively that dementia is best understood as a multidimensional condition to which organic cell damage, genetic or biological factors, life experience, psychological, and current social factors all contribute.

Detailed attention to past history, careful observation in order to identify present preferences and precipitating stressors, positive reinforcement, pleasurable activity, social diversion within a person's capacities, and warm stable caring relationships in which genuine communication occurs can all assist in minimising disruptive behaviour. In this type of care, social workers can play a major role in contributing family and life history details in multi-disciplinary assessments and care planning, supporting other staff and in direct work with people with dementia and their carers (Gibson, 1991;1995;1997).

Communicating with people with dementia

Dementia impairs people's ability to communicate with others and increasing social isolation and frustration are inevitable consequences. Nevertheless, Goldsmith (1996) argues it is possible to communicate with far more people than is commonly assumed but communication takes time. McLaughlin et al (1997), like Goldsmith found that social workers and others often fail to hear the voice of the person with dementia. Facilitating client choice is a central concern in needs assessment and care planning, particularly when clients are regarded by care managers as 'confused' or personal preferences conflict with relatives' wishes.

Various means may assist. Reminiscence and life history work use the capacity to recall more distant memories long after recent memory is seriously impaired which is a feature of dementia. Effective communication requires people to try as best they can to share the world of the person with dementia. By exploring through reminiscence the long and complex journeys which people with dementia have travelled, they can be held in relationships in the present. Reminiscence, either in very small groups or with individuals assists in understanding to some extent what used to be of interest and what might still give pleasure, reassurance and satisfaction (Gibson, 1994; Osborn, 1994).

Reminiscence does not suit everyone, especially those people with an obsessional compulsive preoocupation with a particular aspect of their past. In dementia care it is better to respond to the underlying emotional content of conversation rather than to pursue factual accuracy. Past pain may leak into the present in distorted, coded or symbolic ways (Hunt et al, 1997) and empathetic attentive listening with individuals or in very small groups makes considerable demands. Music, art, drama, dance and movement, story telling, poetry and many other approaches including validation therapy, Sonas, Snoozelen and aromatherapy may all help to focus attention on people as unique individuals who happen to have a particularly pervasive disability but who still deserve, attention, respect and warm affection (Kitwood, 1977).

Service provision

Because dementia is a terminal condition in which the rate and nature of decline varies greatly between individuals, a continuum of care is necessary. In the early stages some people with dementia (and their carers) may not require much if any formal assistance other than information. Others may be extremely anxious and depressed about their deteriorating memory and fearful of the future. Over time domiciliary assistance, day care, respite, and for some people, institutional care may be required. People may need a range of 'normal' services and only relatively late may they require specialist dementia services.

Dementia is rarely a private illness, affecting only the person concerned. It makes increasingly heavy demands on family members, neighbours, friends and formal carers. The majority of people with dementia are sustained in the community by relatives whose stress has been well documented (Levin et al, 1989). Many carers are either elderly spouses who may themselves be frail or else are married children, most often daughters, caught in conflicting obligations to their own families and to their frail aged parents. Support of family carers is as much a responsibility of dementia services as is the direct care of the person with the disease. The often hidden costs include problems with physical health, emotional stress, relationship difficulties, lost employment, social isolation and financial hardship. As a consequence of the Carers' (Recognition and Services) Act 1995 carers are now entitled to a needs assessment in their own right. At the very least they require access to a named worker and opportunity to acquire information in an accessible format. Many need recurring advice, support, respite and for some, skilled counselling.

Support groups (despite the difficulty of participating because of caring responsibilities) provide acceptable support for some carers. They fulfil various functions including exchange of information about dementia and ways of coping (Tosland and Rossiter, 1989; Nichols and Jenkinson, 1991). Social workers, residential and day care workers, and voluntary agencies using skilled volunteers may take the initiative in establishing and running such groups which operate best on a mutual aid, reciprocal groupwork model. Some people believe that such groups are best conducted by people with first hand personal experience (Toseland, Rossiter and Labrecque, 1989). The extent to which carers respond to opportunities for formal instruction is variable but the effects of training early in the caring career appear to produce sustained benefits (Broadarty and Gresham, 1989; Broadarty and Peters, 1991). People who live alone or those without readily available competent carers will require support, surveillance, supervision and practical assistance. Providing adequate care is available and people continue to reside in familiar circumstances, many mange to live alone for many years.

The majority of people with dementia and their carers prefer non-institutional care. Therefore the challenge to social workers, other professionals and informal carers is how to sustain people with dementia in safe, familiar circumstances in ways which are acceptable and affordable. Risk is obviously a central concern. Social workers must be competent in undertaking risk assessment and working with relevant people to develop ideas about acceptable risk and risk management.

Respite care is highly valued by many carers but resisted by others (Levin and Moriarty, 1994). In-home respite is not well developed yet offers less risk of precipitating further disorientation and deterioration. Home support which requires careful tailoring to meet highly idiosyncratic needs increasingly forms a component of care packages whose composition and availability is variable, especially in rural areas where it can be difficult to find suitable staff and travel costs are high.

For many years home helps managed by social work assistants were virtually the only source of domicilary support available except for a small number of incontinence laundry schemes and early outreach work (Gibson, 1991). Over the years the home help service has suffered repeated redefinition of function and financial constraint as funds have been diverted to support more comprehensive domicilary support schemes.

Increasingly voluntary and private agencies are securing contracts for various domiciliary services.

Both generic and dementia specific day care intended to offer carer relief and social and intellectual stimulation for the person with dementia is being developed by both the statutory and independent sectors. The quality is very variable with some day centres offering little more than day minding, a warm meal and a change of scene. These aspects should not, however, be lightly dismissed because they may ameliorate somewhat the bleakness of the lives of some people with dementia and the bondage of some carers (DHSS, 1993; Gibson and Whittington, 1995; Gibson, 1996). Slowly day care is being extended to offer longer hours and weekend opening. Small domestic-scale local neighbourhood day care which provides genuine opportunities to practice daily living skills is a much under developed resource. Such a service offers considerable promise in facilitating take-up, easy access, preserving functional abilities and encouraging socialisation.

There is little information available about the involvement of social workers at the end stage of dementia. In principle hospice type care has much to offer but is rarely available (Cox, 1996). Hospital based social workers in acute and psychogeriatric services offer support but the majority of people with dementia are thought to die in their own homes or in residential or nursing homes unless either acute illness or challenging behaviour has precipitated hospital admission.

Long-stay wards in psychiatric hospitals are no longer considered necessary or appropriate care environments for people with dementia although many are still in use. It is hoped that once sufficient small, domestic-scale, well designed units have been built and staffed by medical, nursing and social care staff these large outmoded hospital wards will close. The majority of people in institutional care in Northern Ireland who have dementia reside in generic nursing or residential homes where their special needs may go unattended. Only a small number are in specialist residential Elderly Mentally Infirm (EMI) facilities, while others are in specialist nursing homes. Residential care, largely informed by social work values, has increasingly tried to create homely, personalised care which stresses individualisation, utilises key workers and seeks to create a small group living ethos.

Only slowly in Northern Ireland are all care sectors beginning to apply the well researched and internationally accepted ideas about architectural design in dementia care. With the impetus provided by the Stirling Dementia Services Development Centre, some Northern Ireland social workers have been actively seeking to influence resource holders and a small number of projects are being developed. Some projects provide housing with care, while others utilise small scale, domestic environments where extraneous stimuli are minimised, the ethos is relaxed, residents are encouraged to participate in domestic tasks and safe wandering is possible. This approach has already been successfully established in various countries (Fleming and Bowles, 1987, Malmberg and Zarit, 1993, Foster, 1994, Pennington, 1996).

A number of EU funded telematics research and development projects are exploring the use of modern information technology and its ethical implications to support physically and cognitively frail older people in their own homes, particularly those who live alone. Responsive ergonomic design and computer assisted technology may be used for various purposes in dementia care including prosthesis, assistance, promotion of independence, support, social and cognitive stimulation, security and surveillance (Martin, 1992, Marshall, 1995; 1996).

The voluntary sector has traditionally been involved in generic residential care provision and in sheltered housing where the number of residents developing dementia is increasing. Interest in specialist dementia services is growing. The private nursing home and residential home sector has greatly expanded in recent years. The voluntary and private sectors together provide more beds than the statutory sector in line with changing policy trends. Funding arrangements have tended to militate against the provision of private sector respite beds.

Dementia specific day care in urban and rural settings has been pioneered by Age Concern Northern Ireland who has also assumed responsibility for one residential home transferred from a Board. The Alzheimer's Disease Society, a region of the National Society has nine branches in the province and has developed 13 carers' support groups, home care and day care and a telephone information and advice service. These two voluntary organisations and Help the Aged have sought to raise the profile of dementia, to offer direct services, to support carers, to run help lines and advocacy schemes, and to campaign to increase public awareness of and the resources committed to dementia care and research. Crossroads and Extra Care offer contractual in-home relief services and a substantial number of community and church groups, largely using ACE workers provide home visiting, sitting, gardening, decorating and other services to older people, some of whom may have dementia or functional mental illnesses.

Social work practice

If high quality responsive services are to be provided many different professions must work co-operatively together. A uni-professional approach, nor any notion of professional monopoly, cannot meet the disparate needs of older people with mental illness, increasing numbers of whom are also physically frail. It is now taken for granted that in a mixed economy of health and social care, the voluntary and private sectors will be increasingly involved as the provider role of statutory agencies contracts. In this managed market, statutory social workers play an important role in inter-professional planning and development teams concerned with purchasing and contracting.

In provider Trusts and other agencies social workers are also important members of specialist multi-disciplinary dementia teams, psychogeriatric teams and ad hoc planning groups where they are well placed to contribute to service development Together with colleagues in uni-professional or multi-professional teams they engage in direct practice with older people and their carers in a variety of settings. Their work is informed by social work values committed to preserving the personhood of those with mental illness through the use of various creative means of verbal and non-verbal communication. They make an important contribution to supporting carers and involving service consumers in service planning. Through care management many will undertake assessment, care planning, monitoring and review. Others work in hospitals or carry supervisory responsibility for staff in community care, including domiciliary, day and residential services.

Because the present organisation and development of services is so varied it is not possible to be prescriptive about the roles and responsibilities of social workers in elderly care generally and dementia care in particular. Compared to children's services, social workers have never been employed in large numbers as direct practitioners with older people (Chapman and Marshall, 1993). With the contemporary emphasis on the primary care team as the focus for professional response, the increase in the number of fundholding practices and the recent establishment of pilot total fundholding schemes, social work practice in elderly care, including dementia, risks becoming even more emasculated.

They have, however, always worked as team leaders and first line managers of social work assistants and social care staff in community, residential and day care services. A small number, including those in health care and approved social workers in mental health settings, have maintained direct practice in complex cases where their involvement has demonstrated clear commitment to considering the unique needs of individuals and families (Gibson, 1991(b), Gibson et al, 1995). There is an important and much neglected psychotherapeutic role for social workers using various models of intervention, particularly those which utilise a family approach (Gardner, 1993, Sherlock and Gardner, 1993, Hunt et al, 1997) and who understand the importance of utilising the resources of the social context and the local community. Skills concerned with assessing and responding to the psychosocial needs of people, developing service responses, working with volunteers, mobilising the opportunities for support provided by social networks and community work are all relevant. Both the response and how it is offered in ways which respect, not demean and promote autonomy, freedom, choice and citizenship rights and obligations of all people, are central. Communication and empathic relationship building skills are pivotal. Securing financial entitlements is vital and social workers have either an obligation to undertake this work themselves or else involve welfare rights workers.

Older people with mental illness, like other vulnerable adults, may be at risk of physical, emotional, sexual and financial abuse, exploitation and neglect in institutional and domestic settings. Boards and Trusts have been required to introduce abuse guidelines for vulnerable adults and training in detection and response.

When seeking to reach decisions requiring the weighing of rights and risks social workers may be helped by considering the respective contributions to decision making of the essential ethical principles of justice, autonomy and beneficence. Each situation will require careful analysis and the likely resolution of competing and often conflicting interests. Such complex decisions with far reaching consequences for the wellbeing and civil liberties of vulnerable citizens should only be taken after full consultation with multi-professional colleagues.

Unlike child protection work, the legislative basis for intervention in the lives of older people is much less defined. A general common law duty to care prevails and there are legal measures to safeguard the estate of people assessed as incapable of managing their own affairs. Provisions to safeguard the person are much less adequate. The criminal law can be evoked when abuse and exploitation is suspected. When care and treatment may be required and informed consent is not forthcoming, action is considerably constrained. Many of the legal issues discussed in chapter 5 concerning the functions of approved social workers are also relevant to social work with older people. A principle of good practice which hinges upon early diagnosis concerns encouraging people to complete an Enduring Power of Attorney (Enduring Power of Attorney (Northern Ireland) Order 1987). This enables people to ensure that their wishes concerning the future management of their estate will be respected if in the future they are medically assessed as incapable. The person appointed as attorney has far reaching powers to manage the estate of the donor but no legal authority to give consent for medical treatment.

Living wills or advanced directives are not legally binding in the United Kingdom but are a device which permits people to express their wishes concerning their care and treatment should they become terminally ill. They provide a guide to families, professionals and concerned others about how the subject person would wish others to proceed in exercising substitute judgement on their behalf.

The Mental Health (Northern Ireland) Order 1986 allows people with severe mental disorder who may be a danger to themselves or others to receive assessment, care and treatment. Article 4 empowers an approved social worker to apply for admission to hospital of a mentally disordered person, regardless of age, for the purpose of assessment.

Article 18 refers to Guardianship, a provision designed primarily to safeguard the welfare of mentally disordered or severely mentally handicapped people. It is a less restrictive, if relatively little used provision. Only 12 people over aged 65 with mental illness were subject to current guardianship orders at the end of 1995 and eight at the end of 1996. A guardian may require a person to reside at a certain place; require a person to attend for medical treatment, occupation, education or training at specific times and places; and require access to be given at any place where the person is residing to a doctor, approved social worker or any other person specified by the Board. Guardianship may be used to transfer a person who has been admitted to a psychiatric hospital for assessment to a residential or nursing home where this is considered to provide a more appropriate and less restrictive care environment.

Article 107 allows for notification to the Office of Care and Protection so that adequate arrangements may be instituted by the court for the protection of property and assets of people incapable of managing their own affairs. Social workers may initiate applications to the Office on behalf of mentally disordered persons and furnish relevant information in support of applications.

Article 37, Health and Personal Social Services (Northern Ireland) Order 1972 allows for the compulsory removal to a place of safety of a person living in conditions so unsatisfactory that their health is endangered but who is insufficiently mentally disordered to allow compulsory admission to hospital under the Mental Health Order. This provision is sometimes considered with reference to people with Diogenes syndrome who are living in conditions of extreme neglect but is rarely, if ever used.

Given the variable and fluctuating nature of dementia, assessing whether or not a person with dementia is capable of giving informed consent or is able to manage their own affairs requires the most careful assessment and is a decision for which medical practitioners are responsible but one in which social workers, as members of multi-disciplinary teams, may often be involved.

The Registered Homes (Northern Ireland) Order 1992 requires Health and Social Services Boards to register and inspect nursing homes and residential homes for persons in need. Registration and Inspection staff, some of whom are social workers are empowered to undertake announced and unannounced visits, have free access to all records and opportunities to interview staff, residents, patients and relatives in private. Serious accidents have to be notified and complaints may be made direct to the registration and inspection units. Registration may be cancelled or conditions imposed if the standards of care and treatment are found to be unsatisfactory. Neither day care nor domiciliary care services are subject to similar regulation. This is likely to become a more pressing concern as the number of vulnerable dependent people living in the community and using these services increases. A legally established body such as a general social services council is urgently needed to protect the public against malpractice and regulate the practice standards of individual social workers and social services staff.

Conclusion

The DHSS has charted clear policy directions for the development of adult mental health services, including those for older people and for people of all ages with dementia. The reality of service provision and the experience of users and professionals does not yet measure up to the policy aspirations. The Scrutiny Report has undoubtedly provided some impetus for change, although anxieties about future provision prevail. These include overtaxed, inadequate existing provision, severe financial constraints, uncertainty and impotence engendered by repeated administrative reorganisations, concern about the capacity of general practice to meet emerging demands, and indecision about future structural arrangements and professional accountability. At a time when policy directions are clear, relevant knowledge is increasing and practice could be dramatically improved, it is greatly to be regretted that increasing numbers of people who may have either a functional mental illness and/or dementia in their later years may fail to receive adequate, let alone high quality care, treatment, and support.

Too many people with dementia are still not identified and diagnosed until late in the course of the disease and only come to the attention of health and social services agencies at a time of crisis. Too many older people with depression go either unrecognised or untreated. Too much is demanded of too many carers. Early diagnosis, relevant timely information and responsive varied accessible services led by well informed skilled people need to become universally available regardless of where people live or their social and financial circumstances. Working with other professional colleagues, social workers have an important contribution to make in developing and providing health and social care, not as short-term 'hit and run' professionals but in enduring responsive creative ways which support older people and their carers throughout the whole long haul of these complex, demanding and protracted mental disorders.

Notes

1. The Psychiatric Census is carried out on the 31st March each year. Information is collected on all long-stay and detained patients resident in Northern Ireland mental illness hospitals, psychiatric units and learning disability hospitals on this date. Inpatients on home leave on this date are also included in the census (DHSS Standard Analysis 1995 Psychiatric Census).

References

Alzheimer's Disease Society Northern Ireland (1997), *No Accounting for Health: A Report for Alzheimers Awareness Week in Northern Ireland,* Alzheimer's Disease Society: London.

Broadarty, H. and Gresham, M. (1989), 'Effects of a training programme to reduce stress in carers of people with dementia', *British Medical Journal,* 299, pp.1375-1379.

Broadarty, H. and Peters, K. (1991), 'Cost effectiveness of a training programme for dementia carers'. *International Psychogeriatrics* 3(1), pp.11-22.

Chapman, A. and Marshall, M. (1993), *Dementia: New Skills for Social Workers,* Jessica Kingsley: London.

Cox, S. (1996), 'Quality care for the dying person with dementia'. *Journal of Dementia Care,* Vol 4, No 4, pp.19-21.

Dementia Services Development Centre (1994), *Dementia A Literature Review for the Northern Ireland Dementia Policy Scrutiny,* University of Stirling: Stirling.

Department of Health and Social Services (1991), *People First: Community Care in Northern Ireland for the 1990s,* HMSO: Belfast.

Department of Health and Social Services SSI (1993), *Inspection of Day Care Services for Dementia Sufferers and Their Carers in Northern Ireland,* HMSO: Belfast.

Department of Health and Social Services (1994), *Dementia in Northern Ireland, Report of the Dementia Policy Scrutiny,* DHSS: Belfast.

Department of Health and Social Services (1995), *Standard Analyses 1995 Psychiatric Census 31 March,* DHSS: Belfast.

Department of Health and Social Services (1997), *Health and Wellbeing Into the Next Millennium, Regional Strategy for Health and Social Wellbeing 1997-2002*, DHSS: Belfast.

Downs, M. (1996), 'The role of general practice and the primary care team in dementia diagnosis and management'. *International Journal of Geriatric Psychiatry*, Vol 11, pp.937-942.

Drinkamer, M. and Lachs, M. (1992), 'Should patients with Alzheimer's disease be told their diagnosis?' *New England Journal of Medicine*, Vol 326, pp.947-951.

Fleming, R. and Bowles, J. (1987), 'Units for the confused and disturbed elderly: development, design, programming and evaluation'. *Australian Journal on Ageing*, Vol 6(4), pp.25-28.

Foster, K. (1994), 'Specialist housing projects for people with dementia', *Health and Social Care in the Community*, Vol 2(1), pp.56-58.

Gardner, I. (1993), 'Psychotherapeutic intervention with individuals and families where dementia is present', pp 16-39 in A. Chapman and M. Marshall (eds) *Dementia :New Skills for Social Workers*, Jessica Kingsley: London.

Gibson, F. (1991), *People with Dementia: the Ferrard Approach to Care*, HMSO: Belfast.

Gibson, F. (ed) (1991), *Working with People with Dementia: A Positive Approach* University of Ulster and Eastern Health and Social Services Board: Belfast.

Gibson, F. (1994), *Reminiscence and Recall*, Ace Books: London.

Gibson, F. (1996), *Dementia Day Care Innovation in Rural Areas: Problems and Opportunities Illustrated by The Rural Action on Dementia Project*, Dementia Services Development Centre: Stirling.

Gibson, F., Marley, J. and McVicker, H. (1995), 'Through the past to the person'. *Journal of Dementia Care* Vol 3, No 6, 18-19.

Gibson, F. and Whittington, D. (1995), 'Day Care in Rural Areas', *Social Care Research Findings, No 72*.

Gibson, F. (1997), 'Owning the past in dementia care: creative engagement with others in the present' pp 134-139 in M. Marshall (ed), *State of the Art in Dementia Care* CPA: London.

Goldsmith, M. (1996), *Hearing the Voice of People with Dementia*, Jessica Kingsley: London.

Griffiths, R. (1988), *Community Care: Agenda for Action, (Griffiths' Report)*, HMSO: London.

HMSO (1994), *Suicide Confronted* HMSO: London.

Hunt, L., Marshall, M. and Rowlings, C. (Eds) (1977), *Past Trauma in Late Life: European Perspectives on Therapeutic Work with Older People*, Kingsley: London.

Jorm, A., Korten, A. and Henderson, A. (1987), 'The prevalence of dementia: A quantitative integration of the literature', *Acta Psychiatrica Scandinavica 76*, 4, pp.65-479.

Kitwood and Bredin (1992), 'Towards a theory of dementia care: Personhood and well-being'. *Ageing and Society*, Vol 12, No 3, 269-287.

Kitwood, T. (1997), *Dementia Reconsidered*, Open University: Milton Keynes.

Levin, E. and Moriarty, J. (1994), *Better for the Break*, HMSO: London.

Levin, E., Sinclair, I.. and Gorbach, P. (1989), *Families, Services and Confusion in Old Age*, Avebury: Aldershot.

McLaughlin, E., Parker, G., Porter, S., Bernard, S. and Boyle, G. (1997), *The Determinants of Residential and Nursing Home Care Among Older People in Northern Ireland: A Report for the Department of Health and Social Services*, Queens University and University of Leicester: Belfast.

Malmberg, B. and Zarit, S. (1993), 'Group homes for people with dementia', *Gerontologist 33*, pp.682-686.

Marshall, M. (1995), 'Technology is the shape of the future'. *Journal of Dementia Care 3*, No 3, pp.12-13.

Marshall, M. (1996), 'Into the future: A smart move for dementia care?' *Journal of Dementia Care 4*, No 6, pp.12-13.

Martin, F. (1992), *Every House You'll Ever Need: A design guide for barrier free housing*, Edinvar: Edinburgh.

Nichols, K. and Jenkinson, J. (1991), *Leading a Support Group*, Chapman and Hall: London.

Osborn, C. *Reminiscence Handbook*, Age Exchange: London.

Pennington, R. (1996), 'Blowing the whistle on bad design', *Journal of Dementia Care 4*, No 2, pp.24-26.

Sherlock, J. and Gardner, I. (1993), 'Systemic family intervention' pp 63-80 in A. Chapman and M. Marshall (eds) *Dementia :New Skills for Social Workers*, Jessica Kingsley: London.

Social Services Inspectorate (1995), *A Multi-disciplinary Inspection of Assessment and Care Management Arrangements*, SSI/DHSS: Belfast.

Toseland, R. and Rossiter, C. (1989), 'Group interventions to support family caregivers: A review and analysis'. *Gerontologist 29* (4), pp.438-448.

Toseland, R., Rossiter, C. and Labrecque, M. (1989), 'The effectiveness of peer-led and professionally-led groups to support family caregivers', *Gerontologist 29* (4), pp.465-471.

12 Mental health social work with older people in the Republic of Ireland

Janet Convery

Introduction

The story of mental health social work with older people in the Republic is, unfortunately, a short story. There is relatively little work being done with older people within the psychiatric services in the Health Boards that have psychiatric social workers. Out of the eight health boards, the Eastern Health Board has the largest number of psychiatric social workers but two health boards have no psychiatric social work posts at all and other health boards have very few posts at present. In the Southern Health Board, a total of three psychiatric social workers work in an area which encompasses Counties Cork and Kerry, with a population of over 530,000. The priority within the general psychiatric services where social workers are employed is work with younger patients. (Keogh and Roche, 1996). Of the four psychiatry of old age services in the country, only two have employed social workers to date.

A survey of senior social work managers in community care showed that there are virtually no health board (or other) social work services available for older people or their families at community level with the notable exception, at the time of writing, of one post (currently unfilled) in Wexford and three dedicated posts in the North Western Health Board. Donegal is the only place where community care social workers (2) are employed to work full-time exclusively with older people, and some work with older people is done in Sligo/Leitrim. Apart from these few posts, it is left to general hospital social workers, where they are employed, to provide whatever limited social work service is available to frail older patients and their families in the Republic. However, there are many hospitals, especially outside of Dublin, where there is no social worker employed, even in cases where the majority of patients are elderly.

This chapter will briefly discuss mental illness and infirmity among the population over age 65 in the Republic and will outline the legal and organisational context within which services for this group are developed and delivered in the statutory, voluntary and private sectors. Developments in mental health services for older people will be discussed. The role that has been defined for social work in relation to older people in the Republic generally and to those with mental health problems specifically will be analysed using references to relevant policy documents in recent years.

Finally reasons for the lack of development of social work services for older people, including the mentally ill and infirm, will be suggested and issues regarding the future of social work with older people in the Republic will be raised.

Mental illness/infirmity in the older Irish population

The 1991 census reported 402,900 people over the age of 65, or 11.4 percent of the total population in the Republic. Projections by the Economic and Social Research Institute estimate that the number of people aged 65 or older will increase by thirty per cent to over 520,000 (or 14.1 percent of the total population of Ireland) by the year 2011 (Fahy, 1995 in Keogh and Roche, 1996). In common with other European countries, the number of very old people (over 80 years) is expected to rise the fastest and increase by almost two-thirds (from 79,000 in 1991 to 130,000 in 2011). This ageing population has serious implications for health and social services in the Republic that are only beginning to be addressed.

There are no accurate figures available on the overall incidence of mental disorders in older people in the Republic. The information systems needed to collect the necessary data have not been developed at a national level. Local or regional studies and case registers suggest "... that between 20 and 25 percent of older Irish people have a mental disorder of some kind at any one time. Roughly five per cent of those over 65 years, and 20% of those over 80 years, suffer from severe dementia." (Keogh and Roche 1996, p. 25) These figures are comparable to the international data and there is no reason to assume that our older population suffers more or less from mental disorders than elderly people elsewhere. Depression is the most common mental illness in old age and, although the information about the numbers of older people suffering from depression in the Republic is similarly incomplete, it is estimated that it affects between 13-23% of the population over age 65. Also of concern are elderly patients with chronic psychiatric illness who have spent much of their lives in psychiatric institutions. It is estimated that "In absolute terms, there are roughly 100,000 older Irish people with a mental disorder of some severity" (Keogh and Roche, 1996, p.25) and an increase to 120,000 by the year 2011, including 25,000 dementia patients, is predicted.

Keogh and Roche note that many cases of mental illness in older people go undiagnosed (as high as 50% of cases of depression in old age) and that even when a diagnosis is made, older people are not referred for treatment as their younger counterparts might be. While it is easy to count the number of cases referred for hospital treatment every year, it is impossible to account for cases of mental illness in the community which are treated by the GP or which are undiagnosed.

A major thrust of mental health policy in recent years has been to generally discourage the admission of patients to psychiatric hospital and to encourage out-patient treatment at local level wherever possible. It was thought to be particularly inappropriate to admit dementia patients to psychiatric hospitals. (Working Party, 1988) In fact, the number of older people being admitted to psychiatric hospital has remained fairly constant, though the rate of admissions of dementia patients has fallen dramatically by 50% between 1984-1994. (Keogh and Roche, 1996, p.196) Older people with mental disorders are treated in 28 psychiatric hospitals, both health board and private, and 13 psychiatric units in general hospitals, and account for 47% of total admissions in 1994. There is a trend toward increased reliance on private hospital admissions of older people. In keeping with the philosophy of de-institutionalisation, patients, including older people, are treated increasingly on an out-patient basis in local mental health centres, day hospitals and day centres, as available.

Elderly mentally ill or infirm patients requiring long-stay care are usually accommodated in either long-stay wards of psychiatric hospitals or units (5,761 EMI patients in long-stay psychiatric care in 1993) or in community psychiatric hostels (no figures available). Non-psychiatric long-stay care facilities for older people in the Republic (numbering 16,200 beds in 1993) include health board geriatric homes and hospitals, health board welfare homes, health board district or community hospitals, voluntary geriatric homes and hospitals and private nursing homes. Approximately 50% of beds are provided by nursing homes, catering for a population of mainly women over 80 years who do not have a high dependency profile. High dependency patients tend to be accommodated in health board homes or hospitals. (Browne, in Keogh and Roche, 1996, Chapter 11).

Legal framework

At present, statutory responsibility for older people with mental disorders is defined by the Mental Health Treatment Act of 1945 which gives the State responsibility for in-patient care and the detainment of persons of 'unsound mind' (including older people) if they are determined to be a danger to themselves or others and unlikely to recover within six months. There is no legislative framework for the provision of out-patients services although medical out-patients services have developed and are a service priority.

Personal social services have not fared so well in the absence of legislation obliging the health boards to support, develop or provide statutory services to vulnerable older people and their families in the community. Section 61 of the Health Act of 1970 allows the health boards to assist in the maintenance at home of people who would otherwise need to be placed in residential care. (National Council for Ageing and Older People forthcoming) Services such as home help, meals on wheels, day care, and other domiciliary services are provided under Section 61, often by voluntary organisations who are grant-aided by the health boards. Since it is well established that most care of the elderly sick or infirm takes place at home (the patient's or the carer's), and since the thrust of recent health policy places emphasis on maintaining older people's independence by allowing them to remain at home, the lack of a legal mandate which requires the statutory provision of social services to support older people to stay in the community must be challenged.

New mental health legislation

In recent years, efforts have been made to bring the mental health laws up to date with current thinking about the treatment and care of psychiatric patients and about patients' rights. The Powers of Attorney Bill, 1995, was a positive step towards protecting the interests of patients who become disabled by dementia or other serious psychiatric disorders. The Bill includes the creation of Enduring Powers of Attorney which allows persons, when they are well, to designate to another person the authority to look after her/his interests even after she/he becomes mentally incapable. (Dept. of Health, 1995) This is of obvious benefit to people who develop dementia or other degenerative brain diseases. Previously, powers of attorney arrangements ceased at the time when they were most needed, that is when the person who granted the power became too ill to manage their own affairs.

The Mental Health Act, which has been in the process of being drafted for the past several years in response to recommendations made in *Planning for the Future* will provide for other important reforms. The new Act supports a shift from hospital to community psychiatric care and gives the protection of patients' rights priority, particularly with respect to detention of patients. (Dept. of Health, 1995) These general initiatives are most welcome and will hopefully benefit patients of all age groups and their families. The provision in the new Act for Wards of Court and for Adult

Care Orders are ones which speak more specifically to the needs of some older people with psychiatric disorders, including dementia.

At present, a person may be made a Ward of Court if she is incapable of managing her own affairs and if she owns property. The process of applying for Wardship is complex and expensive. The applicant must petition the President of the High Court and supply medical evidence that the prospective ward is mentally incompetent. Responsibility for the ward's interests is divided between the High Court and the person appointed to manage the ward's affairs. Under the current legislation, no Ward of Court can be detained or transferred to a hospital or treatment centre without application to the President of the High Court. (Dept. of Health 1995) The White Paper states that procedures governing the admission or transfer of wards is 'slow and ponderous' and proposes that:

> ... Wards of Court be subject to the same procedures governing, admission, either voluntary or involuntary, as other persons but that in the case of each...admission...the clinical director would notify the Registrar of Wards of Court immediately. (op cit p.95)

Presumably this reform will streamline the process and perhaps make it less expensive.

The new Act proposes another change that has far reaching implications for mentally disordered older people and the health and social services which aim to meet their needs. The Act will provide Adult Care Orders in cases where 'mentally disordered older people' are vulnerable to abuse, neglect or exploitation. (Dept. of Health 1995 p. 85) Health boards (or their delegates) will be authorised to apply to the courts for Adult Care Orders with a view to removing vulnerable adults from situations where they are perceived to be at risk and placing them in a place of safety. The adult person requiring care may be placed with relatives, in a health board placement or in the care of a voluntary agency, depending which is most appropriate. Orders will be made for 8 days in emergency situations, or for a longer period as the court sees fit.

The implications of Adult Care Orders for older persons with mental illness are enormous. At present, the State has no legal mandate to take responsibility for older people 'at risk' In isolated cases, older people have been made Wards of Court to protect their financial and property interests from exploitation. But up to now, the State has not taken responsibility for the physical well being or safety of vulnerable adults. Older people with mental disorders may be particularly vulnerable to abuse, neglect or exploitation and the new Act will make the health boards responsible for their protection. There is no provision, however, for the protection of people with addictions, social deviance or personality disorder unless they have an accompanying mental disorder (Dept. of Health 1995, p.85) with the result that some elderly people with behaviour management problems will not be covered by the new legislation.

The Government's proposal for Adult Care Orders is in line with the principle of the 'least restrictive form of care' (Department of Health 1995, p.82) and recognises that, while some adults may need care and protection (from themselves or others), hospital care is not appropriate. It will force the State to develop or support alternative care service alternatives whether in the form of financial assistance to relative carers, the development of boarding out services for adults, the increase in long-stay non-hospital residential places or increased statutory support to the private sector to develop these services. The legislation places responsibility on the health boards or voluntary agencies for providing care for adults needing it but does not specify who exactly (i.e. which professional group in the health boards) should be responsible.

There is no recommendation regarding the inclusion of social workers in the process of assessing risks to adults, obtaining care orders, selecting placements or supervising them, although social workers carry such statutory responsibilities for children at risk. Likewise no suggestions are made regarding the relative appropriateness of locating these workers, whether within the hospital sector or in community care. The fact that psychiatric social workers are the only social workers working with the elderly mentally infirm at present may influence planning decisions in their favour. However, many psychiatric social workers are still attached to hospitals or work in a medical setting, and the shift in policy emphasis towards community treatment and care may lead to support for the further development of community care social work for adults, including older people. Alternatively, social workers may continue to be considered superfluous to mental health services for older people and, as a result, these new tasks may be assigned to others in the system.

The organisation of mental health services for older people

A critical factor in the way that all statutory health services have developed in the Republic is the fact that, unlike Northern Ireland where personal social services are administered separately from medical services, here personal social services have developed within the medical services and the two are administered together. This has led to the medical domination of the health services in the Republic on a large scale; this is almost never discussed in public documents, is taken for granted and rarely challenged. Rehabilitation and community care social services aimed at strengthening old people's independence or at supporting their carers necessarily takes a back seat when medical services continue to consume most of available resources in spite of public policy objectives to the contrary. Personal social services are very much the 'poor relation' of the medical services in such a system; their role continues to be defined by doctors who also define overall priorities within the system and control access to services. This is the background against which we must look at mental health services for older people in the Republic.

Health board responsibility for older people with mental illness or infirmity in the Republic is typically divided between Programme Managers in the Special Hospitals Programme and the Community Care Programme in each health board. Psychiatric services are delivered by the Special Hospitals Programme but the Community Care Programme provides public health nurses and may fund day care services many of which are provided by voluntary organisations, including day centres, home help services and meals on wheels.

In the Western Health Board there is a Programme Manager for Mental Health Services and the Elderly; the North Eastern Health Board has a Regional Manager of Services for the Elderly; and in the Eastern Health Board there is a Co-ordinator of Services for the Elderly who shares responsibility for older psychiatric patients with the Programme Manager for Special Hospitals and a Senior Executive Officer in Community Care who has special responsibility for the elderly. There may be other organisational configurations in other health boards, but in general the responsibility for the relevant services is divided and organisational arrangements varied.

Responsibility for dementia patients is particularly complex. In theory, the recommended model of care (see *Planning for the Future,* 1984 and *The Years Ahead,* 1988) proposes that dementia patients who have psychiatric disorders (including serious behaviour management problems) should be treated by the psychiatric services (old age psychiatry where possible). If they do not have psychiatric symptoms but have a medical problem, patients should be treated by the medical services (preferably geriatric medicine services). Other dementia patients (the majority) should be the main responsibility of the primary care services. The recommended model remains largely theoretical in the absence of the necessary specialist services. There are only four psychiatry of old age services in the Republic, three in Dublin and one in Limerick. Although geriatricians have been appointed in almost all health boards, the Eastern Health Board has 10 out of a national total of 21 geriatricians working in the public sector in the Republic (Department of Health list) which suggests that services are thinly distributed in the other health board areas.

In fact, which service takes responsibility for dementia patients depends mostly on where they happen to be living and what services are, or are not,

177

available. Patients may be taken on by the general psychiatric services in the absence of psychiatry of old age services, they may be seen by the general medical services in the absence of specialist geriatric services or they may remain the responsibility of GPs. Since very, very few specialist dementia services (especially residential services) have been developed in either the medical or psychiatric services especially for dementia patients with behaviour problems such as aggression and wandering, the discussion about the division of responsibility between the services for dementia patients is meaningless. At the end of the day, it is informal carers with support from GPs and under-resourced community care services, who continue to bear most of the responsibility.

Services in the voluntary sector.

Many of the community support services that exist for the elderly mentally ill or infirm are provided in the voluntary sector in the Republic (with or without grant aid funding from the Health Boards). In the largest health board, the Eastern Health Board (pop. 1.25 million people), the home help service, which is pivotal to helping to maintain older people at home, is a voluntary service funded by annual grants from the Health Board; services are run by voluntary management committees who hire supervisors and staff and pay them. In most health boards outside of the Dublin area, the home help services are provided directly by the health boards, but problems exist in both sectors. While the service is highly cost effective, the National Council for the Elderly's report on the home help services (Lundstrom and McKeown, 1994) highlighted the fact that as a discretionary service which the health boards are not legally obliged to provide, there is evidence of problems around distribution of services, access to services, low funding and funding uncertainty, problems which inhibit planning and development, and unsatisfactory work conditions for home helps.

The Alzheimers Society of Ireland (ASI) has played a very significant role in the Republic in raising public consciousness about Alzheimers disease and in providing services to people with dementia and their families. The Society has, for a long time, run support groups (or phone contacts) for carers in the community and there are currently 80 in the Republic. The ASI established the first day centre specifically for dementia patients in Ireland in 1987 which operated for many years with minimal support from the State but now receives occasional once-off grants. Since 1987, the ASI has set up 14 day centres around the country, five full time, and there are plans to open further facilities. Recently, the ASI has been responsible for the creation of Home Support services which currently serve 750-800 families in three regions of the country, with hopes to extend into two more regions. Workers are trained to give personal

178

attention and care to dementia patients living at home in order to provide respite, support and sharing of responsibility with carers. The schemes rely on funding from the Department of Social Welfare under its Community Employment Scheme. In the Western Health Board, the Western Alzheimers Foundation provides similar services to the ASI.

Other voluntary organisations provide services which may be available to mentally frail older people and their families, including day centre and day care services, meals on wheels, transport services, befriending, carers' support groups and holidays for carers. Individual services in the voluntary sector may be very good but are extremely unevenly distributed in the Republic (even within health boards) and depend upon the initiative and enthusiasm of volunteers. Vulnerable older people with the same needs have unequal access to services by virtue of where they happen to live. In some areas, the needs of carers may receive little or no priority compared to other areas. (Lundstrom and McKeown, 1994). Likewise vulnerable older people in one area may be offered residential care because of the lack of community supports that might make it possible for a person in similar circumstances to remain at home in another area. The fact that voluntary organisations must rely on Social Welfare employment schemes to fund their workforce means funding uncertainties. Problems are created by the regulation which requires a large percentage of workers to leave after one year, having been trained, gained work experience and developed a relationship with those receiving the service.

Dementia services information and development centre

In 1993 the National Council for the Elderly facilitated discussions about the development of a dementia services information and development centre based on the Scottish model, aimed at service providers. A proposal has been accepted by the Department of Health to place the new centre in Mercers Institute for Research on Ageing, St. James' Hospital, Dublin under the direction of consultant geriatricians in the Meath Hospital and St. James'. It is expected that the centre will be operational by the end of 1997; the emphasis will be on the education and training of health professionals to keep them up to date with the latest knowledge and developments on the treatment and management of dementia patients.

Services in the statutory sector for older people

In general, the prevention of hospitalisation, the quick return of patients who have been admitted and the desire to maintain most patients in the community are the driving forces of mental health strategies today. (Dept of Health 1992, 1995) In keeping with this principle, there is much more

179

outreach work being done than previously; home assessments are routine in many areas and carers' needs are increasingly considered. Community psychiatric nurses (CPNs) are often involved in this type of work in the absence of social workers.

Literature from four of the eight Health Boards shows that older people with mental illness are on the agenda and have been targeted as needing special services, however much of the policy discussion is still aspirational. One goal that has been achieved is that there has been a significant decrease in the number of dementia patients admitted for long-stay care in psychiatric hospitals. But there is still a heavy reliance on the hospitalisation of older psychiatric patients generally, with varying rates of admission across the different health boards, (Keogh and Roche, 1996, Introduction) and the development of alternative specialist services has been slow and patchy. Assessment/diagnostic services have improved considerably with the appointment of geriatricians and especially with the development of the very small number of consultants in the psychiatry of old age.

Specialist units for older people and for dementia patients in particular are at least in the planning stages in several health boards. These may be situated in a general hospital setting, in psychiatric hospitals or in the community. In the Eastern Health Board, 20-50 bedded Community Units are being developed to provide a range of services including day care, respite, convalescent and long-stay beds for vulnerable elderly people including the elderly mentally infirm who do not present with serious behaviour problems. Remarkably (considering the record of social work input to services for the elderly in the Republic), the units will all also have social workers in half-time posts. The Co-ordinator of Services for the Elderly (an administrator) has responsibility for the new units and it is perhaps significant that the person is not a doctor.

Respite beds, usually but not always in health board hospitals, have been made available, including (in the Eastern Health Board at least) 'floating beds' whereby patients are brought into hospital for respite for 2-3 days per fortnight. In some health boards a certain number of day care places in private nursing homes are allocated to medical card patients and funded by the health board. These are recent positive developments, although these new services are still spread thinly and unevenly.

Prior to the writing of this paper, the views of professionals in the mental health services for older people were solicited by correspondence followed up by interviews where possible. There is a consensus among those interviewed (doctors, administrators and social workers) that dementia patients with serious behaviour problems pose the biggest challenge to service providers in the Republic.

As suggested earlier, there are few short-stay or long-stay residential places for these patients (very, very few places that might be deemed appropriate to needs). Although mental health policy dictates that these patients should be the responsibility of the psychiatric services, ideally a psychiatry of old age, there is a feeling of reluctance to accept this responsibility even where specialist services exist. This reluctance is most likely because of the unsuitability of present services to this particular group. Likewise, resources in the medical services have not been channeled into the development of appropriate services for dementia patients either. Other reported service deficiencies include the general lack of community care services, including social work services for the elderly mentally frail and their families, the lack of day care places for dementia patients, and the lack of respite care.

Services in the private sector

Perusal of any of the newspapers in the Republic suggests a boom in the development of private domiciliary and residential services for older people. Private nursing services, private day care, meals services, night sitting and private home help services have mushroomed, especially in urban areas. Likewise the private nursing home sector has grown considerably in recent years. The implementation of the Nursing Homes Act 1990 resulted in major changes in the system of state subvention to private nursing homes (including an increase in the maximum nursing home subvention from £42.00 per week to £120.00 per week).These changes in funding have contributed to a significant increase in the amount of public money going into private nursing home care in the Republic in the wake of a decrease in the number of public long stay beds. However, even with the increased subvention, the high cost of private nursing home care, especially in the Dublin area, puts this option beyond older people whose only income is the state pension. Lack of financial resources is cited as a major problem by staff charged with finding residential care for older patients with psychiatric problems.

Keogh and Roche (1996) raise the issue of the appropriateness of non-specialist residential care, including private nursing home care, for older people with mental health problems. One senior health board manager shared this view and made the point that, in spite of public policy stating the desirability of the de-institutionalisation of older people, the state is now spending huge amounts of money to put people into what is simply a different type of institution (i.e. private nursing homes). A consultant geriatrician expressed the fear that reliance on services offered for profit in the private sector works against the development of quality, high cost services for patients. A representative of the Alzheimers Society of Ireland observed that, in her experience, when private nursing home proprietors advertise special units for dementia patients, it can sometimes mean that facilities for these patients are segregated from the rest of the residents, in a basement or at the back of the main unit. There may be, in fact, no extra specialist activities or therapies for the residents with dementia which would be costly to provide.

Mental health social work with older people: policy and practice

Social work with older people has not been generally acknowledged or developed as a service that is needed in Ireland in spite of policy recommendations to the contrary. The *Care of the Aged Report* published in 1968, was the first important policy document on services for the elderly in Ireland. Although the emphasis in the Report is on medical and hospital services, a recommendation is made for trained social workers to be available to assist public health nurses to look after the "complex' needs of elderly people living in the community and especially, those living alone. (Inter-departmental Committee 1968, p. 65-66). The Report goes on to suggest that social workers be employed to help in the full assessment of social and environmental factors when the question of long-term residential care is being considered. Even after older people were institutionalised, the Report envisioned a role for social workers who would help the older resident to maintain contact with her family who might ultimately take her home again. The *Care of the Aged Report* recommends '...that each health authority should employ, or should make arrangements for the employment by voluntary bodies, of sufficient trained social workers to meet the needs of the aged in its area.' (op cit p. 66).

The Report observes that, "... in practice, public health nurses in rural areas are already providing many of the services normally provided by social workers." (op cit). There is only brief mention of psycho-geriatric patients and no mention of psychiatric social work services for older people.

The Years Ahead is the most recent major policy document for the elderly in Ireland. (Working Party 1988) While this report puts more emphasis on non-institutional care, most of the prescriptions offered are still medical This is not surprising given the fact that the Working Party Committee was comprised almost exclusively of doctors and administrators. Social work again merits only a very brief discussion (the same length as the discussion on alarm systems in the same chapter!) and the potential role assigned to social workers is actually narrower than that envisioned by the Care of the Aged Committee. *The Years Ahead* sees social workers as the appropriate professionals to deal with relationship problems in the families of older people (p.98). In the general discussion of care at home, it notes that hospital social workers and a very few social workers employed by voluntary organisations, as well as some members of religious orders, are already engaged in this work in Ireland. The Report recommends that community care social work services be expanded to become available to dependent elderly people and their families on a similar basis to the situation in Northern Ireland. However, recognition is made of the fact that community care social work departments were already stretched in 1988 due to the large volume of work with children at risk and their families.

In the chapter on Care of the Elderly Mentally Infirm, *The Years Ahead document* cites the South Belfast district of the Eastern Health and Social Services Board in Northern Ireland (p154) which depends heavily upon the involvement of the social services, including social work, as a model of good practice and service provision. *The Years Ahead*, while applauding the comprehensive, interdisciplinary approach adopted in South Belfast, uses differences in the organisation of health services between Northern Ireland and the Republic to justify the proposal of a service development model which is exclusively medical in its approach. Specifically, the fact that our social services have not, up to now, taken responsibility for the delivery of welfare services to the elderly, is used as justification for continuing on the same course of responsibility for the elderly mentally infirm, including dementia patients, remaining the exclusive domain of the medical services, to be shared between general practitioners, consultants, and public health nurses. Scant mention is made of the social and psychological needs of dementia patients, the relationship problems and difficulties in family dynamics experienced by families who must deal with dementia or issues regarding the vulnerability of some dementia patients to abuse or exploitation. Nor are there recommendations regarding how best to deal with these issues.

Planning for the Future (Study Group 1984), the major policy document which deals with the psychiatric services, devotes one chapter to services for the elderly mentally infirm. This report strongly recommends the development of specialist psycho-geriatric services, noting the prevalence of disabling conditions in old age including mental deterioration. (op cit p 83).

Recommendations are made for better preventive services, including domicilary support services, support for families, assessment facilities, and specialist medical services including hospital treatment services. The document notes the inappropriateness of placing the elderly mentally infirm, particularly those with severe behaviour problems, in psychiatric hospitals. Psychiatric social workers are mentioned as essential to the assessment of elderly people presenting with medical or social problems. References are also made to the need for involvement of the community care team in providing services to elderly patients and their families, although social workers are not specifically mentioned.

The *Green Paper on Mental Health* (Dept. of Health 1992), in its discussion on the elderly mentally infirm, reiterates recommendations in *The Years Ahead* for the development of a specialist psychiatry of old age services, the provision of community based services for dementia patients and their families, and less reliance on psychiatric hospitals to meet the needs of dementia patients with severe behaviour problems. Emphasis is placed on the appropriateness of placing the major responsibility for dementia patients in the Primary Care services, without specific mention of social work services. In the chapter on Personnel, the authors note the small numbers of psychologists, social workers and occupational therapists working in the psychiatric services with all age groups. They go on to say that 'social workers, psychologists and occupational therapists have a distinctive contribution to make to the care of the mentally ill. These professions should have a greater involvement in the psychiatric service of the future.' (op cit, p.59)

As outlined earlier, the *White Paper* (Dept. of Health 1995) proposes the introduction of Adult Care Orders which have possible implications for social workers, although social work is not specifically mentioned. In Keogh and Roche's study of *Mental Disorders in Older Irish People* (1996), a document which will presumably inform future policy decisions regarding the care and treatment of older psychiatric patients, social work is considered to be an essential service. It is recommended that social workers be included as members of psychiatry of old age teams (with occupational therapists and psychologists) to' ...provide care and specific intervention programmes in the individual's own home as well as in other care settings'(p. 176). In discussion about dementia services, social work services are included (with other community care services) as essential to the provision of '...a comprehensive range of support services for people with dementia living at home and their carers (p. 189)'. Finally, in their conclusions, Keogh and Roche note that

> While it is recommended that multidisciplinary teams should be in place in each district, in practice these teams usually consist of doctors and nurses with limited input from psychiatric social workers, occupational therapists and psychologists because there are so few in the services. This restricts the range of treatment options available to patients. Also the different range of skills available from psychologists, occupational therapists and social workers are not available to care teams. The inclusion of these professionals in psychiatric care teams would go some way in providing the widest

possible range of treatments to older people with mental disorders. (op cit, p.250).

The future of mental health social work with older people in the Republic of Ireland

Psychiatric social workers, hospital social workers and the very few community care social workers who are currently working with older people and their families in the area of mental health in the Republic are doing excellent work with skill and commitment. They are involved in patient assessment work. They are working to rehabilitate young elderly psychiatric hospital patients into the community. They are working with old people and their families to make decisions about residential placement and giving advice and information. Social workers are doing counselling and therapy with individual old people, and give psychological support to carers and help to arrange practical support. Finally, social workers undertake advocacy work and assist in finding legal solutions to protect vulnerable old people and their assets from abuse or exploitation. One geriatrician interviewed noted the importance of social work expertise in helping to bridge the hospital/community interface; he felt social work skills were useful in solving problems in the areas of elder abuse, the co-ordination of family support, in minimising discord within families, and in helping to assess priorities in a context of scarce resources. However, the very limited involvement of social workers in work with mentally frail older people and in the Republic should be a source of concern to social workers if not to others. Below some of the factors contributing to this situation are discussed.

Organisation of services The low priority placed on non-medical services generally, including social work, which are either situated within the medical services or controlled by them accounts in part for the present situation in which social workers find themselves in the Republic. This situation is characterised by very few job opportunities, especially in adult services, and with little or no opportunity for career advancement. The division of statutory responsibility for frail older patients between health board programmes is another factor militating against the planning, development and delivery of comprehensive, co-ordinated social services to this client group.

Attitudes to work with older people The needs of older people in Ireland continue to be defined in physical terms mainly, and this is a function of the medical domination of both medical and social services here and of public and professional attitudes towards older people who are seen as sick

185

and dependent. This has inhibited the development of social services for the elderly. Social workers in the Republic, with a few exceptions, have not sought out work with older people. There has been little interest shown in work with older people and little pressure from within the social work profession in this country to develop new services for older people. There is a Dublin based Special Interest Group in the Irish Association of Social Workers (composed exclusively of hospital social workers) who are committed to the improvement of social work services to older people. This small group has conscientiously made submissions whenever possible to present a social work perspective to existing services and service developments in the Republic, but there is little evidence of active support from within the profession for what it is trying to achieve.

Psychiatric social work posts have actually been lost over the years and replaced by community psychiatric nursing posts and, in some cases, addiction counselling posts and there does not appear to have been any protest from within the social work profession. In recent years, with growing public consciousness about child abuse and the health boards' need to be publicly accountable, any new community care social work posts have gone to child protection and any health board social workers in community care who previously had the opportunity to work with adults, including older people, are no longer able to do so.

Attitudes toward social work and social workers Interviews with senior health board managers, consultant doctors and psychiatric social workers around the country suggest that there are negative attitudes towards social workers among those who make policy and plan services. These negative attitudes keep social work very low on the list of service development priorities in the mental health services in the Republic.

A view was put forward that social workers make problems rather than solve them (for doctors and for health boards) and that social workers had little understanding of the scarcity of resources in the system. There were suggestions of inappropriate behaviour on the part of some social workers. There was the view that social workers had not proved their effectiveness and still have to earn respect and trust from within the system. Others simply had no experience of working with social workers and felt that they were doing fine without them.

Community psychiatric nurses and public health nurses are the groups who are particularly valued by medical directors and administrators in the mental health services, possibly at the expense of social work. One psychiatric social worker observed that nurses are trained to know their place in the medical hierarchy and nurses speak the same language as doctors. There is the perception that nurses work well with doctors and have proved their worth. As a result, increasingly, CPNs are being asked to

186

take on social work roles for which they are not trained, such as home assessments, behavioural and family therapy and support to families (Dept. of Health 1992, p. 58). The Green Paper, while including social work services in the list of essential community based services for dementia patients goes on to recommend extra training in the above skills for nurses who will now be working increasingly in the community (ibid, p.58) rather than emphasising the need for the employment of social workers either in the psychiatric services or in community care.

Demand for social work services In places where social workers were never a feature, the people who control resources within the system are not lobbying for their employment. Where social work posts do exist the expansion of these services is definitely not a development priority for service planners. However, surveys of field workers around the country suggest that there is a perceived demand for new or improved social work services for older people, including the elderly mentally ill or infirm, amongst those actually working with this client group. The demand is coming from public health nurses, co-ordinators themselves, directors of community care, physiotherapists, and from hospital social workers. There is particular concern among public health nurses and area medical officers about elder abuse which is seen as an appropriate brief for social workers. Protocols are only beginning to be developed at local level; this might be the issue which prompts the employment of social workers at community level to work with older people. Other roles that respondents felt were appropriate to social work included giving advice and information about services, family relationship work, crisis counselling, advocacy, boarding out, carer support, work with dementia patients, housing, and residential placement.

Adult Care Orders If and when the new Mental Health Act is implemented, issues will arise regarding the staffing implications. Specifically, decisions will have to be made about who in the health boards will be responsible for taking out Adult Care Orders and about the development of statutory or other (relative carers or boarding out) residential places for adults at risk. Again, there may be an opportunity for the development of social work services in this area since the required training and skills are already part of social work education although they have not been applied to work with older people in the Republic as yet. There is an opportunity for psychiatric social workers to initiate discussion on the subject so that social work involvement will be on the agenda when the Act is implemented.

Conclusion

Social workers interested in working with vulnerable older people in the Republic need to find opportunities to convince decision makers of the relevance of social work skills to work with older people. Those already working with older people desperately need to show that their work is important and effective. They have a responsibility to be professionally accountable to the agencies that employ them as well as to their clients. Much work needs to be done to prove the worth of social work in the mental health services for older people and the time may be right to do so, given the increasing emphasis on de-hospitalisation and care in the community.

References

Department of Health (1992), *Green Paper on Mental Health*, Stationery Office: Dublin.

Department of Health (1995), *White Paper: A New Mental Health Act*, Stationery Office: Dublin.

Department of Health (1995), *Shaping a Healthier Future: a strategy for effective healthcare in the 1990's*, Stationery Office: Dublin.

Eastern Health Board (1995), *Review of Services for the Elderly and Four Year Action Plan 1995-1998*, Eastern Health Board: Dublin.

Eastern Health Board Review Group (1992), *Social Work and Psychiatry*, Eastern Health Board: Dublin.

Fahey, T. (1995), *Health and Social Care Implications of Population Ageing in Ireland*, National Council for the Elderly, Report No. 42: Dublin.

Inter-disciplinary Committee on Care of the Aged (1968), *The Care of the Aged*, Stationery Office: Dublin.

Keogh, F. and Roche, A. (1996), *Mental Disorders in Older Irish People: incidence, prevalence and treatment*, National Council for the Elderly, Report No. 45: Dublin

Lundstrom, F. and K. McKeown (1994), *Home Help Services for Elderly People in Ireland*, National Council for the Elderly, Report No. 36: Dublin.

Mid-Western Health Board (1997), *Health Expenditure and Service Plans*, Mid-Western Health Board: Limerick.

National Council for Ageing and Older People (forthcoming), *Legal Information Handbook*, Dublin.

Study Group on the Development of the Psychiatric Services (1984), *The Psychiatric Services - Planning for the Future,* Stationery Office: Dublin.

Working Party on Services for the Elderly (1988), *The Years Ahead - a Policy for the Elderly,* Stationery Office: Dublin.